THE
STOP

HOW THE FIGHT
FOR GOOD FOOD
TRANSFORMED
A COMMUNITY
AND INSPIRED
A MOVEMENT

NICK SAUL *and*
ANDREA CURTIS

MELVILLE HOUSE
BROOKLYN · LONDON

THE STOP

Copyright © 2013 by Nicholas Saul and Andrea Curtis

First Melville House printing: September 2013

Melville House Publishing   8 Blackstock Mews
    145 Plymouth Street   and   Islington
    Brooklyn, NY 11201   London N4 2BT

mhpbooks.com   facebook.com/mhpbooks   @melvillehouse

Cover photographs: ©iStockphoto.com/flyfloor (spoon);
    ©iStockphoto.com/MarkSwallow (pitchfork)

Library of Congress Cataloging-in-Publication Data

Saul, Nick.
  The Stop : how the fight for good food transformed a
community and inspired a movement / Nick Saul and Andrea
Curtis. — 1st ed.
      p.   cm.
  Includes bibliographical references and index.
  ISBN 978-1-61219-349-6
  1. Food banks—Ontario—Toronto.   2. Community
gardens—Ontario—Toronto.   3. Food security—Ontario—
Toronto.   I. Curtis, Andrea.   II. Title.
  HV696.F6S28 2013
  363.8'509713541—dc23

                                      2013026867

Printed in the United States of America
    1 3 5 7 9 10 8 6 4 2

For Cliff Gayer and the Davenport West community

"The fundamental job of the imagination in ordinary life, then, is to produce, out of the society we have to live in, a vision of the society we want to live in."

NORTHROP FRYE, *THE EDUCATED IMAGINATION*

ALTHOUGH WE WROTE THIS BOOK together, it is written in Nick's voice, as the story that follows charts his fourteen years at The Stop Community Food Centre.

In Canada and the U.K., food bank refers to both the smaller organizations handing out donated food, as well as the larger distribution centres that organize, store and dispense this food. In the U.S., these smaller organizations are often called food pantries; the larger distribution hubs are known as food banks. For the purposes of the book, food bank is used to refer to all interchangeably.

CONTENTS

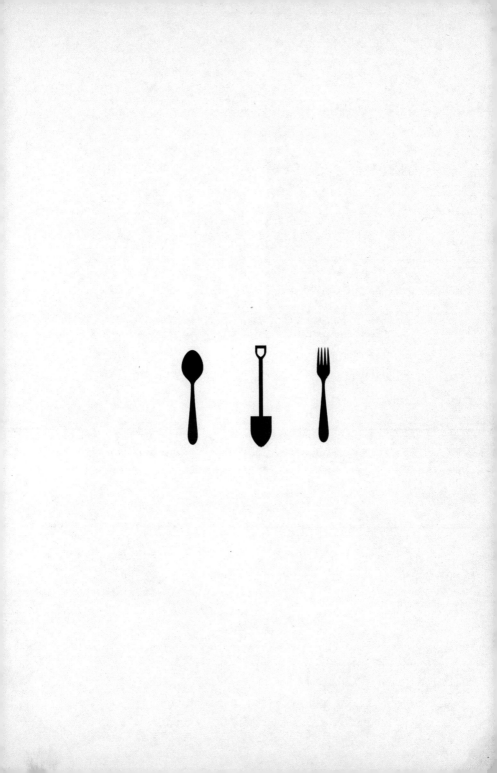

NEVER UNDERESTIMATE
THE POWER OF A
GREAT MEAL

HE'S LATE AND THE GREEN BARN is buzzing. Sunlight streams in the big south-facing windows as kids chop mangoes and cucumbers, giggling and chatting with the staff and each other. TV crews and radio hosts wander the refurbished industrial space, checking their cellphones and hunting for the best position to set up.

Finally, a big, black SUV pulls up. I leave the frenetic energy of the Barn and head outside. The fall air is crisp but clear. Moisture clouds the windows of the car. When one of the world's biggest celebrities unfurls himself from the back seat and puts out his hand to shake mine, I hardly recognize him.

Jamie Oliver—international superchef, restaurateur, TV star, activist and entrepreneur—looks exhausted and a bit puffy around the eyes, his purple hoodie faded, his bed-head perfectly mussed. We walk toward the Green Barn making small talk. He's charming, down to earth and immediately likeable. But he's been up half the night battling jetlag, so he's not quite ready to face the cameras. In fact, he'd like to chat out here for a bit before he meets the children and the media.

We sit on a fence in the community garden outside the greenhouse. I tell Jamie how the Green Barn is one of The Stop's two locations, a satellite of our main centre. The Barn is part of the historic conversion of an old transit-vehicle maintenance site in the heart of Toronto. The buildings lay derelict for some twenty years—until proposals for reimagining them were requested and The Stop threw its hat in the ring with several other organizations. Of course, as he can see, the Green Barn is not a barn at all—it's a long brick structure built to fit streetcars inside. Today, our weekly farmers' market, sustainable food education programs for kids, bake oven, greenhouse, outdoor gardens and food enterprise—catering and fundraising dinners served beneath the stars in the greenhouse, among other things—have made it one of the city's favourite destinations. When The Stop opened the Green Barn doors in 2009, it seemed like an overnight success, but it was a project nearly a decade in the making.

This garden where we're sitting is one of the newest initiatives here, a program in which downtown seniors and youth connect by growing plants that represent their diverse cultures. We've got a Latin American plot filled with corn and squash, a South Asian plot planted with bitter melon and okra, a plot devoted to tomatoes and basil and garlic for the substantial Italian contingent. The young and older people get together to plant and tend the gardens and learn about each other's lives. Every week, one cultural group cooks a meal for the others. The gardeners recently held a big harvest festival where they shared the fruits of their labours.

Jamie listens carefully and seems genuinely interested. In fact, he quickly turns the tables and puts me on the hot seat:

What do we do at the farmers' market? Who uses the green-house? How much government support do we receive?

The truth is, it's not hard to get me talking about this place. I'm proud of it. It wasn't easy for a relatively small antipoverty organization to jump through all the hoops—including raising five million dollars—to get here. But operating the Green Barn is only part of our work. I tell Jamie that next time he's in Toronto, I'd love to show him our other site; it's not too far away, but in a much different neighbourhood. You don't really know The Stop until you've been there. The Green Barn is the pretty face of the organization, new and fresh and bright, drenched with sunlight and goodwill. But our main space, a sprawling community centre in the bottom floor of Symington Place, a public housing development in one of the city's poorest and most underserviced neighbourhoods, is the gritty heart of The Stop's operations.

It's there that The Stop does the tough slog of emergency food programming, engaging thousands of hungry, isolated people who need food, a friend, a referral or a safe place to land. We have a big outdoor garden, communal dining and cooking initiatives, a weekly health and nutrition group for low-income pregnant women, breakfast and lunch drop-ins, civic engagement projects and the program that started it all: a food bank.

We're still chatting when one of Jamie's people comes up and indicates that the children and media can't wait much longer. The chef rests one hand on my shoulder and says, "You know what, brother? I've been all around the world and I've never seen anything like this place."

Jamie puts on a big smile and pushes through the door into the busy room where the kids from our school-age program are preparing a special lunch. There are camera flashes, oohs and aahs. He's a rock star.

Amazingly, the kids don't seem star-struck at all. They keep up their chopping and dicing and mixing the ingredients at stations set up on big wooden tables. This is their space, a place where children from low-income families come after school three times a week (and on school holidays like today) to learn about cooking, growing and healthy eating, as well as the big issues in the food system like inequality and climate change.

Jamie crouches down at kids' eye level to ask questions, offer a bit of sage advice about dicing mangoes, laugh, even sign a few autographs, all while sneaking in messages about the importance of healthy eating.

"You're the best chefs I've worked with in a long time," he tells the children when we sit down to eat their pancakes, fruit salad and homemade chicken nuggets. The kids revel in it, apparently oblivious to the cameras, microphones and digital recorders crowding all around them. When Jamie asks the kids to raise a hand if they love The Stop, they all reach for the sky. One boy asks Jamie if he loves it, too. "Yes!" he says. "Well, then put up your hand!" the child laughs, and Jamie shoots his hand into the air like a chastened schoolboy.

After the meal, I take Jamie on a full tour of the Green Barn, cameras in tow. We pause at the commercial kitchen, the sheltered outdoor garden and bake oven, the greenhouse and compost demonstration area. We're talking about the impact that loss of food skills has on society, and the problems of growing inequality and poor health, when he's swept off to do more interviews. A half-hour drop-in has turned into a nearly two-hour visit.

That evening Jamie tweets to his millions of Twitter followers that The Stop is "Toronto's food mecca" and that every community would be lucky to have an organization like ours.

The response in the rat-a-tat-tat world of social media is overwhelming. The Stop is all over the blogosphere and Twitterverse within minutes. Jamie Oliver has unbelievable exposure and influence—from politicians to restaurateurs to celebrities and Food Channel–loving home cooks.

It tells you something when one of the biggest celebrities in the world is a chef. This lad from Essex who grew up at the stove of his parents' pub has become one of Britain's biggest exports and a worldwide phenom. The Stop, too, has been riding an ever-increasing wave of interest in what and how we eat. Food is huge. Whether it's diet-related health problems, food safety issues, organic-versus-conventional debates, fruit gleaning, urban gardening, farm subsidies, food miles, the worldwide food price crisis, environmental degradation caused by industrial farming or any of the other myriad questions about the complex and ailing system through which we produce, distribute and consume food, you can't escape it on the news, in schools or on the internet. People are interested, but also deeply worried—and with just cause. In fact, as fuel prices rise and our fuel-intensive society shows its cracks ever more vividly, we're likely to find the problems of the food system even more of a public priority.

Still, with all this talk about food, it's astonishingly rare for anyone to touch on issues of justice or equality. Even when The Stop is featured in newspaper articles or online, our main work—that is, advocating for and with low-income people on food issues—sometimes doesn't even get mentioned. Reporters will write or talk about our education programs for kids, the bounty of our gardens or the delicious offerings of our chefs, but not the reasons we must do what we do.

The reality is, the poor, marginalized and hungry rarely get a place at the discussion table. Most people don't even bother to ask why there is so much hunger and poverty in one of the world's wealthiest cities. Maybe it's too uncomfortable or depressing; maybe they think people who are poor deserve their lot in life. Maybe they believe that food banks and soup kitchens are dealing with the problem adequately. But whatever they think, the bottom line is if you're poor you're expected to stand in lines and take the cheap, unhealthy, processed food from the charity that offers it and be grateful.

I've never thought this kind of response is good enough. And at The Stop, we've never believed that such handouts are going to solve anything. That's why the organization has been building a new approach. We call it a Community Food Centre, and the model is based on the belief that we're never going to build a healthy, just and sustainable food system unless good food that's gentle on the planet is available to everyone—rich and poor alike.

But The Stop is about a lot more than just *access* to healthy food. It's also about using the power of this good food to transform lives and our community. In Healthy Beginnings, our program for low-income pregnant women, low birth weights have been dramatically reduced because these moms-to-be have an opportunity to access nutritious food and learn about how to make it, all while sharing their fears, anxieties and wisdom about babies, birthing and healthy eating.

In our community gardens, new immigrants from Afghanistan, Brazil and China learn about the kinds of veggies that grow in this climate and bring home both new friendships and new knowledge to their apartment balconies, window ledges and backyards.

In our civic engagement project, people who may never have considered voting or writing a letter to their political representatives—who never felt that they had a voice at all—come together over a meal to talk about how to fight for their right to good food and other key services.

Every day at The Stop I see that you can never underestimate the power of a great meal—prepared with love and eaten with others—whether it's the one our After School Program kids offered to Jamie Oliver or the community meals served daily to hundreds of people at our main site at Symington Place. I've seen it over and over: food has the ability to bring people together and to challenge the barriers that divide us.

Of course, it isn't always like this sunny Jamie Oliver love-in. Building The Stop has been a hard-won journey with many bumps and bruises, false starts, even a few fist fights and at least one bomb threat. Many people who come to our centre bring with them their difficult lives and everyday problems. And not everyone in the world of emergency food has welcomed our challenge to the traditional food bank. A lot of people and organizations are very invested in the old way of doing things.

But every social transformation needs a bit of grit to get traction, and challenging the old paradigm of emergency food handouts and the fraught territory of charitable giving is critical. After all, the way we've been doing things for the last thirty years has done little to end hunger. Food bank use continues to rise dramatically. And hundreds of thousands of people—including many children—in towns and cities across the continent report that they don't know where their next meal will come from.

In fact, hunger is on the rise all around the world as the gap between rich and poor widens into a crevasse. The food system is in tatters. We need twenty-first-century responses to a twenty-first-century problem—and organizations that model the fair, healthy, inclusive and resilient communities we want to see. The Community Food Centre approach we are forging at The Stop is a big part of this response. Instead of considering hunger in isolation—a problem solved by a food bank hand-out—at The Stop we understand it as intimately connected to poverty, inequality, health, the environment and social relationships. We create programs that reflect this holistic, integrated view, supporting low-income people in determining the course of their own lives.

Along with many, many others fighting for a good food revolution—one of the fastest-growing social movements on earth—The Stop is issuing a clarion call: we must change this food system that is damaging the planet, making us sick and dividing us as citizens. For we are more than just consumers. We are friends, neighbours, brothers, sisters. The Stop's story is one of how an impoverished inner-city community asserted that truth, harnessing the power of food to build a better neighbourhood and a better world.

ONE

NO ONE WANTS A HANDOUT

MAY 1998. The food bank doesn't open for another hour, but already a lineup has formed at the double steel doors opening into a back street. I lean out and see a middle-aged Korean woman at the front of the line. Bright pink lipstick is smeared across her lips and she's carrying on an animated conversation with herself while two younger men speaking Spanish pace back and forth behind her, kicking the ground, jumpy. I nod at one of the guys, someone I recognize, and he looks back at me hopefully. I shake my head and point to my wrist. Not yet.

Inside, three volunteers are busy stacking canned goods and sorting the skids of donated food, mostly the sort of thing nobody else wants: damaged tins of creamed corn, mislabelled boxes of macaroni and cheese, a few perishables like chicken nuggets with a serious case of freezer burn that we'll store in hand-me-down chest freezers. But we did just get a donation of toilet paper: food bank gold. It'll be scooped up faster than you can say single-ply.

Richard Thompson, a solidly built man, his grey hair like a helmet around his ears, walks in carrying plastic bags bursting with fruits and vegetables. He plops them down on the folding table that divides the food from the people who line up to get it. Once a week, Richard volunteers to go around to the greengrocers that cluster near an intersection in his tony neighbourhood, and collects the produce they can no longer sell. There are bruised apples, tomatoes with splotches of brown, and bananas—some a bit overripe, others so soft you could drink them. He brings them to the food bank so we can give them out. It's often the only fresh food we have to offer.

I clap Richard on the back. "Thanks."

Richard is beloved around here. He's volunteered at the food bank for nearly a decade, and he came up with this delivery scheme a few years ago after his church adopted us as their community project.

Compared to Richard, I'm new on the scene—and green enough to wonder if such bruised fruit and dented cans are as good as it gets. I was hired in March to be the executive director, but I also work two days a week handing out food in our food bank.

Cliff Gayer, our sole food bank staffer, spends part of his time cleaning the space. The demand for food is so great, we could both be working day and night every single day—sorting and organizing the food, talking to people, doing intake interviews, handing out the food hampers—and we'd still not meet the need in this community.

I think I'm up for the challenge of running this place, but there are still times when I wonder why I applied for the job— let alone why they hired me. I've never managed anyone in my life and have zero experience working with food. And the truth is, I've never cared much for the idea of food banks. They've always seemed to me like a band-aid solution.

I have, however, done quite a bit of community organizing. I worked with homeless men in a downtown shelter at my last job, and in a public housing complex before that. I've knocked on doors in several political campaigns, and worked in the Ontario premier's office, where I was an assistant to one of the premier's advisers and had a fascinating inside view on decision making.

Still it's clear—to me and everyone else—that hiring a young guy without a history in food banking was a bit of a flyer for The Stop's board. The organization, I've learned pretty quickly since arriving, was in trouble—with staff not talking to each other, board members trying to cobble together the pieces, and funding barely at a subsistence level. I think they must have figured it would be hard for me to make things much worse.

Before the job interview, I rode my bike up to Symington Place to check out the space. It was a ride through Toronto's history and the waves of immigration that have transformed the city over the last hundred years. I passed the old factories now made into thousands of condos and townhomes, the formerly Jewish neighbourhood now predominantly Chinese, pockets of Caribbean and Portuguese and Italian all jumbled up, houses and cars and gardens close together. When I arrived in Davenport West, I realized it was a neighbourhood I'd driven through on the way to the highway, but I'd never noticed.

Squeezed between railway tracks on the northwestern edge of the city core, it's a kind of liminal space with no real centre. Davenport Road—a long east-west artery that cuts through the western half of downtown like a narrow utilitarian belt—is the closest this neighbourhood gets to a main street.

The Stop's tiny office is located on Davenport itself, on the ground floor of the Symington Place public housing building where Toronto Public Health also has a large office. The food bank takes up a smallish room in the same building, but it faces the back street and the townhouses that are also part of the complex. Both Stop spaces are cramped and rundown, but the rent is subsidized by the public housing authority and many of the people who come here live nearby. They need us. A lot.

The area used to be known for its factories—General Electric, American Standard, a large baked goods plant—but many of them have shut down in the last decade and people in this neighbourhood have been struggling to find a footing in the new economy. Davenport-Perth Neighbourhood and Community Health Centre, a respected multiservice agency that delivers both medical and neighbourhood programs (immigrant settlement, youth programs, adult drop-ins, crisis intervention) is right next door. There are a few marginal shops—convenience stores and TV repair, the windows crammed with random bits and pieces of ancient electronica coated in a thick layer of dust—but not much in the way of other businesses. It's more of a residential and industrial area, the kind new immigrants have flocked to for generations, attracted by the relatively cheap housing and nearby jobs. Today, Davenport West still has lots of immigrants, noise and pollution, but most of the jobs are gone—and the ones that remain are largely low-wage, service sector and, as a result, vulnerable.

To make matters worse for this struggling neighbourhood, a few years ago a new conservative provincial government, brandishing a platform they called the Common Sense Revolution, was elected with a lot of rhetoric about lazy poor people and a mandate to slash and burn the social welfare system. One of their first orders of business was chopping welfare rates by 21.6

percent. They also eliminated rent control and cancelled the building of new affordable housing.

For the already vulnerable families in Davenport West— where 20 percent of households live on social assistance and nearly two-thirds of single adults struggle below the poverty line—this "revolution" has been anything but common sense. Families here are frequently on the edge of losing their housing, forced to choose between paying the rent and feeding themselves or their children. There are no specific food assistance programs like the school meals offered in other industrialized nations or food stamps available to low-income people in the U.S. Our community members have few places to turn for help with food.

I saw the terrible impact of these cuts in my previous job at a homeless shelter, which was tucked beside a highway underpass in the east end. There, our numbers went through the roof as men from all over the city jostled in the lineup for one of the sixty or so thin plastic mats that we offered to put down on the floor. Before lights out, the guys—a mixed bag of the recently unemployed or separated, refugees, men with addiction issues and those struggling with mental illness—would sit in the smoke-filled room playing cards and watching TV. It was like a warehouse for people: stressful, dirty and depressing. There were arguments, fights, lice, tuberculosis and some severe foot problems (try walking all day every day in ill-fitting hand-me-down shoes and you'll understand).

Since then, Toronto has even sprouted a tent city on prime waterfront real estate, a sprawling, self-regulating enclave of homeless people that looks something like a refugee camp. Working with some of the most at-risk people in the city, it sometimes feels to me as if my hometown—once known as Toronto the Good—is falling to pieces.

Two of our other volunteers have just arrived at the food bank, and I wave hello. They're older women from a downtown church, both carefully coiffed and wearing white smocks over their clothes.

I push past the wobbly, fabric-covered divider that separates the bathroom door from what will shortly be the food bank lineup, and notice a fluorescent light flickering in the low ceiling. It's stressful enough here without the added irritation of flashing lights, so I drag out a ladder. One of the volunteers, a guy doing community service after being released from jail, points at me and laughs, "Hey, Nick! You're the chief cook and bottle washer!"

Nice. I smile at him grimly, then pull aside the ceiling tile. Something dark shifts overhead. I've got just enough warning to close my mouth before mouse turds shower down all over me.

—•—

IT SEEMS TO MANY OF US as if food banks have always been with us. But the truth is, food banking only became a widespread phenomenon in North America during the economic recession of the early 1980s. They were designed to be temporary, a stop-gap emergency measure to help people manage during the crisis, a supplement to the soup kitchens run by churches and missions, the meal delivery projects designed to get food to seniors, and the ad hoc school nutrition programs that could no longer meet the need.

It was John van Hengel, a volunteer at a St. Vincent de Paul community dining hall in Phoenix, Arizona, who is credited with inventing the concept in the 1960s. He discovered that while the people using the St. Vincent de Paul resources were going hungry, grocery stores around his area were throwing out edible food that had damaged packaging or was close to its expiration date. He began approaching grocery managers to donate this unsaleable but still edible food, and found that he actually had far more than his St. Vincent de Paul could use on its own.

Van Hengel began to look for a central location for what he called a "food bank." The way he conceived it, companies and individuals could make "deposits" of either food or funds, and community agencies could make "withdrawals" for their members. In their first year, van Hengel and other volunteers handed out more than 250,000 pounds of food to local agencies—shelters, soup kitchens, community programs and food pantries. The program was so successful that van Hengel himself became a proselytizer for the idea, serving as a consultant to the food banks that began to spring up all over.

In Canada, Edmonton claims the distinction of opening the nation's first official food bank. The city had been faced with a massive tide of people looking for work in the oil patch. But there weren't enough jobs to go around, and the social service system was overwhelmed. In 1981, some nonprofit organizations got together and created a food bank to serve the dual purpose of helping feed the hungry and of gleaning edible food from corporations and restaurants that would otherwise go to waste.

By 1985, there were ninety-four food banks across the country. In 1989, food banks from nine provinces banded together to establish a national organization to represent them on the public policy front. The Canadian Association of Food Banks, as the group then called itself (it's now Food Banks Canada), wrote a sunset clause into its constitution that called for the organization to wrap up within three years—once the crisis, presumably, was over. But eventually the clause had to be eliminated. By the early 1990s there were 292 food banks across Canada. A similar explosion of emergency food providers occurred in the U.S. during the same period. Between 1980 and 1989 in New York City, the number of emergency food programs grew from 30 to 487. The problem of hunger was only getting worse.

There are many reasons why the food bank idea appeals to people so much. There's the basic humanitarian belief that in a wealthy society like our own—let alone anywhere else—people shouldn't go hungry. There is also the added attraction of preventing unnecessary waste—a thrifty urge that tends to cut across political lines. Who doesn't remember their parents admonishing them to clean their plates because there are children starving in . . . (fill in the blank with whatever country is currently in turmoil)?

Food banks also help food corporations avoid hefty fees for getting rid of their unsaleable food. Instead of dumping, they can donate. Good Samaritan laws that make it difficult, if not impossible, for people to sue if the donated food causes health problems turn donating food into an especially attractive option. In a few jurisdictions, companies are even offered a tax credit for passing on their unsaleable food items.

With a powerful appeal that seems to cut across political and social lines, the notion of food banking has spread like wildfire. Today, there are food banks in countries from Canada and the United States to Britain, India, France and Japan. No longer considered temporary, food banks have become part of our international economy, our political landscape and our social fabric.

The Stop's story is not unlike that of other food banks, though in the beginning it didn't set out to be a food bank at all. It all started at the Church of Saint Stephen-in-the Fields in the vibrant downtown Toronto area known as Kensington

Market, a place where generations of immigrants—Jewish, Chinese, Caribbean, Latin American—have flavoured the narrow streets with their food and culture. In the early 1970s, Father Cam Russell and his family moved into the beautiful old rectory south of the church, and found they were on what he calls "the circuit." Unemployed or otherwise down-and-out people (mostly men) would travel the city looking for a meal, and his door was one of their stops. He and his family would regularly hear a knock and open up to find someone who asked, please (always please, he recalls), for a sandwich. Father Russell and his wife, Shirley, would invariably comply, producing so many baloney sandwiches they lost count.

After a few months, Father Russell started to ask people inside, and found that hunger wasn't the only problem people brought to his door—and often it wasn't even their biggest concern. They needed housing and help with the welfare system, they had lost their job or didn't know the language, they had mental health problems and/or trouble with their families or the law.

Father Russell started doing advocacy work, helping connect people with housing, lawyers or language classes. Eventually the need for his services outgrew his ability to manage both this work and his ministry at St. Stephen's. His largely Caribbean congregation was sympathetic but they couldn't finance expanding his advocacy work on their own, so Father Russell approached other churches in the neighbourhood and elsewhere in the city. Some came up with money. The Order of the Holy Cross, an Anglican monastic community, offered to provide staff. The group decided to continue what Father Russell had started and minister to those who had fallen through the cracks in society and the social service system. One thing all of the people involved agreed upon: they didn't want to become a food bank, simply handing out food and then shutting the door.

The new organization set up three days a week in St. Stephen's parish hall. It called itself Stop 103 for the street number on the door of the church and the legendary sign on Harry S. Truman's Oval Office desk that read "The buck stops here." (Even then most people just called it The Stop.) They offered coffee, advocacy and support to help people get back on their feet, as well as a bit of food from the cupboard if necessary.

By the mid-1980s, the organization had grown and moved to a storefront further uptown, and a recently ordained Anglican priest named Dennis Drainville (now the Bishop of Quebec) took over. Despite the original intentions, by the early 1990s Stop 103 had established itself as a food bank, feeding two thousand people every month. Still, it retained its activist roots. Rev. Rick Myer, who ran it for a number of years in that period, was dubbed the "warrior priest" in the local media for his outspoken questioning of food banks as an institution. He called them a band-aid and said he spent as much time trying to mobilize the poor as he did handing out emergency food hampers.

Other food banks were doing the same. A city task force on emergency food produced a tough, no-holds-barred paper around that time called "Not by bread alone: a strategy to eliminate the need for food banks." It sounded the alarm against food banks becoming "institutionalized."

During Rev. Myer's tenure at Stop 103, a large private donation allowed the organization to offer microgrants to people in the community, spawning start-up businesses from shoemaking and leather repair to handmade sweaters. Stop 103 even developed some nonprofit housing in Parkdale—a grand old neighbourhood in the west end of the city where huge Victorian homes had been colonized by artists and low-income

renters—to help people struggling with exorbitant housing costs.

By the time I arrived in 1998, the organization had dropped
its religious affiliation altogether (though many churches were
still involved) along with its tagline "Ministering Among People."
But like many other food banks overwhelmed by the need in
their community, it had also lost much of its original zeal for
advocacy and working on solutions to poverty and hunger. The
nonprofit housing had been spun off into a separate organization and the large donation had been spent. Plus, Stop 103 had
been forced to move twice in three years because of problems
with landlords. The small staff was exhausted, the organization
tired. Although it called itself an antipoverty agency, Stop 103
no longer directed resources toward challenging the policies and
politics that cause poverty in the first place.

Gillian Hewitt Smith, who joined the board of directors as
a twenty-three-year-old, almost two years before I came on the
scene, remembers that time at The Stop as focused entirely on
keeping the doors open. "It was a subsistence-level organization
focused on subsistence issues," she says. There was a budget of
$220,000, two full-time staff (as well as two part-timers) running
two programs: the food bank and Healthy Beginnings, a perinatal health and nutrition program for low-income women. The
food bank was considered the organization's main work; Healthy
Beginnings, though it had helped to dramatically improve birth
outcomes in the neighbourhood, was treated in many ways as
an extra.

The board, Gillian recalls, acted as an extension of the
staff, pitching in as required and making decisions about
finances, human resources, communications and fundraising.
It was a small and vulnerable organization working with very
vulnerable people.

There was, however, a fighting spirit left—I think of it as a kind of passion for social justice in the organization's DNA—and a desire among members of the board, especially, to change. When I took on the job, it was this potential that attracted me.

●—

I WAS BORN IN DAR ES SALAAM, Tanzania, five years after the East African nation declared its independence from Britain and during the heyday of its socialist experiment. It was a radical time, with President Julius Nyerere taking over industry and banking, and making all land common property. The University of East Africa (later the University of Dar es Salaam), where my Toronto-born parents worked—my father as a professor of African studies, my mother teaching English and doing her master's in history—was an intellectual hothouse, full of people from all over East Africa and the world who were committed to a new era of independence on the continent.

I don't remember a lot from those childhood years, though the experience shaped my own and my family's life. Even after we came back to Toronto when I was six years old, the wars for independence in Africa and the fight against apartheid in South Africa were everyday talk in our home (along with the basketball and baseball box scores). My parents were deeply engaged in the anti-apartheid movement through academic work, writing, mobilizing others and direct action. I was nine when my dad was arrested—thrown face-first onto a cricket pitch, the image captured on the front page of a national news-paper—while protesting the appearance of a South African cricket team in Toronto when the country's sports teams were supposed to be part of a boycott.

When I was fifteen, my parents decided we'd return to East

Africa to live and work in Mozambique for a year. I was a typical middle-class teenager at the time, convinced of my own invincibility. I don't remember being terribly concerned about leaving; it's my younger sister who, family legend has it, had to be pried from the tree in front of our house when we left. But Mozambique was like nothing I'd ever known. The country had recently declared independence from Portugal, but a war with agents of South Africa's apartheid regime meant bombings and terrorism in the countryside as well as regular news of rape and mass killing, and in Maputo, where we lived, shortages of everything from fuel to bread. I remember turning on the tap and no water would come out. I'd go to the market and there would be no food.

One of my chores was to stand in the bread line for our ration of milk and starchy buns—*pão* in Portuguese—the kind that became hard as a soccer ball after a couple of days. Several times a week, I'd head to a nearby apartment tower with a rationing station on the bottom floor and stand in line for what seemed like hours. There would be Mozambican women with babies on their backs, children much younger than I was, and a healthy collection of expats, some of whom arrived in chauffeur-driven limousines and seemed to think they deserved their *pão* before the rest of us. These self-important jerks would push to the front of the line while we all stood waiting like cattle. It was infuriating, but I felt completely powerless.

A few days before we left Mozambique to return to Canada for good, my parents' friend and my dad's colleague at the university, Ruth First—a South African exile and prominent opponent of the apartheid regime—was assassinated by a letter bomb sent by the South African police. She had just been preparing to host a farewell party for my dad.

It was a year that changed me in ways I'm still sorting out. I know I came back a very different kid than I left. My younger sister—whose passions and loyalty run strong—had to be pried from the tree in front of our place in Maputo, too.

Parts of that seminal experience returned to me when I began working in The Stop's food bank and saw the long lines of people snaking out the back door by the large garbage bins. People would start to line up hours before we opened the food bank: hungry people, people with nowhere to go, people worried we'd run out of food. Seeing it, I was thrown right back to those lines in Mozambique, remembering the humiliation and sense of powerlessness I felt.

Even though I'd just arrived at the organization and knew little about food banks, I felt certain it didn't have to be that way.

SEPTEMBER 1998. I park my bike near our Davenport office and go around the back of the apartment building toward the food bank doors. I pass two men sitting on the concrete raised flower beds just outside the window, eating straight from their food bank hamper. They're too hungry to wait until they get home. They don't look up as I walk by.

Inside, the tiny space is packed with people. I nod to the intake volunteer, who's listening carefully to an animated woman in a wheelchair explain why she needs to be served her hamper first. There are crying children and elderly people, a man standing near the bathroom riffling through a collection of plastic bags stuffed with papers.

I squeeze between two freestanding dividers, holding them still as I pass so they don't fall over, and head into the back. Electrical cords wind all over the floor and a collection of freezers punctuates the small area. A stack of flattened cardboard boxes and several towers of milk crates teeter in one corner; a wooden pallet loaded with canned goods and pasta sits in the middle of the floor.

Cliff is helping someone collect a food hamper, but he looks at me and holds up a finger. We need to talk.

Dorothy, a volunteer who's been at The Stop for years, bustles by carrying a cardboard box full of canned soup. "You wouldn't believe it in here, today," she says, shaking her head. "Crazy."

I knew it was going to be a challenging day when I saw the almost-full moon last night. It seems absurd, though I've heard doctors and nurses say the same thing: a full moon invariably means there's going to be trouble—arguments, even fights, general mayhem.

When Cliff finishes, he motions with his head for me to follow him next door to the large community room that we barely use. The space has a small kitchenette with intense dark blue walls, windows on one side and a raised area at one end that can act as a stage but is usually packed with broken chairs and other debris. It's supposed to be a community space for the residents of the apartment building, but they rarely use it. We host Healthy Beginnings here because we need the space, and provide a free lunch for volunteers at the tables after their food bank shift is over. It seems insane to have six or seven people in this huge room while we pack hundreds of people into the tiny food bank on the other side of the door. But we are so under-resourced, we don't have enough people to program it or make it safe.

Cliff is solidly built with a prematurely receding hairline, a thick moustache and a zany sense of humour. He's five years younger than I am, though he'd already been working at the organization for five years when I arrived. He started as a placement student in a local college's community worker program. But Cliff's experience with poverty began long before he joined

The Stop. He describes himself as a neglected kid, growing up in the city's east end with his mom and twin sister, who is developmentally challenged. He remembers the day when he and his family were forced to use a food bank for the first time. He was seven or eight, and his mom had just been served notice of eviction. The food bank was in the basement of their local Salvation Army. He remembers five or six lines of people, each about ten deep, leading toward a curtain. He watched his mother disappear behind the cloth and emerge with a food hamper. It meant they'd have dinner that night.

The people who use our food bank recognize in Cliff a kindred spirit, and they're devoted to him because he's fair and compassionate and works really hard. Fortunately, he's also open to changing things. We have recently created a new number system that's taken the place of the much-loathed lineup, we're training volunteers more thoroughly and, after hearing one too many complaints about the interview and food hamper hand-out process, we're making it less invasive and more consistent. Unlike at some British food banks where hungry people must be referred by "care professionals" such as a doctor, social worker or police, anyone who lives in our catchment area can come in our door. We don't want people to be deterred from seeking help by what could be a difficult need-assessment process.

We've also been thinking carefully about the language and terminology we use. Instead of "users" or "clients," people who use the food bank are now *members*. Once you come in the door, you join the organization and receive a membership card that entitles you to certain rights (to be treated with respect, to receive a food hamper once a month) and also to certain responsibilities (to treat others with respect, to not engage in sexist or racist behaviour).

Cliff and I both know that changing a few words and introducing a number system instead of a lineup isn't going to solve the problems of hunger and poverty in a community, but it does do something important to the way people feel here. There are people who would scoff at these kinds of subtle changes—different word choices, a coat of paint—as red herrings, detracting from the real issues at stake. But after a stint organizing tenants in a downtown public housing community called Alexandra Park in the mid-1990s, I became convinced that the physical (the way a place looks and feels) could determine the social (how people feel and behave in that space).

Alex Park was built in the late 1960s. Like many public housing projects created at the time, it had no through roads, lots of common space (though little of it green) and loads of dead ends. It was intended to be a safe place for children to play, free from having to worry about cars. By the 1990s, when I worked there, the common spaces were in ruins, the townhouses were rundown, and the neighbourhood was known for drugs and violence.

Still, as I discovered rather quickly, many people in the community were profoundly connected to the place and to each other. There was Sonny Atkinson, a long-time resident who became the neighbourhood voice for safety and community advocacy. A big man with huge hands and an air of authority, he argued that the brick and concrete barriers separating one back door from the other and the townhouses from the street were actually security threats, providing not privacy for residents but, instead, cover for drug dealers. After he and others in the community received permission to tear down some of the walls, crime activity was swiftly reduced. Their initiative became a powerful symbol of the potential for change in Alex Park, and Atkinson and others began to take charge of their environment and their community. They argued that tenants deserved better than to wait months, even years, for simple repairs from the municipal housing authority, and that residents who could do such repairs themselves should be paid for their labour. Soon, the idea of taking over and running the place as a self-governing co-operative began to form.

My job, paid for by the tenants' association, was to help them get there. I worked in Alex Park for a year talking to people, organizing and facilitating community meetings, and asking residents to voice their concerns about the buildings and the potential for a co-op. At the referendum to decide if the co-operative had the necessary backing, hundreds of previously disenfranchised people came out. The support for conversion to a self-managing co-op was decisive. It would take many more years to actually make the change, but something essential had returned to Alexandra Park: dignity.

It was a formative experience for me. People at the housing authority had told me before I began that such pavement pounding wouldn't be worth the wear on my sneakers, that people in Alex Park didn't care about their community and wouldn't be interested in a co-operative. But knocking on doors, sharing tea and stories with residents, getting to know people there, I found something quite different. Not a single one of them wanted to be poor or was even remotely ambivalent about their circumstances. Instead, the residents cared deeply about their homes, their lives and a better future for themselves and their kids.

So when I arrived at The Stop, changing our physical environment to make our members' experience more respectful and dignified seemed like an obvious place to begin. Things like building a real barrier between the bathroom door and the wide-open food bank space so it no longer felt like everyone knows your business. Like painting the dirty grey walls and replacing the water-stained ceiling tiles. Like building interview rooms where people who needed support, advice or referrals could talk in privacy.

Having a more welcoming space and better systems for getting people the food they need shifts the emphasis away from charitable handouts toward something more interactive, engaged and respectful. It's difficult enough to come and ask for help without being treated like a second-class citizen when you do. The people who use food banks shouldn't feel they have to check their dignity at the door. Cliff understands this intuitively. Still, some of the changes we're making are raising questions in the community, and he's on the front lines of the complaints.

"It's the clothing depot this time," he says once we close the door, not bothering with pleasantries. "People are angry we got rid of it. Sally was here again making a big fuss. She brought this."

He hands me a letter. It's written in pencil and runs over three pages, moving from neat cursive to big, emphatic block letters with lots of exclamation marks. It's written by a single working mother with two children who explains that she relies on the clothing depot to clothe her children, and relies on Sally, a community member and volunteer, to pick the clothes up during work hours and bring them to her. "What will I do now?" she writes. "HOW WILL I MANAGE???"

It's a heartbreaking letter. But we got rid of the clothing depot because it was a nightmare for the organization. Some mornings we'd come in and find the food bank door blocked with torn black garbage bags stuffed with clothes, random bits and bobs strewn about the street. And once we got the stuff inside, we didn't have washing machines or anywhere to store it in an orderly fashion. There was supposed to be a system so that each person who needed something would have an opportunity to look through the stash, but it was nearly impossible to implement. Sally and others would often leave with several garbage bags full. They said that they were distributing the clothes to family members and friends, but we had no way of making sure it was fair or that there was enough for other people who also needed help.

Managing this ad hoc clothing exchange was taking over our small, already crowded space and distracting volunteers, as well as taking Cliff and me from our main work: food. We decided that in order to focus on doing what we do properly, the clothing depot had to go.

"I'll speak to her," I say, holding up the letter. "And we'll find her a referral for an agency that can help her with clothes for herself and the kids."

"And Sally? She's furious. She thinks we're getting rid of it because we don't trust her."

"I'll talk to Sally, too."

Cliff shrugs and heads back into the food bank. I'm left alone in the community room. It's cavernous in here compared to next door, with its long bank of windows on the north side looking out onto the townhouses. But in addition to hiring more staff, we'll also have to convince the residents' association to share it if we are going to use the space more often. Some of the more vocal tenants have been complaining that the food bank brings a "bad element" into Symington Place.

As I'm heading out the door, Dorothy, the volunteer, intercepts me. "Can I talk to you?"

It's always like this. People want to talk. Volunteers, community members, staff. It means it takes a lot longer to do everything, but it's one of the things I like most about my job. Dorothy and I sit down at one of the folding tables. She's sixtyish, with no-nonsense straight hair, a simple white shirt and clean white running shoes. She connected with The Stop through her uptown Anglican church, which is a long-time funder, and she's been around here for years. But today she looks nervous, as if she's been steeling herself to say something and now that the opportunity is here, she's not sure if she can go through with it.

"What's up?" I say.

Dorothy takes a deep breath. "Well. I'm not happy with some of the new policies. And I'm not the only one. Not happy." She takes another deep breath.

"Volunteers come here because they want to be of use," she continues. "They want to help. And they are used to being trusted—trusted to make judgment calls. And now, with all the new systems, it's not like that anymore."

"Did something happen?"

"Well, no. I mean, yes. Something always happens. The new geographic boundaries, for instance. People come in and they're confused about why we can't give them food," she says.

"You know why we did that, don't you?" I ask her. "We were getting people from all over the city. We'd never refuse someone on their first visit. But we're a neighbourhood-based organization. We need to make sure we can serve our neighbourhood. There are other organizations in other areas."

"I know," she says. "But when someone comes all the way here to get food, do you really want us to turn them away? I can't do it. Just because they don't live around here doesn't mean they're not hungry. I mean, we used to use our judgment. We could make a call if it made sense or not. Aren't we supposed to be helping the needy? They *are* the needy—it doesn't matter where they live."

Dorothy and I continue to talk, but she just gets more upset.

The changes we're making are rocking the boat across the organization—for community members and volunteers. Even changes that seem unequivocally positive have been greeted with concern by some. After members take a number and wait to be called for the food bank, for instance, they are now given an opportunity to *choose* their food from among various options on the shelves. We still aim to provide a three-day supply of emergency food once a month. But whereas volunteers used to simply pack the hampers and hand them out, now members can decide between, say, a can of tuna or salmon, rice or pasta—according to the number of people in their family and what we have in stock that day. We think it's a more respectful way of meeting people's needs. But there have been complaints that it isn't efficient. It takes too much time, some volunteers say, and anyway, it's not as if we're operating a grocery store—shouldn't people just be happy with whatever we give them?

The new membership cards and interview process we've created are also contentious, mostly, as Dorothy noted, because they enforce clearer rules around who can access the food bank and how often. In the past, when someone seemed really stressed out or knew the volunteer or had a very emotional (and no doubt true) story, they might get more, or something extra, maybe even a second hamper that month. Now, we're working hard to ensure the quantities are equitable, our procedures transparent, and we don't make exceptions. Period.

Of course, it's not easy for any of us to say no to someone who's obviously struggling, but some long-time volunteers—and those community members who benefited from the looser rules—are genuinely angry about the change. Volunteers who come to us because they like the idea of helping the less fortunate or because they see charity as part of their role in the world, often for religious reasons, find it especially bewildering.

But as we've tried to explain, you have to ask yourself what you're going to say to the next person who *does* meet the criteria when there's nothing left. And who decides who should be an exception and who shouldn't? Creating clear, consistent systems is the only way we can maintain any sort of fairness and integrity, not to mention establish trust with our community.

But the most important, overarching point of all of the changes we've been making is to move The Stop away from the old charitable model, where one group of privileged people helps the underprivileged, perpetuating an us-and-them atmosphere.

A few years ago, I heard a radio program in which a reporter talked to men in a lineup for a downtown soup kitchen and asked them how it felt to be waiting there. One guy paused and then expressed himself so eloquently that his words continue to haunt me. He said it was demeaning. He told the reporter that it feels like the volunteers giving out the soup have a halo around their heads and he's coming up to them, hands out—a taker. It might make the volunteers feel good about themselves, he said, but it makes him feel terrible. No one wants a handout.

Dorothy and I don't come to a resolution. She leaves the food bank feeling, I think, that even though I listened I didn't really hear her.

The truth is, the more time I spend in the food bank, the more convinced I am that the changes we are making are essential. And the more certain I am of the failure of a charitable approach to hunger and poverty that serves the interests of food corporations and some volunteers better than it does the poor themselves.

Instead of simply "helping the needy" by handing out food—a one-off transaction—there is incredible potential here at The Stop to engage with the people of this neighbourhood to take charge of their own lives. To provide support as they articulate and work toward their own dreams for the future.

Anyway, it's clear from those members who come back every month and the new people who turn up every week that giving out cans of soup or beans once a month does nothing to make poverty and hunger go away. And as Father Russell noticed in the early days in Kensington Market, people may need something to eat, but those who come to us also need support or a referral, safe housing, advocacy, health care, new skills, even friendship.

When Dorothy is gone, I go outside for some fresh air before spelling off Cliff in the food bank. People are still trickling in and there's a small cluster congregating by a chain-link fence nearby. I go around the side of the building and head into the parking lot that separates Symington Place from the health centre next door. A few mattresses and other large pieces of cast-off furniture have been thrown alongside the building, awaiting garbage day. Plastic bags flutter from the nearly barren trees.

I see two women I recognize from the food bank. One is in her late twenties with short, slicked-back blond hair pulled into a tight little ponytail. She's wearing an oversized Toronto Maple Leafs jacket and protectively gripping the handle of her stroller while she talks to an older woman in sweats who is clasping a bundle buggy. As I approach, I see the older woman throw up her free hand in exasperation and the younger one step back a bit.

"Hey," I say when they see me. "How's it going?"

"Fine," they each say with small pinched smiles. I peer inside the younger woman's stroller, but there's no baby. It's full of plastic bags with food from the food bank.

"We're swapping," she says.

"I'll give her these bananas and the canned corn if she gives me her laundry soap," the older woman explains.

"That's quite a choice," I say.

The younger woman passes the box of soap out of the stroller with a shrug. She accepts a small plastic bag with bananas poking out the top in return. She shakes her head and looks at me. "Yeah—some choice," she says.

TWO

GARDENS WON'T SAVE THE PLANET, BUT THEY'LL MAKE IT A WHOLE LOT NICER PLACE TO LIVE

OCTOBER 1998. We've just finished setting up the food bank for the day when a white parks department truck pulls up at the doors. Cliff and I go outside to see what's up. It's unseasonably warm, one of those bright fall days when it seems as if the winter will never come. Brian Green, our local parks supervisor, hops out of the driver's side. He's tanned, with a slightly daydreamy air that belies the fact that he really knows how to make things happen. He's the kind of guy who understands his parks job is about far more than cutting grass and keeping up playground equipment. One of his young staffers steps down from the passenger seat. She's smiling, too.

They don't say much, just open the back flap of the truck to reveal a full load of zucchini and tomatoes, some leafy greens, yellow and green beans and small, deep purple eggplants. Cliff and I look at them and then each other in disbelief.

"It's yours. From Earlscourt. All of it," Brian says proudly.

I'm not sure what I expected when he came into my office last spring and proposed using the overgrown bocce court in nearby Earlscourt Park for a vegetable plot. It helped, certainly, that he offered a staff member to work on the garden with our volunteers and community members over the spring and summer. It wouldn't have been possible with just our tiny, already overextended staff. I said yes to Brian's idea without thinking twice.

When I started at The Stop, one of the first things I saw was a food access audit done in the neighbourhood several years before. The report mentioned an interest in community gardens in Davenport West but, as the author noted in what I read as a sardonic tone, "in our surveys of agency staff and users, the option of the community garden came up frequently, but predominantly as a good idea for someone else."

The idea of a garden associated with our food bank made a lot of sense to me. Participants and our food bank would get fresh veggies, and it would be a great way to connect with community members. We've seen a few tomatoes and cucumbers here and there since the middle of the summer, but the bounty now is a shock. A truckload of vegetable goodness (and more to come) for the food bank—and at a time when there's a near crisis in the sector with low levels of food available for distribution. It couldn't have arrived at a better moment.

It's hard to believe, in fact, that it came at all. When we first started to dig, the garden didn't look like much. A flat patch of churned-up grass, some sandy soil. The 3,500-square-foot plot was sandwiched between a neglected running track to the west and a little-used alleyway to the east. The bocce court had been made obsolete several years before when an indoor one was built at the recreation centre that stretches across the top of the park. The abandoned spot seemed distinctly unpromising.

But the day we started to dig the holes to install fencing around the patch, there were lots of volunteers interested in helping out: Gordon, a regular at The Stop who is always willing to pitch in; Kiet, a long-time volunteer who is blind and deaf but manages quite well thanks to his determination and the help of his full-time support worker. Park neighbours gathered around, too, wondering what we were doing. Everyone had an opinion. Dig deeper, go wider; the post is straight, it's crooked.

And everyone wanted to know what we were going to plant. An older Italian gentleman in a sweater with patched elbows who used to play bocce on the court offered some tomato seedlings. A Portuguese grandma chasing her tiny, excited granddaughter said she'd bring by some kale seeds. "For *caldo verde!*"

Another man watched us skeptically from his backyard, which overlooks the garden. He hung on the back of his fence staring at us as if we were competitors in a garden contest. And, in fact, I could see he had quite a plot himself, the soil rich-looking and prepped for planting, a jumble of wooden sticks and plastic pots lying here and there like the aftermath of a battle. But over the summer, that man, Herman, surprised us all by becoming instrumental in maintaining the space. Laid off from his long-time job at a nearby factory, he had time on his hands. And with a perfect view of the garden from his backyard, he was able to shoo away pesky animals and people who ventured too close to the fledgling plants. He also started taking a deep personal interest, building a more secure fence and a new storage cabinet for the garden, putting in tomato plants, watering and weeding. And he didn't neglect his own patch either. His enormous tomato plants and thriving beans are the envy of our gardeners.

With the help of our local public health unit, Brian and his staffer got local schoolchildren involved as well, planting seedlings in their classrooms to be transplanted into the garden, and talking to them not only about gardening and the environment but also about the poverty and hunger that exists in their neighbourhood.

A crowd from the food bank and neighbours from the townhouses that look onto the entrance have started to gather around the parks department truck. From the oohs and aahs you'd think no one had ever seen fresh eggplant or tomatoes before. There's no question they make the canned ham on our food bank shelves look a lot less appetizing. We don't even have to ask: everyone helps to bring the overflowing boxes inside.

PEOPLE HAVE BEEN GROWING FOOD in urban areas since the beginning of cities themselves. But greater density and the idea that cities are for industry and production while rural areas are for growing food—as well as the notion that food is grown by specialized people in a specialized process—has conspired to make urban farming unusual. City vegetable plots have never died, though, especially among certain immigrant communities.

In the neighbourhood where I live, the Italians and Portuguese are well known for their creative gardens—apple and pear trees on postage-stamp lawns, zucchinis draped from old steel pipes and hockey sticks, tomatoes growing in apple baskets and plastic buckets on any available surface. We're across the street from a Portuguese man named Tony whose entire side lawn running the length of the house is cultivated with tomatoes, kale, beans and various fruit trees. He could feed many of our neighbours in the summer months.

Tony remains an anomaly, but more and more people around the world are beginning to see the potential of growing food in cities. Chefs and environmentalists cultivate bees in parks, on rooftops and in backyards. In Detroit, long-neglected lots are being turned into massive urban farms. Supermarkets like Toronto's Big Carrot and London's Thornton's Budgens grow vegetables on their roofs. In Delhi and Mombasa and Hong Kong, people are cultivating alleys, balconies and abandoned lots to grow food.

Our community garden is part of this explosion in urban growing, but even while our harvests become more and more bountiful and our garden programming becomes more varied and fulsome, we have never considered that the goal of these projects is to bring an end to hunger in Davenport West. Considering the short growing season and the relatively small area, they simply couldn't do the job. Food policy pioneer Rod MacRae and the co-authors of a paper on the potential for urban agriculture in Toronto estimate that—taking into account available land and rooftop space—the city could produce just 10 percent of the fresh vegetables currently consumed. It's an important goal, certainly, and one we're working toward and supporting as part of the city's urban agriculture community. But at The Stop, our garden is primarily a way to build community, engage people with their food and foster new skills.

One-on-one, through informal sessions, town hall meetings, surveys and programs, community members talk about the shame and humiliation they feel having to use food banks and receive charity. Gardens don't prevent that feeling, of course, but they help alter the conversation. People might become involved in planting or weeding and have a chance to bring home some of the food. And when they share the work and the produce, their connection to what they eat, to each other and to the organization changes. It's no longer a "we give, they take" proposition. It's collaborative—and something to build on.

Bookshelves groan with the theory behind this "community development" approach to supporting people to improve their lives. The late Brazilian intellectual Paulo Freire—with his seminal work, *Pedagogy of the Oppressed*—has been especially influential. His focus was education because he saw it as inherently political; Freire believed in fostering social change through working with the poor and marginalized. He advocated for valuing lived experience, for people being agents of change in their own communities (as opposed to having it imposed from outside), for dialogue and working together as a function of mutual respect.

I read Freire while doing my master's degree in sociology, studying the potential for popular education in labour organizations, and found his writing inspirational. But for me, none of what we're trying to accomplish at The Stop is truly about theory or strategy; it's more a way of being in the world. Listening to people—whether it's in the garden, kitchen, food bank or classroom—is the root. It's a glass-half-full approach that begins from the premise that people are the experts on their own lives and, given the right support, have wise and intelligent ideas about how to improve them.

Of course, like everything worth doing, community development requires patience and a certain amount of optimism. There are bound to be frequent setbacks and detours. When I worked at the homeless shelter, one of our initiatives was helping to create a shared business—a community economic development project.

A colleague and I put up posters and convinced some guys to come to a meeting to discuss the kinds of businesses they'd like to be involved in. About ten men showed up—some for the free coffee and doughnuts, others because they wanted to work. There was Ron, a stringy older guy with a quick wit, who'd spent his life on the move, riding the rails and criss-crossing the country; James, a teenager from Grenada waiting on his refugee claim; and Mike, a forty-something First Nations man who spent his days waiting for work from the contractors who troll the downtown streets hiring cheap manual labour.

Once we started talking, we discovered that all of the guys had some skill and experience working with wood—some had been contractors, others general labourers or carpenters. We decided that together we'd create a woodworking co-operative. We applied for and received a small city grant to buy some tools, and looked around for a wood shop to rent or borrow. We found space at a local community centre and launched Inch by Inch Woodworking Co-operative by making small cedar garden boxes for container planting. From there we moved on to wooden rocking horses and garden chairs. We were even commissioned to build a cabinet for a popular downtown restaurant.

A lot of the time, we were making it up as we went along, but the guys were pleased with the work, proud to be connected with something constructive, and glad to have some extra money. Not everyone stuck around, and sometimes it was diffi-cult to find them when we needed them. Many of these men were living dangerous and itinerant lives. One of the guys who passed through Inch by Inch turned up dead, killed on the street. But there were also triumphs, like Ron, who managed to gain enough stability in his life that he entered supportive housing and eventually moved into his own apartment.

My colleague and I often joked that we were doing pretty well at the community development part of it—but not so much the *economic* element. None of the men were going to become rich by building rocking horses, they might not even become self-supporting, but the co-operative helped push back the four walls of the shelter or rooming house they were living in, giving them a positive place to be with others. For all of them, it was a better spot to begin the long, difficult work of changing their lives.

At The Stop, we see the garden as a similar stake in the ground—a beginning, rather than an end in itself.

SEPTEMBER 1999. Tania Julien is a slight young woman with a big smile. She's sitting at the Healthy Beginnings registration desk in the community space chatting with the women, handing out public transit tokens and a small grocery voucher to help the moms buy healthy food.

When she first turned up at The Stop seven years ago, Tania was twenty-one and pregnant for the first time. She was shy and frightened. Her strict parents thought she was too young to have a child and didn't like her Trinidadian boyfriend, Geddes. The couple had moved out and found an apartment on Davenport Road, but they were barely getting by. They had little money or support. Tania's doctor at a local health clinic was so concerned that she wasn't gaining weight that he recommended she go to Healthy Beginnings and pick up a voucher and a food hamper.

Tania had never been to a food bank before. But she's a self-described "people person," and it wasn't long after she started attending the Healthy Beginnings program that she'd made friends. Geddes got involved, too, making Caribbean dishes in the small kitchen for the moms. The other women especially loved his peanut butter punch—a hearty peanut butter milkshake spiced with nutmeg.

Tania liked talking to the public health nurses and the other women who'd already been through childbirth. They swapped stories and advice, baby equipment and laughter. The nurses were happy to answer her questions about what was happening to her body and how to make sure she and her baby remained healthy. Attending workshops—on everything from prenatal yoga and labour pain to postpartum depression—Tania began to make sense of the barrage of confusing new information she'd been hit with since learning she was pregnant. At first, she wasn't sure about breastfeeding, but the more she learned about it and talked to the other moms, the more convinced she was that nursing was right for her.

After Ashley was born, Tania returned, seeking help from the nurses when she had trouble getting the baby to latch, volunteering and helping to start a Young Moms Program. It was a relief to have a place to go during the day, because at home by herself with the baby she was bored and lonely.

When Mercedes, Tania and Geddes' second child, was born a few years later, Tania came back again and found support at Healthy Beginnings. She became involved with the advisory committee for the program and even joined The Stop's board of directors.

I've known Tania since I started here. I stop at the desk to say hello, but she's too busy to talk. She's volunteering in the food bank these days, but still helps out at Healthy Beginnings when they're swamped. There are lots of new women today. You can always tell the new participants: they're hesitant, uncertain where to land their eyes.

Shirley Eto, one of the nurses from the public health unit in the building, is circulating, her reassuring voice and presence calming to everyone there. They've organized a workshop on making your own baby food. The nurses will do a hands-on demonstration where the women can give it a try.

I often eat lunch with Shirley and the rest of the public health team in their offices—partly because their space is bigger and more comfortable than our tiny, poorly ventilated office, and partly because it's nice to share a meal with them. They eat communally on a regular basis, organizing potluck lunches and telling stories. The nurses know this neighbourhood inside and out, and understand intimately the toll that poverty takes on families. They tell me about the nearby apartment building where prostitutes turn tricks and smoke crack in the hallways and people are beaten up for looking at someone the wrong way; they tell me about the public housing townhouses to the west where people live in close quarters with their extended families, but the places are so neat you could eat off the floor.

I walk around the community space, chatting with the women in the program, checking out the new babies. It's noisy and full of life in here. Some women are barely showing, others look ready to give birth at any moment. I see some older moms casting gentle been-there, done-that glances at an exhausted-looking pregnant woman who's trying to convince her older daughter to go into the free childcare room next door. One of the women I've known since I came to The Stop asks me about my own newborn son. Everyone knows about Ben, who arrived by emergency Caesarean two months before his due date this past summer, weighing just three and a half pounds. He was in hospital for a month, and had to stay in an incubator for the first two weeks. My wife, Andrea, and I weren't even allowed to hold him until a week after he was born.

"He's great," I tell the moms. "Keeping us up at night. But growing and smiling. Laughing, too."

The women ask me for pictures and I promise to bring one next week. I fold up one of the baby-food handouts I find on a table and tuck it in my pocket for the day Ben is old enough for solids. I always like dropping in on Healthy Beginnings. It never fails to make me feel hopeful about what we're doing.

It was back in 1989 when prescient public health nurses noticed the prevalence of low-birth-weight babies in Davenport West. Toronto has a higher rate of these births compared to the rest of the country, and it's places like our neighbourhood, one of the poorest in the city, that skew the stats upward. Poverty, poor nutrition—both before and during pregnancy—teenage parenting, violence in the home, smoking, stress, and drug and alcohol use are the kinds of risk factors the nurses were seeing in their daily practice.

These infants, some born early, some small for their gestational age, have increased rates of illness and death, and often require hospital care after birth—which has high emotional and psychological costs for the moms and families, and high financial costs for the health care system. The U.S. Institute of Medicine has calculated the average price tag to care for a premature baby's first year at more than $50,000. And that's not even taking into account the possible long-term health problems such as learning and developmental challenges, respiratory problems and other chronic health issues these children sometimes experience.

Having gone through our own struggles with a premature baby, I know the toll it takes. We had lots of resources at our disposal—including the support of family and friends—and it was still one of the hardest, most emotionally draining experiences of my life.

The nurses and their partners made the case to government funders that early intervention—supporting low-income women throughout their pregnancy with healthy food, education and peer support—could readily alter the negative outcomes and save the health care system a huge amount. It made sense to team up with The Stop because many low-income pregnant women in the area were using our food bank, yet their special dietary needs still weren't being met.

Healthy Beginnings, with its collaboration between The Stop, public health and a number of other local agencies, became a model for perinatal nutrition and support programs across the province and, later, the country. Every Wednesday since the program began, The Stop has hosted as many as fifty or sixty women. Nearly 100 percent of infants born to women in the program are delivered at normal weights, and almost all of the women breastfeed for their baby's first six months.

With this kind of track record and so much that is working about the program, it was strange to me that when I arrived at The Stop, Healthy Beginnings was treated as unconnected to the organization's "real" work in the food bank. I'm not sure it was intentional, exactly; instead it was a function of the insatiable demand for emergency food. As I'm learning first-hand, when there is so much need, it takes a Herculean effort to focus energy anywhere other than food bank handouts. Healthy Beginnings simply didn't fit into The Stop's emergency response approach to the problem.

Seeing the women here—from Jamaica, Guatemala, China, Southern Africa and Canada—eating together and sharing their knowledge, as well as learning from the staff, it looks to me like exactly the kind of program people in Davenport West have asked for. Like the Earlscourt community garden, it's not just about supporting people once they've hit rock bottom, but about helping people prevent themselves from getting there. Healthy Beginnings uses food as a bouncing-off point to connect with community members, and is structured so that it can be shaped according to what the women want and need.

Shirley calls the Healthy Beginnings moms over to the tiny kitchen where they're doing the demonstration on homemade baby food. As I head into the food bank area, I hear the whirr of the food processor filling the air.

OCTOBER 1999. George is a marmalade cat who showed up one day a few months ago and never left. He rubs his warm tabby fur against my pant leg as I stand at the food bank intake table. George is a mouser, the only reason I tolerate him, though sometimes it seems as if the other staff and volunteers at The Stop would gladly open an animal shelter if I showed the slightest hint of interest. I shake him off my leg and walk over to the shelves where Cliff is stacking cans of tomato sauce. Don the box man— an elderly volunteer who comes in once a week and does nothing but break down boxes—gives me a wave. The food bank isn't open until noon but it's already busy in here.

In fact, The Stop is getting busier all the time. In addition to the new paint and new interview rooms, we've been working to create a more comfortable atmosphere. There's always coffee available and we encourage people who come for hampers to stick around for housing referrals and advocacy on their immigration, legal or welfare issues. All of this is helping to take the edge off some of the desperation as people linger and receive help on the other issues that bring them to our door.

And there are a lot of issues. In a recent survey, we discovered that 65 percent of food bank users spent more than half of their income on rent. One-third of families in our neighbourhood live below the poverty line. Over and over, people describe how hard it is to manage with high rental costs and low incomes—food always comes last on their list of priorities. And there's little hope for most people, especially families, looking for public housing in this city: there's already a five- to ten-year wait. Many families and singles in Davenport West are doubling up, living in cramped quarters, or couch-surfing. It isn't the hard-core homelessness I saw with the men at the shelter. It's not what you picture when you think of people living in ravines, underpasses or shelters. This homelessness is much more hidden—but it's homelessness all the same.

So we've partnered with two other organizations—Davenport-Perth next door and the local legal clinic—to create a Homelessness Prevention Project. Designed to support people on the edge of losing their accommodation, the project allows us to train and hire regular housing advocates who help settle disputes with landlords or deal with social-assistance problems that threaten housing. These are people from the community who have experience living marginally. Armed with training, knowledge and information, as well as legal support, they are helping their neighbours. We're also hosting community forums to educate people about their rights around landlord-tenant and social-assistance issues.

Through the small, dirty window on the north end of the food bank, I spot a car pulling up at the doors. It's Richard Thompson, the man who picks up food from his local greengrocers. My heart sinks. There's no question he's a well-intentioned man who's devoted a huge amount of time to this organization. But we've introduced veggies from the garden, started buying fresh food when we can, and have more good-quality perishable items coming in thanks to a relationship with Second Harvest, a local food reclamation organization. The bruised fruit and overripe vegetables he collects have no place at The Stop.

We've been turning down damaged cans and opened packages since I've been here—partly because of safety concerns, but also because being given such throwaways makes food bank recipients feel like second-class citizens. Cliff and I have also been talking about putting our collective foot down and saying no to the super-processed food and failed experiments—hot chili–flavoured mac and cheese, zesty taco chicken nuggets, lemon and herb potato-coating powder that is actually glorified salt—that find their way into the food bank slipstream. If these industrial food rejects don't have a place in the market, why should the poor have to eat them?

The food bank experience is so often a slow, painful death of the spirit—forcing yourself to visit a crowded, ill-equipped, makeshift place, answer personal questions, swallow your pride as you wait in a lineup. Reaching the front of the line only to be offered bizarre processed food products or slimy, wilted lettuce that couldn't be revived with electric shock treatment is the final nail in the coffin.

I'm going to have to talk to Richard about it.

"How's it going?" I ask as I help him carry in the boxes from his trunk.

"Alright," he says. "Some of my regulars weren't around today. But I got a lot of peppers for some reason. And most of them aren't in bad shape. Not too soft. I know you asked about that."

We make another trip out to the car. It's now or never.

"Richard," I begin, "you know we really appreciate all your work."

"Yes?" he says, already suspicious.

"But I think that you should stop going to your stores. We shouldn't be giving out this food. Some of it's okay, but most of it isn't. Look at this—" I pick up a gnarly carrot and it bends over like a piece of fresh licorice. "Would you eat this?"

Richard's generally ruddy face turns redder. He sets down the box and turns to face me. "Why not? It's just a bit soft. It's not going to kill anyone. Aren't the people who come here hungry? Isn't it better than nothing?"

"Well," I say, knowing there's no way this conversation is going to go well, "I think people who use the food bank deserve to eat good food."

"Of course," he says. "I'm not saying they don't. It's just I've worked really hard to develop these relationships with the shops. They didn't want to give the food to me at first, but I convinced them it was a waste to throw it out. That they were helping people. That I was helping people. Do you want me to just throw it in the garbage?"

Richard is looking more upset, which is not what I want. He is a great volunteer. He's also sent us lots of other volunteers from his church and his group of friends and neighbours. And the fact is, Richard isn't alone in his feelings. The old "beggars can't be choosers" maxim is deeply ingrained in our society. We say it—and think it—without much consideration of what it means, or what applying this punitive logic to real people does to them or to our sense of responsibility and connection to each other.

"You *have* been helping people, Richard. You do great work for us here," I say. "I hope you'll continue to volunteer."

"So why was all this"—he gestures a hand at the box in his trunk—"okay before *you* got here?"

I'm a bit surprised, since we've always gotten on well, but I'm not going to take the bait. I know he's angry and probably embarrassed. It might feel like an attack on him, but it's actually about a sea change in our approach. People like Dorothy (who tendered her resignation as a volunteer not long after our conversation) and Richard, as well as others who don't voice their concerns to me, no doubt see me as some young upstart coming in and changing everything. Things that were working just fine, thank you very much.

Except they weren't working. Not the electrical cords winding their dangerous way through the entire space, not the squishy red peppers or the dented cans of pork and beans, not the once-a-week volunteers deciding who gets extra and who doesn't. And not the focus on emergency handouts, like a row of sandbags in front of the tidal wave of need in our community.

After a pause that feels endless, Richard finally says, "I guess you don't need me." He gives a shrug.

"It's not that . . . Richard . . ."

But he isn't listening anymore. Richard places the last of the boxes in my arms, and goes around to the driver's side of his car. I stand there watching, the heavy box digging into my forearms while he drives away.

WHEN I WAS IN MY FIRST YEAR at the University of Toronto, I tried out for the varsity basketball team and was one of the last men chosen. I'd played all through high school and helped my team win the city championship twice. I played point guard and was crazy about the game. But I wasn't recruited by

U of T and had a lot to prove to secure my spot on the squad.

So when I slept through my alarm to meet the team bus for our first weekend tournament out of town, I wasn't surprised that the coach didn't wait for me. I figured I'd screwed up my basketball career forever. But then I remembered that my high school team was playing a tournament in the same place, four hours away, that weekend. I called up my old coach and begged him for a lift. When I showed up at the hotel where the varsity team was staying, ready to practice, the coach didn't say much. But that night, with ten minutes to go in a close game, he called down the bench, "Saul. Take off your warm-ups."

I stripped down and ran onto the court, and even though I was terrified—it was my first game in what I saw as the big leagues—I held my own and even scored a few points. I was thrilled, of course, and that thrill carried me through most of the season, though I continued to spend a lot of time on the bench. It would take a lot more work, and many, many more early morning bus trips, but I eventually earned my place on the roster. By my fourth year, I was co-captain of the team.

All of which is to say, I'm dogged, some would probably say stubborn. I drew on this quality and thought of the basketball story often as we faced resistance making those big changes at The Stop. To people like Richard Thompson, the changes seemed personal. Feelings were hurt, toes were stepped upon. There were those who became caught up in defending programs or ideas simply because that's the way they'd always done things.

And yet it was clear—to me and to our board of directors—that change was desperately needed. We had to whip the food bank into shape, find more solid funding, focus our mission, achieve greater consistency, and emphasize the programs that actually meet the community needs. And to do this we needed dedicated staff and a degree of professionalism that made some people in the previously volunteer-based organization uncomfortable.

Volunteers are the lifeblood of The Stop, critical in day-to-day operations. We rely on them to manage the sheer amount of food (who else but Don the box man could spend all day breaking down boxes?) and support the thousands of people who come through our doors every month. They are deeply committed to our work and dedicate a huge amount of time, energy and passion to The Stop.

But, like food banks everywhere, depending almost entirely on unpaid labour means The Stop didn't have the capacity to do much more than move food from delivery truck to food bank hampers. There wasn't the time, opportunity or impetus to look more deeply at improving the quality of food or service or even to consider, frankly, if the food bank was doing much good in the lives of the people who used it.

Father Russell's original commitment to looking at the political and social reasons behind hunger and poverty didn't stand a chance in such an environment. Fighting for the kinds of public policy that can lead to long-term solutions requires the sustained attention and resources that only staff who are committed to social change can bring to bear in any consistent way.

Of course, hiring staff costs money—something in short supply at many not-for-profits, including The Stop. Most of our funding in the early days came from private donors and foundations, as well as churches, with Healthy Beginnings running partly on government grants. To make matters more challenging, the donor database was a Mickey Mouse operation, and we had inconsistent communication with the people and organizations we relied on to keep our doors open.

It shows the extent of my own lack of fundraising sophisti-
cation that when I learned a foundation we were considering
applying to had offices not far from Davenport Road (if several
kilometres and tax brackets away from Symington Place), I took
it upon myself to go and say hello. I had experience knocking on
doors in Alexandra Park and working on many political campaigns, so I wasn't especially nervous cold-calling at the George
Cedric Metcalf Charitable Foundation, a private family foundation with an interest in poverty reduction, as well as the arts
and environment.

"You're near Davenport, we're *on* Davenport," I told Sandy
Houston, the affable executive director, when his assistant called
him to the door. (A bit of a stretch as an opening salvo, I'll admit.)
Sandy laughed and invited me inside. I discovered he was new at
the foundation, the only employee other than an administrative
assistant, and he was there just one day a week while working as
a partner at a law firm specializing in alternative dispute resolution. Clean-cut, with black-rimmed glasses and a freshly pressed
shirt, Sandy came across like a favourite young professor, the
sort of generous and erudite teacher who asks good questions
and delights in his student's responses. We talked about the
foundation and its interests. The Metcalf Foundation, I learned,
was similar to other family-run funders, with board members
gathering around a table to decide how their money would be
distributed—not arbitrary, but not necessarily strategic in its
choices. Sandy was beginning to think about how he might
shape and professionalize the foundation. He realized that the
withdrawal of government from the arts, environment and social
services had created a vacuum, and there was a place for foundations like Metcalf to be more deliberate about what kinds of
projects they invest in. He figured that leveraging their money in

the right way could mean the foundation would have a genuine impact on people and, potentially, on public policy.

I left feeling excited about the possibility of collaborating with Sandy and the foundation. Soon after, we applied for and received a Metcalf grant that made it possible for us to hire Rhonda Teitel-Payne as a garden and kitchen coordinator, taking over from parks and rec staff, and beginning to roll out new programs. Rhonda had trained as a social worker, then became involved in organizing the Metro Days of Action, a massive protest against the poor-bashing regime of the Common Sense Revolution. Though she had little experience gardening, she brought a love of baking, political street theatre and community organizing. She jumped into the position with both feet.

We also made the decision to forego an administrative assistant and instead hire a full-time fundraiser. When our first fundraiser began, she inherited a filing cabinet full of paper and an ancient, extremely limited computer program for tracking donors. But she quickly created new systems and organizational flow. Within a few months she'd replaced the old computer software program with a much more effective one that allowed us to examine trends and patterns and make sense of how to target our fundraising. It was a major investment of money and time (she had to manually input all of the donor names), but when it comes to fundraising there's no other way to do it: you have to spend money to make money.

Our first priority as we unearthed new funding sources was for Cliff to drop his cleaning duties and work full-time in the food bank. He also took on the responsibility of training volunteers, freeing me to focus on fundraising, developing contacts in the community sector, managing the organization, leading our first strategic plan and building a new vision for The Stop.

The effect of this modest uptick in staff resources was transformative. Having full-time staff meant consistent faces for our community members. It meant that tasks were completed on time, and we could have regular hours five days a week. (Most church basement food bank operations have irregular hours dependent on holiday schedules and volunteer commitment.) We hosted training in negotiating conflict, and implemented antidiscrimination policies. It also meant we could be more accountable: if community members felt they'd been treated disrespectfully, they could register their complaint and we would respond. It's a far cry from some volunteer-led organizations that run on the like-it-or-lump-it approach.

Staff members make volunteer positions more rewarding, too, since one key staff responsibility is to support people in managing tricky situations, power dynamics and their own stresses. Not everyone is cut out to do front-line volunteer work with people living in poverty. It can be difficult to manage the many competing needs; judgments are made and food bank members can be humiliated and stigmatized in the process. For the most part, volunteers really liked having staff consistently available to support them. It also made it possible to encourage food bank members and other Davenport West residents to work as volunteers too. Supporting others in their own community, these volunteers put the boot to the idea that low-income people are lazy or don't want to contribute. A mutually supportive atmosphere began to form at The Stop, blurring the line between those who give and receive, helping us move from charity toward solidarity.

Even Richard Thompson came back a little while after our conversation in the parking lot. He was a bit standoffish with me, but that didn't stop him from continuing to volunteer and send friends and other contacts our way.

One of Richard's referrals even turned into an important voice of support. A retired school principal who volunteered in the food bank, he had the gravitas of someone who's navigated many difficult situations—personal and political—and I trusted him to tell it like it is. I wasn't officially working in the back anymore, but I was often drawn into the fray and went to the food bank to talk to people several times a day. I heard my own fair share of the complaints, and the school principal helped keep it in perspective. When he eventually left his volunteer position, he wrote me a letter. He said that what we were doing, making the food bank a more dignified, efficient and fair place, was the right thing to do. He reminded me that change is hard—but worth it. I tucked that letter away. I figured I might need the encouragement again.

MAY 2000. It's cool and slightly breezy in Earlscourt garden. The daffodils planted last fall have come up along the sunny west-facing fence line, and I can see the green leaves of snowbells that have already had their day. Herman is crouched over inside the fence in blue coveralls and a black winter cap, planting seeds. Rhonda and Herman have hit it off. To his delight, she introduces him to everyone as the plot's guardian angel, and she teases him that he's on a first-name basis with every plant in the garden.

Francesca and Dorino are here, too. An older Italian couple from the neighbourhood whose knowledge about planting and tending the garden has been invaluable to Rhonda, they're tilling the soil in two neat lines. Rarely without his big dark sunglasses and a white dress shirt buttoned to the very top, Dorino doesn't seem to be breaking a sweat despite his labour. We're doubling the size of the garden this spring, and there is a lot to do.

Most mornings since the ground thawed, Rhonda comes into the office for a short time before loading up like a pack mule, carting enormous garbage bags full of stuff up to the park. Despite her lack of gardening experience when she was hired, she's learned a huge amount. She started a native plant program, produced a quarterly newsletter for volunteers and initiated a collaboration with our church supporters, involving them in planting seedlings at home to be transplanted into our garden.

She's also continued work with local schools. In fact, today she's got a group of kids gathered by the compost bins near the alleyway, where garages tagged with graffiti face the park. All the children are wearing mustard-yellow T-shirts with the name of their school on the front. They're rambunctious, excited to be outdoors after a long winter. Rhonda, in one of her bright blue batik shirts, is laid-back as usual, leaning into the compost pile and grabbing a handful of soil to show the kids the jagged remnants of an eggshell with a worm crawling through it.

With only a few plants growing and straw still covering many of the beds, the space looks tidy, but it will soon be a riot of plants, flowers, art and homemade scarecrows. Last summer, Rhonda and her volunteers built twig trellises for climbing plants that they set up in various spots around the garden like small teepees. Some kids painted a massive mural of butterflies and daisies, bees and sunflowers all tangled together on a piece of wood that will act as the new gate for the expanded plot. Rhonda is already organizing planting parties and harvest parties, barbecues and other events. We've also planned farm visits—a strawberry-picking trip for the spring, corn for the fall—to make the link between what we're doing in the park and what farmers do in the country. People living in Symington Place and

Davenport West love it. Many of them say th...
the last time they had a chance to get out of th...

Already, the garden has become much mor...
source for The Stop's programs. It has started to...
organization altogether: from a place focused on a sing... ...or-
alizing transaction—food hamper handouts—it is becoming a
community resource where people know they'll be treated
respectfully and offered opportunities to succeed.

I'm grateful that The Stop's board of directors understands
the importance of these changes. They were glad to move away
from putting out fires on the front lines—mediating human
resources problems, stuffing envelopes—to working on big-
picture issues. By creating a plan for change and growth, they've
helped transition The Stop away from the old just-getting-by
approach. Part of this shift has included moving from an oral
culture to a written one, with clear systems, bylaws and policies. We created written expectations for board and staff, job
descriptions and procedures, the kinds of things that bigger
organizations take for granted and that are the essential groundwork for growth.

We're also forging a new name and mission statement. The
name Stop 103 always seemed clunky to me and the street
number has lost its meaning after numerous relocations. But
many people responded to the idea that our name referred to
stopping poverty and hunger, and The Stop continues to have
currency among community members and many supporters.
We've decided that we can't risk losing that connection, and will
officially become The Stop.

Crafting a mission statement is more complicated. We
don't want it to be just a collection of words or jargon. We want
it to be useful and meaningful to staff and community members,

to potential funders and people at large. It needs to speak to our larger social goals of greater justice and equality, and help us move forward—a statement that can capture both what we are and what we hope to become. It's a lot of weight to place on a single sentence.

We finally decided on "The Stop strives to increase access to healthy food in a manner that maintains dignity, builds community and challenges inequality." The "challenging inequality" part is mostly aspirational at this stage, but it's an attempt to embed an antipoverty ethos into the bones of the organization, a guiding principle for us as we consciously engage community members in reshaping the organization. That means talking to people who use the food bank and garden about what they want and need, listening to their concerns at community input sessions and the annual general meeting, and in regular evaluations and surveys, as well as ensuring staff are receptive to feedback during programs.

Of course, not everyone wants to attend community feedback dinners or spend hours in a hot space talking about translating program materials into Turkish or even go on marches or demonstrations against policies that negatively affect them—but that doesn't mean they don't care about improving their lives. It's our role to create many different entry points for people, respecting where they're coming from and meeting them where they're at.

As part of this mandate to challenge inequality, Stop staff have also begun attending local antipoverty and community-based meetings. I've found that many people and organizations in the city had never heard of The Stop before. Just showing up has been enough to change the way the organization is perceived in the sector and in our neighbourhood. Most importantly, becoming involved puts us in a position where our members can have a say in the issues relevant to their lives.

With people like Rhonda—who understands the importance of talking about justice and inequality both in programs and outside the organization—and with new initiatives that members are helping to shape from the beginning, The Stop is not just about service delivery anymore. We've set our sights at no less than community and social change.

One day not long after she started, I went back behind the building to find that Rhonda had gathered some women together and gone outside to bang on pots and pans in a gesture of solidarity with the World March of Women event. At first the women felt silly, but people kept joining in until it was loud and fun and purposeful. There's a photo taken that day of three of the women standing by a brick wall behind The Stop. On the right, a woman in traditional Ethiopian dress is holding a large aluminum tray, about to hit it with a stainless steel soup-serving spoon. A tall Jamaican woman, whose rum cakes are famous in the neighbourhood, stands next to her wearing a pink T-shirt and cardigan, holding a colander and ladle. The woman on her left has her eyebrows furrowed and is pounding so furiously on the lid of a plastic bin with her kitchen tongs, her hand is a blur.

Back at the Earlscourt garden, before I return to Symington Place, I join the group of schoolchildren now sitting under a tree on a grassy rise beside the garden. They're in grades two and three, and Rhonda's talking to them about how growing your own food can help families eat more healthily. One child shoots up his hand. "My grandmother grows tomatoes in our backyard," he says. "We have zucchini," a girl pipes up, "but I don't like it." The group starts chattering about the vegetables they eat and the ones they hate.

Rhonda lets it go for a minute before bringing them back, explaining that growing food and plants without chemicals can help the health of the environment, too. She asks them to think about what they'd say if they were to write a letter to the planet. Why is its health important? What do they like? The kids throw out suggestions. "I like bugs!" shouts one little boy. Their teacher hands out small pieces of card stock and markers. Rhonda asks them to write a message to the planet that they'll hang from the fence. I look over the shoulder of a little boy lying on his stomach concentrating hard on his drawing. He sometimes came to the food bank with his mother and little sister last summer. He's written JAMES in capital letters at the top and beside it, he's carefully drawing a circle. I ask him about it. "It's an apple," he says with a hint of disdain, as if I'm a fool for not knowing.

Once they're finished their messages, Rhonda and the teacher usher the kids back into the garden. She's getting them to plant lettuce seeds in the rows that Francesca and Dorino have hoed. It's the perfect plant for this group because it grows quickly and will be ready to eat before they finish school in June. They'll come back to harvest and eat together. I head across the park to Symington Place, but before the garden is out of sight, I look back. All the little yellow shirts are in a row, crouched low over the soil, completely absorbed in their work.

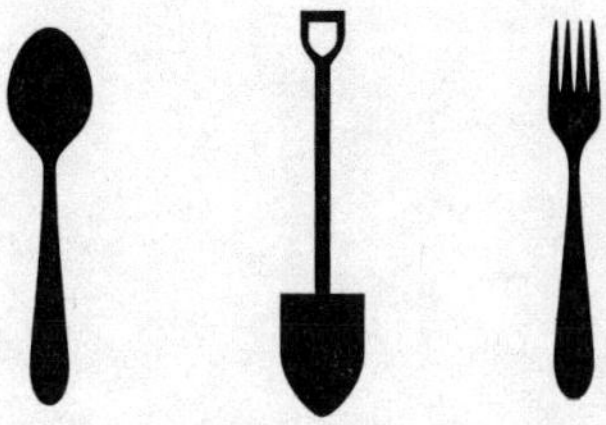

THREE

ALL GOOD PARTIES
END UP IN THE
KITCHEN

▷───▶

SEPTEMBER 2000. Our office at the front of Symington Place is tiny and cramped, host to a motley crew of mismatched hand-me-down desks and chairs. The glass door and a small window let in the only natural light. A folding table where we eat lunch, have meetings and stack papers sits in the centre of the room. With new staff and programs, we're bursting at the seams with books, folders, boxes, coffee mugs and garden supplies. I spend more time than I'd like to sifting through the detritus, as well as dealing with the ancient office equipment—printer, fax, photocopier—that never seems to work properly.

Rhonda's desk is against the wall, near the folding table. Paper pots and potting trays litter the table's surface; a large fig that someone donated is tucked alongside its legs. A fern hangs over a black filing cabinet, fronds dripping into an old soda can. Rhonda hasn't spent a lot of time here recently because she's been working nearly every day in the garden with new community volunteers and a garden assistant we managed to find the money to hire for the summer. We've also convinced a local high school with an underused second-floor greenhouse to lend us some space to expand our program into winter and spring and grow seedlings for the garden. And Rhonda's been asked to work with homeless First Nations men to help set up another local garden. Through all of this activity, we've also been involved in writing a proposal for a new urban agriculture education space in an old industrial building a few kilometres from Symington Place. We're in the dream phase right now but we're imagining gardens, a greenhouse, maybe even an aquaponics demonstration area where we'll raise edible fish and vegetables together in an integrated system—a public space highlighting food, the environment, social justice and community.

There's so much potential. I became even more excited about the possibilities in our garden when I visited some friends in Rochester, New York, and had a tour of city farms run by NENA (NorthEast Neighborhood Alliance). I met up with Hank Herrera at the bustling outdoor farmers' market. A psychiatrist turned urban agriculture crusader, he took me around the streets of the city's beautiful but decayed core to empty lots that he and his organization have cultivated with vegetables.

The project started in the early 1990s when the local supermarket in the low-income northeast section of the city burned down, and no stores were interested in taking its place. The community eventually convinced a commercial supermarket to set up shop, but in the intervening years, local people and community activists like Herrera found other ways to take charge of their neighbourhood food system.

NENA began with two garden plots, one of them at a major Rochester intersection, and they recently added a small farm outside the city that had been dormant for twenty years. They sell the produce to restaurants and at the farmers' market, using volunteers and (thanks to a city grant) employing a posse of young people in planting, tending, weeding and harvesting the vegetables and fruits. They also offer the youth entrepreneurial training. Any profits from produce sales are poured back into the gardens. Herrera is focused mainly on market-based activities, with the intention of bringing greater wealth to his low-income community through jobs and new businesses. Some of his ideas include selling the project's produce (say, habanero peppers or certain herbs) to ethnic-food processors, even getting into institutional markets such as schools.

Creating employment opportunities and income for community members isn't the main purpose of our garden—though Rhonda and her volunteers did make a huge batch of pesto from the bumper crop of basil they grew last summer and one of the churches that supports us sold it, with the modest proceeds going back into the garden. Still, it's inspiring to see what other low-income neighbourhoods are doing to reclaim urban spaces for food production and alternative distribution models.

One of the things that people in our neighbourhood often lament—as they do in northeast Rochester—is the lack of affordable full-service grocery stores. Davenport West has lots of convenience stores, their shelves stuffed with cigarettes, soda and processed foods, but few grocery stores. It's not exactly a "food desert" as you find in some American inner cities, where it's next to impossible to buy healthy food because the grocery stores have shut down or refused to open. But it is challenging. The closest discount grocery store to Symington Place is a twenty- to thirty-minute walk away. It's possible to travel there more quickly on public transit, but it's not always easy to get around with groceries—especially for older people, parents with children in strollers or people with physical challenges. And in a city that goes into deep freeze four months of the year, it's especially difficult.

As a result of feedback we've gathered, we've been thinking about creating a community grocery store. It might be in the same space as the food bank, but offer some essential items that don't usually appear in donations (cleaning products, toiletries, pet food, meat, diapers) at a wholesale cost. Another possibility is to lease a storefront near our front office to function as a low-cost food store, maybe even a co-operative. All of these ideas are just talk right now, part of reimagining our community's access to food and the food bank. The truth is, we're maxed out with the new programs we're starting and with trying to raise money to fund them.

My hands are covered in toner from our finicky photo-copying machine when the garden assistant opens the door, the sounds of the busy street racing inside with her. Everyone in the open space looks up. She's tanned after a summer in the sun and seems excited.

"You have to come into the back," she says. "We're making callaloo."

I've never heard the word, but I'm glad of a reprieve from the maddening machine. We head out the door, around the side of the apartment building and into the food bank. Rhonda is inside the community space. With more staff, we're now able to use it regularly, including for the new community kitchen groups that Rhonda has started.

A cluster of people is sitting at one of the round tables. And I can see through the small pass-through into the cramped kitchen that there are more inside. The smell wafting out is thick with garlic. We all sit down, and Herman, our garden neighbour, emerges wearing an apron, carrying a tray covered in leafy greens that he's steamed and cooked with salt fish, garlic, onions, salt and pepper, and sweet red peppers. "Callaloo," he says proudly.

Rhonda tells us the story as we take our tentative first bites. One day recently Herman came into the garden and saw some volunteers pulling out what they thought was a weed. "That's no weed," he told Rhonda. "It's callaloo." So she asked Herman to show everyone how the Caribbean specialty is cooked and eaten, and today a group of volunteers is trying out his favourite vegetable.

The verdict is good. It looks and tastes a lot like spinach or kale. Herman is pleased, proud to show off his Jamaican roots.

Rhonda did a bit of digging and discovered that Jamaicans aren't the only ones who love this plant. People all over the world know it and its different varieties as "amaranth" and eagerly eat the tender leaves, stalks and seeds. She also found that farmers north of the city call one variety of the plant "pigweed" and consider it a scourge. The seeds spread easily in the wind and they struggle to contain it on their farms.

I look at the faces around the table—Herman and Rhonda; Francesca and Dorino; Gordon, who's been working at the plot since the first day we dug the fence posts; a woman who lives in a rooming house nearby and suffers from severe diabetes.

One person's weed, it seems, is another's delicacy. In fact, as I'm beginning to realize, food is never just food.

WHEN I WAS WORKING at the homeless shelter, my colleagues and I offered the men whatever was quickest and easiest to distribute in the morning before they were sent back onto the street—ham sandwiches and coffee, vats and vats of coffee. I would never have said that I thought the food was great, but we figured it did the job of helping the guys get through at least part of their day.

When I took the position at The Stop, I still thought that any food was good food: not that poor people *deserved* whatever unhealthy thing was thrown at them, but that something was better than nothing. Food, after all, is supposed to be a basic human right enshrined in the 1976 United Nations Covenant on Economic, Social and Cultural Rights, signed and ratified by some 160 countries around the world. But I didn't distinguish between different types of food. To me, it was all the same: essential fuel for the mind and body.

Many people—especially those of us who grew up in cities— share such a take on the role of food in our lives. My family bought our food at a grocery store. As far as I was concerned, tomatoes grew on the shelves at the Super Save. Later, when I went to university and moved out, I ate on the run, squeezing it in between school and basketball, work and play. I had learned my way around the kitchen from watching my dad, who was the chief cook in our family because of his relatively flexible university schedule, but I never became a huge experimenter. I cooked basic things because I had to and ate to keep my engine running.

Once I started working in the food bank, though, all those ideas about food being incidental, peripheral—even benign— went out the window. I saw shelves packed with canned pork and beans, salt-laden soup and lots of processed food with ingredient lists the length of my arm, stuff that few people with a choice in the matter would want to buy or eat (hence the donation). We often had pasta, rice, and tins of tuna fish, but almost no fresh food. Milk was a rarity, though we had lots of dried-out chicken fingers, instant mashed potatoes, and mysterious coating powders intended to dress up cheap cuts of meat.

It quickly became obvious to me that the kind of food we were providing in the monthly hampers *wasn't* better than nothing. Serving some of the things we had on our shelves was degrading. And we didn't even attempt to offer culturally appropriate foods to our largely immigrant neighbourhood (staples like dried beans for the large Central American contingent or leafy greens for the Portuguese community)—though to do so would mean people would eat more healthily and with more dignity.

The changes we made at The Stop's food bank—refusing soupy bananas and cast-off industrial experiments, as well as adding fresh produce to the hampers—were intended as a way to deliver food respectfully, but I started to realize there were health benefits, too.

Our neighbourhood—like low-income communities elsewhere—is a hotbed of diet-related health issues like diabetes and heart disease. As the public health nurses saw every day in Davenport West, and health researchers the world over have shown, income is a key determinant of health. While prosperity doesn't guarantee wellness, low incomes are nearly always associated with poor health. Quite simply, poverty makes people sick. Over 7 percent of people in our area have diabetes—more than double the rate in wealthier parts of the city. The cheap, highly processed, packaged foods available in our food bank began to seem to me like a health care crisis on a plate. How could we think this food was actually helping anyone?

Others had begun to make the links between processed, packaged industrial food and individual and community health before I did. I didn't know it when I took the job at The Stop, but I was arriving on the scene as a growing number of activists around the world were coming together to question the dominant system of food production, distribution, marketing and consumption. The links between food and health, poverty and hunger were just the beginning. Those early food movement thinkers began to look, also, to what the supply chain and processing of such food meant for the environment and for the people who produce the food.

It was the early 1990s when activists with an antipoverty and right-to-food approach first joined forces with those interested in environmentally sustainable agriculture. Together they birthed the idea of "community food security"—a phrase that refers to a broad-based and systemic approach that aims to reconnect sustainable food production and consumption with equitable access to good, healthy food.

Rod MacRae was one of the early voices championing this new approach. As the first coordinator of the pioneering Toronto Food Policy Council, a subcommittee of the Board of Health, he helped forge links between people in the food, farming, health and community sectors on issues that matter to everyone. He was also instrumental in creating the city's Food and Hunger Action Committee, which advised the municipal government about addressing inadequate nutrition and hunger, and produced an action plan aimed at increasing community food security in Toronto.

Wayne Roberts, a food policy analyst and writer, who took over as the Food Policy Council coordinator in 2000, was also a key proponent, helping to craft the influential Toronto Food Charter, a declaration of citizens' rights and government's responsibilities that put sustainability, health and access front and centre. It was the first such food charter adopted by a major city, and it inspired many other municipalities across the continent to follow suit. The charter advocated use of city lands for community gardens, healthy government-subsidized snacks and meals for school-aged children, and relationships between farmers and community groups, among other initiatives.

On the wider stage, it was the creation of the North American Community Food Security Coalition in the early 1990s that began to bring attention to the potential of neighbourhood-based programs like gardens and kitchens, and to the possibility of creating small-scale food projects (such as produce markets) that could generate income for community members. As the movement grew and gathered momentum, the coalition and others in the nascent community food security sector were also influenced by the "food sovereignty" movement emerging from the global South.

Rural peasant farmer organizations, such as La Via Campesina (founded in 1993 by farmers from four continents), were starting to actively resist the efforts of the World Trade Organization (WTO) to institute new global trade rules related to food, fishing and farming. La Via Campesina and others argued that such changes—including government deregulation, an end to protections for local companies, the privatization of public lands and certain trade restrictions—favoured large producers and agribusiness over small-scale farmers. They claimed that such trade rules threatened not only cultural values but also their very survival.

These farmers rejected the initiatives of the WTO, a powerful but unelected body, arguing that the people most affected by policies on food and agriculture should be the ones creating and implementing them. They called for democracy and a redistribution of power away from corporations and into the hands of the people who produce and consume the food.

As in any other burgeoning social movement, tensions in the community food security movement formed as ideas and individuals bumped up against each other. There were anti-poverty activists who argued that community kitchens and gardens, like the ones we were starting to create at The Stop, did nothing to alleviate hunger or address the structural reasons for poverty. In fact, they claimed, such efforts even help mask the real problems of inadequate wages, social assistance and housing with a feel-good hot lunch.

Groups that advocated for such programs pointed to success stories like the *comedores populares* (roughly translated as community kitchens) in Peru, where impoverished women get together to cook for their children and their communities, helping to alleviate hunger, ending their own isolation and forging a new space for collective action. Where some activists saw only the failure of government to ensure access to food, advocates argued that *comedores populares* and similar programs can increase self-reliance, rebuild local food systems, encourage long-term self-sufficiency and even act as a platform for mobilizing toward larger social change.

Despite such (largely internal) quibbles, a hybrid food movement began to take root, building on the emerging analysis of food insecurity and food sovereignty. In his book *The No-Nonsense Guide to World Food*, Wayne Roberts calls it a "fusion" movement. It's about seeing antipoverty work as intertwined with environmental sustainability and health, talking not only about access to food but also about the importance of cultural values and community connectedness. "The common ground . . . [is] valuing food as a cultural more than an agro-industrial product," Roberts writes.

But as much as anything, this fusion food movement is about seeing what's on the table—or on the food bank shelves—as connected to the farmers and growers producing the raw product, the big corporations processing, packaging, transporting and selling it, and the health of the planet and of the people consuming the food.

Toronto-based FoodShare was an early adopter of such fusion or "food systems" thinking—looking at food as part of an integrated whole. Founded in 1985, the organization began as an effort to coordinate emergency food services such as food banks and soup kitchens, as well as to collect and distribute food. But after a few years—during which they founded the Hunger Hotline as a referral service for people looking for food—FoodShare leadership and staff became frustrated by the fact that, despite their efforts, hunger was not diminishing in the city. The organization started to branch out, exploring self-help models that addressed immediate hunger but also created more stability, security and better health in communities—things like group buying clubs, collective kitchens and gardens. Executive director Debbie Field, a passionate promoter of access to good food for everyone, became a go-to voice of this emerging food movement.

I visited FoodShare's Field to Table Centre a few years before I started at The Stop. I'd been talking to Kathryn Scharf, a FoodShare staffer, about involving the men at the homeless shelter in community kitchens, and I wanted to check out their facilities. The building I visited was an old warehouse on a sketchy dead-end street jammed between two highways not far from the shelter. And yet it was an impressive place, with a huge variety of food activities, from a street-front herb garden and compost area to a full industrial kitchen in the basement and a greenhouse on the roof. They didn't serve a specific low-income community with programs or services; instead, they acted as an incubator and training ground for good food ideas and programs. The Field to Table Centre had beehives in the back lot and a sprout-growing operation in the warehouse. Inside, volunteers worked an assembly line packing fresh fruits and vegetables (sourced as much as possible from local farmers) for their Good Food Box program, a wholesale nonprofit food distribution scheme intended to make nutritious produce accessible to everyone. The signature green boxes—some organic, others with convention-ally grown produce—would be delivered to central sites all over the city where people who'd ordered them could pick them up.

The centre was busy and boisterous, full of volunteers and activity, and when I started to reimagine what we could do at The Stop, it would serve as inspiration for the potential of food to animate our programs and our community. Over the next few years, I regularly ran into Kathryn. A West Coast native with an interest in organic growing, migrant workers and social history, she'd started at FoodShare as a volunteer and eventually became involved as staff in nearly every aspect of the organization, from community kitchens to the Good Food Box network to heading up their communications work. When I met her, she was already deeply involved in food systems thinking, serving as community co-chair of the Food Policy Council and active in the Food and Hunger Action Committee. Articulate and razor sharp, Kathryn helped guide my own thinking about food programming. She understood clearly the potential for marrying the food systems approach with support for low-income people at the neigh-bourhood level. Eventually I convinced her to join The Stop's board of directors, and she became an important advocate for this holistic thinking within the organization as well.

We'd already started to insist that the food we offered in our hampers be healthier. But with this new philosophy acting as a guiding principle, we also began to make more conscious links— in the programs we created and the vision we pursued—between The Stop's work and the rest of the food system. That meant purchasing food from farmers who use sustainable growing methods, and committing to organic growing techniques in our own garden. In the new community kitchen groups that Rhonda initiated, we began to explore the benefits—health, financial and environmental—of cooking from scratch. We also talked to the volunteers and schoolchildren who worked in our garden about the value—for their own health and that of the planet—of making compost, eating local food and saving seeds.

Rhonda discovered that when she tried to talk about global environmental issues like climate change, volunteers and participants would ask her what those topics have to do with growing veggies in a city park or cooking in a community kitchen. Such connections can be hard to wrap your mind around, especially for a generation of people who've been raised on big box stores and Big Macs—and it's particularly difficult in an urban environment where the source of what we eat can be distant and food is something simply to be bought and sold. But this growing recognition of the interconnected parts of the food system began to lay the groundwork—for me, staff and community members—for other questions and discoveries about the power of food.

●—

ROSA LAMANNA LIVES IN ONE of the red-brick, two-storey townhouses opposite the back entrance to The Stop. She's a fixture in our programs, a familiar face to staff, volunteers and participants. But she remembers well the lonely summer when she arrived in the neighbourhood, a young bride from Calabria, Italy, unable to speak English and not knowing a soul.

It was the early 1970s, and the Lamannas were part of the postwar influx of immigrants to Toronto who turned the city into one of the largest Italian communities outside of Italy. Davenport West, with its factory jobs and relatively inexpensive housing, was a prime landing spot for these newcomers. For Rosa, the big city and its culture were bewildering. "I felt like I was nothing because I didn't understand anything. It was frustrating. I felt people were laughing at me," she recalls. "I felt small—like a little bird."

But over time, Rosa, her husband, Angelo, and their son, Tony, made a life for themselves. They enrolled in English as a Second Language classes, Angelo worked as a tailor and Rosa got a job at a nearby fabric factory. When Tony was five years old, they moved into the rented townhouse with brown horizontal siding and a small backyard where they still live.

The way they remember it, Symington Place in those days was "one big *famiglia.*" "Lots of kids," Rosa says, her brown eyes twinkling. "And lots of nicky nicky nine doors!" People looked out for each other. There were new immigrants from Egypt and Jamaica, from England and India, an Italian contingent and some Portuguese families. Nonna Mary, an older woman with glasses and a walker, lived nearby. Not long after the Lamannas moved in, Nonna Mary made sure, according to one oft-told family story, that Tony got back his beloved tricycle when another child "borrowed" it and disappeared. After that, Tony would plant himself on the trike and refuse to move. Only a year later, Tony took apart a bicycle for the first time and put the whole thing back together again.

In the late 1990s, Angelo, out for a walk, discovered The Stop, newly ensconced in the bottom floor of the Symington Place apartment building. When Rosa went by to check it out, she was surprised to see that she recognized some of the volunteers. She'd been a volunteer herself at The Stop's food bank when the organization was in a church basement a few streets away, and hadn't realized it had moved.

Angelo wasn't well in those days. He had diabetes and wasn't able to work much of the time. With Tony too young for Rosa to leave at home and Angelo ill, money was very tight. Rosa decided to go to The Stop to collect a monthly food bank hamper to buy them a few extra days. She'd also go over in the muggy heat of the Toronto summer just to sit in the air-conditioned room and cool off.

By the time I arrived at The Stop, Rosa was a regular. A fabulous cook, she was glad to become involved in Meals Made Easy, a community kitchen program that an enterprising pair of Stop volunteers, one a baker, the other a nutritionist, had started. A core group of people—Francesca and Dorino, Luigi, who spent thirty years cooking in Toronto nursing homes before retiring, an Indian grandmother and her Caribbean neighbour, among others—would gather each week around a big table with chopping boards and utensils, divvying up the tasks as they made simple, inexpensive and nutritious meals to eat together. Sometimes they'd make enough to take home, but more often they'd cook the meal, then sit at one of the tables in the community space and enjoy the chance to socialize.

When Rhonda was hired, she took up where the volunteers left off, and ramped up the number and variety of community kitchens where participants would cook and then eat together. She kept up Meals Made Easy and also established a Cook with

What You've Got program aimed at people using the food bank, a cooking drop-in for seniors, and a Women's Cooking Group that focused on health concerns such as diabetes and osteoporosis.

Rosa enjoyed Meals Made Easy, but her family also liked it when she brought home extras from the food they'd made. And they liked it even more when she refined the recipe at home, adding a carrot or some meat and making the dish her own. She would file away the recipes, with her own additions and other tweaks, in a special binder. One day Rosa taught the kitchen group her tomato sauce recipe. The verdict was unanimous: perfect.

"It's fun. People are so happy to be in that place. I've made many friends there," she says. They joke and argue, sometimes complain, but they also look after each other, checking in if someone is sick or absent. Everyone takes a lot of pride and ownership in the group. It never fails to remind me when I go to see them how every good party seems to end up in the kitchen. Food isn't just food. It's not just fuel for the body. It's a way to show love and generosity, an opportunity for connection.

For Rosa, this sense of community is the most important part of Meals Made Easy. But for many people at The Stop who've never learned to cook, the opportunity to learn cooking skills is also essential. They are hardly alone in their lack of knowledge about how to make a home-cooked meal. I would wager, in fact, that on any given day in North America more people are watching chefs on TV than cooking themselves. With convenience foods so readily available, time at a premium and priorities elsewhere, many people—and this cuts across racial, cultural and class lines—have never learned how to cook or prepare raw vegetables, fruits, whole grains or meat.

Nutritionists and physicians identify lack of food skills as the cause of many diet-related health issues including diabetes and obesity. After all, when you don't know how to cook, there's little choice but to rely on packaged food—complete with high salt, hydrogenated fat, refined sugar and cereals, and food additives—or the calorie-dense and often unhealthy offerings of fast-food restaurants.

Some people have argued that teaching people to cook from scratch is actually the answer to hunger and poor health in North America. Such cookery advocates argue that cost, or income, is not the major barrier to eating nutritious food. Frugal food bloggers chronicle their attempts to live on a dollar a day; Slow Food USA hosted the $5 Challenge with the cheeky tag-line "Take back the 'value meal.'" Mark Bittman, the celebrated *New York Times* columnist and cookbook author, writes regularly about health and sustainability as linked to "the all-but-vanished craft of cooking and associated thrift."

They're right, of course. Acquiring food skills is essential for anyone who wants to break the habit of relying on processed food. But for many people at The Stop, like those on low incomes everywhere, it's not so simple. Lack of income *is* a major barrier to buying fresh food and making meals out of it. Shopping, prepping and cooking time is often extremely limited for people who might be working several minimum wage jobs just to make ends meet. And many who use our programs don't even have a stove or a kitchen to cook in. Trying to live on a welfare cheque of less than six hundred dollars a month in a rooming house or jammed in with others in a one-bedroom apartment means proper cooking facilities are frequently unavailable.

And you can't discount the social exclusion faced by people living in poverty. Sharing a great meal with others can help you feel connected and alive, as it does for Rosa and the rest of the Meals Made Easy crew, but if you're on your own in a dingy, miserable room, cooking a meal by yourself can simply serve to highlight your solitude.

While we can't claim community kitchens—and the food skills learned there—are going to end the poverty or hunger of participants, they can definitely help low-income community members eat more healthily, have greater control over their personal circumstances and break out of their isolation.

For Rosa and her family, the kitchen was a gateway to The Stop's other programs. They soon became involved in the Earlscourt garden. Rosa had some farming experience from back home in Italy, and they already grew beautiful roses as well as some vegetables and herbs in their backyard. Their mint even won a gardening contest Rhonda organized. As he's grown older, Tony has become involved, too. "I have two green thumbs," he says proudly, holding up his hands.

"Except when you first started, you couldn't plant straight," his mother laughs. "I tell him, 'Plant it like the CN Tower, not the Tower of Pisa!'"

Tony shrugs. "Now I know."

The Stop has become a huge part of Tony and Rosa's family life (Angelo passed away in 2003). They volunteer and also drop in for meals, taking part in programs whenever they can. "I was raised in this place," says Tony, who lives at home and works for a major big box retailer. "I'm one of The Stop kids."

Some staff and volunteers, in fact, know Rosa as Mamma. She hasn't forgotten what it felt like to be a newcomer in the big city and she's glad to help those people who come from far away and still feel like "little birds." When she's introduced to people new to The Stop, those who are scared and nervous and worried about saying the wrong thing, she offers up her big, warm smile and says, "Welcome home."

·———

IF I CAME TO THE STOP suspecting food banks were an inadequate response to hunger, it didn't take long to become certain of it. Forty-five percent of the adults who use our food bank still go hungry at least once a week; 25 percent of the children from families who rely on these handouts say the same. And as a result of shortages, many food banks have to turn people away, close early or cut back on hamper sizes. Nearly 90 percent of people who use food banks still have to go into debt just to buy food or other necessities.

Meanwhile, use keeps rising as poverty increases exponentially. In the U.K., the number of people seeking food aid has nearly tripled as government benefits have been cut and unemployment has increased. But we've seen food bank use grow even during periods of growth. And I don't think it's a coincidence. In fact, I've come to believe the very existence of food banks has played a role—however inadvertently—in making hunger worse.

I know from first-hand experience that people working or volunteering their time in food banks have the very best intentions. In fact, they've done their work so well that they've made it look to the outside observer that this system of food handouts—with its massive distribution chains and elaborate corporate relationships, the warehouses and food drives and walkathons—has dealt with the issue of hunger. Food banks have stepped into the breach as governments around the world have withdrawn their social safety nets, failed to establish adequate minimum wages, cut back on affordable housing and childcare, and lowered social assistance rates. And the good people working in the food banks have become so consumed by the day-to-day pressures of delivering food to desperate people that they have no time to ask larger questions about what brings the hungry to their doors in the first place.

One of my touchstones in thinking about all of this is American sociologist Janet Poppendieck's book *Sweet Charity? Emergency Food and the End of Entitlement.* Poppendieck uses a parable to make her point about the folly of getting so caught up in short-term solutions you forget about the long-term ones. She tells a story about a village beside a river. One day, someone sees a baby floating by. Frantic, the Good Samaritan wades in to save the infant. Once on the riverbank she alerts her neighbours and together they find everything the baby needs: crib, food, clothing, blankets and more. But the next day there are more babies. They rescue those, too. And soon there are babies in the river all the time. People organize themselves and everyone becomes involved, until saving babies becomes a regular part of life. They hardly remember a time when they didn't have to rescue them. Then, one day, someone suggests they look upstream to figure out why the babies are in the river in the first place. There is much discussion, but no one is willing to take the time or resources away from rescuing the children. They're worried that one of the babies will drown while they're away.

I find the parable a useful way of thinking about the problem of charity in general, and of food banks in particular. We spend all our time rescuing the babies—feeding people in emergency circumstances—and forget to work at preventing what is causing the emergency in the first place. As a result, government—supposedly responsible for the health and welfare of its citizens—is let off the hook. It can safely ignore hunger because it's not on the agenda. In the meantime, citizens and government point to the busy food banks and distribution centres, volunteers and donations as evidence that the problem is solved, the hungry fed.

But the problem is only growing worse. (More than 50 million people in the U.S. don't know where their next meal will come from.) Indeed, instead of regarding food banks as the embodiment of a good deed—a compassionate response to hunger in an affluent society—I think we should view these small, ephemeral, volunteer-run places serving up unhealthy food as symbols of the breakdown of our social fabric, the end of whatever collective understanding we have about our responsibility to each other.

My opinion is not a popular one, not least among many food banks themselves. It's odd, considering that when food banks first started popping up across the continent, no food bank leader would say they believed their handouts were doing any more than providing temporary relief. Many would have argued, in fact, that they hoped that through advocacy for better social supports they'd "put themselves out of business." In the early days of food banks, an Ontario government standing committee issued a report that highlighted "the urgency of discovering strategies for transferring back to the government the responsibility for feeding the hungry."

But these days, we rarely hear a peep about government responsibility for ensuring citizens' access to healthy food—let alone the basic right to food. Despite efforts to the contrary, food banks have indeed been institutionalized, with thousands of volunteers and staff sorting, distributing and handing out food, national organizations, conferences, buildings, transportation networks, donors and fundraisers. And large corporations have taken them on as pet philanthropic projects. Author of *Food Banks and the Welfare Crisis*, Graham Riches put it succinctly in an article for the Canadian Centre for Policy Alternatives: "Big business—and in particular the food and transportation industries, professional sports organizations, and the TV and radio news media, have become persuasive educators of food philanthropy." Such education occurs on billboards and courier vans supporting food drives, in TV, radio and internet ads, and in massive cross-country media campaigns urging people to donate more food. The result, Riches argues, is the pervasive idea that hunger is "a matter for charity."

Given this environment, to question the existence of food banks, let alone suggest government has a role to play, is to court controversy. Middle-class volunteers feel personally affronted when they're told food banks aren't working. Companies are angry and confused when their philanthropy and intentions are brought into question. And some people in the sector—even those who see food banks' inadequacy every day—become defensive when their work is challenged. "There is no alternative"—one of Margaret Thatcher's famous slogans, the acronym for which became one of her nicknames, TINA—has become the default response.

One of the first times the fault lines became really clear to me was at a public forum I was invited to about two years after I arrived at The Stop. The panel discussion was held at Timothy Eaton Memorial Church, an imposing grey-stone structure on the lip of a hill in one of the city's wealthiest neighbourhoods. The congregation had long been funders of our work, and I had been asked there previously to talk to the outreach committee. For a few years, in fact, I was invited to speak to church groups most Sunday mornings, offering a speech from the pulpit or to smaller assemblies about hunger, poverty and our work. Church was hardly my natural habitat. Before I took the job at The Stop, I'd rarely darkened the door of a religious institution. But I didn't have to recite scripture that day (or any other). My job was to speak on a panel with several others about the future direction of food banks.

When I arrived, the crowd was already gathered on chairs pulled up to circular tables in a large, fluorescent-lit meeting room. There were some familiar faces, older men and women mostly, who volunteered at The Stop.

Sue Cox, then executive director of Daily Bread Food Bank, the city's main emergency food distribution organization—which has a large warehouse to collect and then distribute most of the food to the city's food banks—was already settling in at the front. I didn't know her very well then, though I would come to like and respect her. Still, I knew already that we had different takes on food banking. At the time, in fact, some of her staff was having conversations with Cliff, saying they wanted us to offer food at The Stop food bank twice instead of once a month. Daily Bread doesn't have administrative authority over us or the other food banks they distribute food to, but we all sign an annual code of conduct spelling out how we will oversee the food that they bring to us. And since we all rely on Daily Bread for a significant portion of the food we hand out, they have quite a bit of influence over the sector in general. Cliff and I discussed their request, but held firm to our conviction that we needed to place limits on the resources we put toward the food bank or it would consume us entirely. We'd seen it happen before, both at The Stop and elsewhere. And after witnessing the success of our new initiatives in the garden and kitchen programs, we already saw the incredible potential there. We knew food banking wouldn't be our focus any longer.

Cliff told Daily Bread that we weren't giving the food bank short shrift—in fact, we'd made our monthly hampers healthier and the experience more dignified for our members—but the food bank was embedded in a larger roster of food programs. Daily Bread wasn't thrilled, and it wouldn't be the last time we were asked to discuss this contentious issue.

Before joining Sue at the table, I made a detour to chat with the evening's organizer, a long-time Stop supporter. Sheila Allen was sixtyish at the time, energetic and tanned. She gave me a firm handshake and confessed that she was nervous about the panel. She was worried I was going to throw down the gauntlet about getting rid of food banks, and the forum would degenerate into something unpleasant.

Sheila and I had talked about all of this before. It was a subject close to home at Timothy Eaton, since the congregation there had partnered with other nearby churches to start a food bank in the basement a few years earlier. It operated on volunteer power several days a week, for limited hours with limited food supplies. Before my time, The Stop had even been involved in helping establish it. I had told Sheila before that it didn't make sense to me to have a smattering of small, under-resourced food banks all over the city, rather than channelling energy into organizations that have the capacity to support people consistently and efficiently, and also look at bigger-picture issues—like how we're going to make sure food banks are no longer necessary. But the congregation wanted to continue their food bank.

"Don't worry," I whispered to Sheila before I made my way over to the table, "I won't call for abolishing food banks. At least not today."

By the time we started, there was standing room only. I was surprised. We routinely hear that church attendance is on the decline in Canada. Financial contributions from churches are also declining, as donors grow older and fewer young people take their place. For many social service organizations, it's one of the great fundraising dilemmas of our time. And yet, there we were in a busy church in the middle of one of the city's poshest neighbourhoods with a packed house eager to get into the nitty-gritty about poverty and food banks.

Sue went first. Food banks exist, she said, because of government's failure to support the poor. They might have started as short-term solutions, but they've become an integral part of the world we live in. Daily Bread, she told the crowd, was even talking about buying a larger building—a symbol of permanence that she and others in the organization never would have wished for. "We've been institutionalized," she said. But, Sue argued, there's no quick fix. Increasing income is the only way we'll see food bank use decrease. She talked about the work she and her staff were doing to advocate for an increased minimum wage, good jobs, better welfare rates and affordable housing, but admitted that such change wasn't likely to happen any time soon.

I was glad to hear Sue's strong words about the root causes of poverty. But I also felt impatient with the sentiment (to be echoed by many others over the ensuing years) that until we see an increase in incomes, food banking is the only way forward. We were already seeing the positive impact of more participatory, less stigmatizing food initiatives at The Stop. And the idea that what we were offering was not just a handout but a hand up was starting to transform the organization. Plus, the integrated food systems thinking and community development focus of our work meant that Stop members were building relationships not just with each other and staff, but increasingly with farmers, gardeners, chefs, environmentalists, health care workers and anyone else who cares about food.

When it was my turn to speak, I tried to convey all of this. I said that what we're doing with food banks isn't working and we must find alternatives. And I said that at The Stop we don't think simply handing out food and sending people on their way is good enough—not now or ever. The Stop encourages engagement in everything from guiding and shaping the programs and services to setting our course for the future. I said that from this platform it becomes possible for people to move beyond their community to articulate their needs on a larger stage. That's how social change happens—from the ground up, not only because middle-class activists and leaders lobby government on behalf of the poor.

The panel didn't degenerate into an argument, as Sheila had feared. It was civil and useful, and a rare opportunity to discuss these issues in a public space. In fact, the panel offered me new insight into how much of a paradigm shift we were proposing. It was that day, describing our new programs and the renewed vigour at The Stop, that I began to say that what we were building was not a new kind of food bank, but a new species altogether: a Community Food Centre.

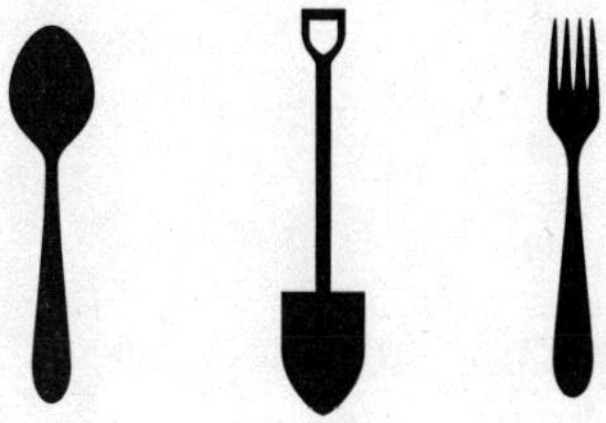

FOUR

POVERTY IS RUTHLESS

GLENN KITCHENER HAS WORKED HARD all his life. Gentle and soft-spoken, with a remarkable memory for numbers and dates, he was born in a small town on the outskirts of Toronto. When he was a child, he moved with his family to a farm east of the city. The day he turned sixteen, his parents—rural people with little time for formal education—pulled him out of high school and told him to start looking for a job. He went to the local employment centre, plucked a job description off the wall, and has been working ever since, sometimes two or three jobs at a time—everything from labouring at a mining camp in the Far North to driving a truck and doing maintenance at a sports facility.

By the time he was a teenager, Glenn was already an alcoholic. He drank beer 24/7 and bought tequila by the case, even lacing his coffee or juice with liquor. He didn't stop until he was twenty-three—burned out, living on the street, his kidneys and liver so diseased he had to be hospitalized.

"The doctors told me if I hadn't come into hospital I'd be dead," he recalls.

But he managed to quit altogether, eschewing AA for out-patient therapy and public speaking lessons. Booze made Glenn, a natural introvert, more gregarious, and learning to express himself in public gave him new confidence. (He hasn't had a drink since September 26, 1980.)

Sober and still a young man, Glenn continued to take on whatever work he could find with a grade nine education. He did maintenance jobs at the university, worked as a groom at a local racetrack, even fished for sole and plaice on a forty-metre trawler in the North Sea off Denmark. When he was thirty-three, he and his then-girlfriend moved west to British Columbia so they could be near her family. There, Glenn found stability and happiness, building a successful landscaping company. He and his girlfriend created a solid middle-class life for themselves, with two houses, three cars and a thriving business with several part-time employees. But when the army base in their area shut down, work dried up, his relationship fell apart, and Glenn's world came tumbling down around him.

A few years later, in the early 2000s, he landed in Davenport West, broken and alone. Toronto, where he'd spent many years as a young adult, had been transformed in his absence. On streets where he used to know everyone—Poles, Italians and other small-town transplants like himself—he saw only unfamiliar faces. "I started to feel really isolated," he says.

Still, Glenn is nothing if not a survivor. He found a job at Home Depot and a place to stay, though all he could afford was a decrepit, bedbug-ridden rooming house not far from The Stop. He began coming by to pick up food once a month at our food bank.

"It was a really hard time for me," he recalls. "Going from being self-sufficient with money in the bank to waiting for a food handout was a real kick in the teeth. I didn't want to make eye contact with anyone. I'd just go in and out. When someone offered me a plate of food to eat at the drop-in, I said 'No, thank you.' I was too embarrassed to take it."

But then Glenn had a serious angina attack in the middle of his Home Depot shift one day, and was forced to take time off work. When he returned, his hours had been cut back dramatically. Lonely and reluctantly living on welfare, he started coming to The Stop more often.

The drop-in meal program was relatively new at the time. We'd applied for and received a small municipal grant to do a bare-bones renovation of the tiny kitchen, knocking out a wall so it was more open and accessible, building an island for food prep, and fixing up the community room with new lights and a mural. It had made a big difference to programming possibilities, allowing us to add regular drop-in meals for people who visited the food bank. At first it was just breakfast three times a week, though we also offered community information, workshops, a nurse practitioner once a month and even haircuts. Then, when we found funding for more staff time, we added an afternoon drop-in with coffee and snacks during food bank hours—plus resource referrals, more workshops and a weekly movie. Twice a week, lunch was served through a partnership with Second Harvest, the food reclamation organization (which supplied the food), and a local skills training group (which prepared the meal). Responding to suggestions from members, we called it The Stop Café. The menu—with a vegetarian option—was posted and volunteers served food to the tables.

At first, Glenn mostly kept to himself. There were people just out of jail and guys—some alcoholic, others with serious mental health issues—living outside or in homeless shelters who'd come in for a meal. Glenn purposefully kept his nose out of their business. He remembers only too well getting beaten up when he was the overweight kid in the schoolyard. He'd also become a practising Buddhist not long after moving back to Toronto. Still, he says, it's not easy to stay out of trouble when you're living on the margins, because vulnerable people attract those who want to take advantage. Once, after leaving a cheap all-you-can-eat restaurant in Chinatown, he was jumped by a couple of guys and left for dead. All he had was fifty cents in his pocket. Doctors in the emergency ward put sixteen staples in his head before the freezing even took effect. He says they knew he was on welfare and he was so out of it after the beating they must have figured he was drunk. He was patched up and sent on his way—battered and bruised—as soon as they were done.

"Poverty is ruthless," Glenn says. "People are negative. Everything is just negative. People disrespect and abuse you all the time. When I first went on welfare I had fights with my caseworker. Those doctors in the hospital wrote me off as a welfare case. I felt like I had no recourse. Poverty is a very deep hole to get out of."

But eventually Glenn started volunteering in the kitchen, and it became a lifeline. He'd learned to cook when he was a kid. He remembers his mother's skills as classically English—everything fried or boiled—but his Italian neighbours always had delicious-smelling meals made with fresh produce pulled straight from the garden. He loved what they were eating and learned by watching them. Later, one of his many lines of work would be handling the stove at small restaurants.

Glenn was finally in the right place at the right time. We'd decided that we needed to hire our own part-time cook for the drop-in to make food from scratch in-house. As a result, there was lots of work to be done by kitchen volunteers. Glenn began volunteering twice a week, chopping and dicing, mixing and prepping. Those days quickly became the highlight of his week. He liked that staff relied on him. It was the only time, Glenn says, that he felt treated with respect. And it was nice to be not just a participant but part of a team. For a guy who'd worked his entire life, it just felt more normal.

As we discovered rather quickly, however, not everyone loved the menu that our kitchen was producing. It was fresh, healthy and varied—costing us somewhere between $1.50 and $1.75 per meal, with about half of the food donated—but many people complained about being offered salads, too many vegetables and foods they didn't know. They wanted their french fries and cheesy frozen lasagnas back. Our suggestion box filled up with complaints. "I hated lunch today" was a common refrain.

It wasn't easy for our staff or Glenn and the other volunteers to hear. They were working hard, and it wasn't as if they were serving tempeh and using unfamiliar spices. This wasn't about forcing everyone to be vegetarian. The food was genuinely tasty, fresh and interesting. We even offered dessert, sometimes fruit, sometimes homemade cakes and sweets. But it wasn't what people were used to. Most soup kitchens and drop-in meals are heavy on starch and stew with lots of potatoes and bread, or processed convenience food that's easy to prepare. These kinds of dishes have become comfort food for a lot of people—filling and easy on the stomach.

Reading the comments and hearing the complaints made us wince. But we had seen the health impact of the alternative and remained committed to providing healthy food cooked from scratch in all our programs. So we worked hard to find the balance between nutritious and delicious. We offered alternatives to the salad dressing vinaigrettes that some people said hurt their bellies. There were some duds, like one kale and quinoa salad that will go down in infamy, but eventually the switch was flipped. Regulars began coming for lunch or breakfast four days a week, enjoying the meal, connecting with each other and with staff who helped them access other supports.

Things also began looking up for Glenn. He still had to lean on the food bank once a month, and was happy to have two solid meals a week following his volunteer kitchen shift, but he started feeling better about himself. Even his body language was different. He looked people in the eye, his voice was louder, his words clearer. This change, and the way the atmosphere at The Stop made such a transformation possible really came home for him, he says, when an older homeless man who lives in a nearby shelter came up to him on the street to shake his hand and say thank you. The man wanted to tell him he didn't think he would like it, but the salad Glenn had made for The Stop's lunch drop-in was delicious. Glenn was so surprised by this thanks—by hearing something unabashedly positive— that he hardly knew what to say.

OCTOBER 2003. Community centres aren't always easy places to be. People are often in crisis, and they can be angry and without hope. There are communication breakdowns because of language and cultural barriers. Many of the people who need our programs at The Stop lead stressful, difficult lives. As Glenn realized, the drop-in breakfast and lunch programs, especially, can often seem like a great big family dining room with the screaming kids, crazy uncle, sister with addiction issues and a demanding mother-in-law all forced to eat together. Sometimes it's a happy circus and sometimes there are fights.

We work hard to keep a lid on tensions, and the table service and welcoming staff presence go a long way toward making it less stressful. But, occasionally, someone pops off. One day not too long ago, I returned to my office after an especially crazy morning to find a voicemail waiting for me. The message was clear, even if the muffled voice on the other end of the line was not. I should watch my back.

It all started at breakfast when Bobby—a short, strong, wiry guy—was causing problems, yelling and complaining, and he refused to leave when asked. Then he told a drop-in staffer to fuck off. I was called into the community space to deal with him.

When I arrived, Bobby was up near the island in front of the kitchen area, a clutch of volunteers and our drop-in staff nearby. The room was still busy; a few tables of people were playing games, some were eating, and the whole place smelled vaguely of pancakes and coffee. Bobby, a long-time street fighter, was bouncing around on the balls of his feet as if he were in a boxing ring. I had about six inches on him, but he looked fit in his navy blue K-Way jacket and tight jeans, with the body of a teenager and the face of someone who'd lived through hell.

He was the aggressor, no doubt about it, but I also knew there was a lot of stress in his life. Drugs, money problems, violence. He needed us. Still, we can't have someone going around threatening staff or community members. "Sir," I said, in an effort at civility, "I'm afraid you're going to have to leave."

With the entire room watching, Bobby walked right up to me and pushed me—an angry two-hands-to-the-chest shove. I took a deep breath and stepped back, swallowing my own rage. "I'm going to have to call the police if you don't leave right now," I said.

Eventually, after some jawing and a few choice words from Bobby about the sorry state of my manhood, he left. We told him he was barred from The Stop indefinitely, but we all knew it wouldn't be the last we heard from him. When I got the voice-mail later that day, I was certain it was Bobby.

We didn't hear from him for a while after that. Maybe he left town, went to jail for some other issue, or just decided we weren't worth the bother. But then he turned up again, and conveniently seemed to have forgotten his threat. We told him he was still barred from our programs, but knowing he was desperate agreed that we'd provide him with a food hamper as long as he came only to the front door.

It's so easy to get off balance here: despite all our efforts to make the drop-in a more supportive and safe place, one out-of-control person can tip the scales. We're always on alert. In fact, the drop-in staff know the community so well that they are aware of what sets certain people off, who needs to be escorted out the back door for a cigarette to calm down, and who is all talk but won't actually start anything. Often all it takes is to say to the disruptive person that there are frightened children in the room, or that their angry behaviour is affecting everyone. The scariest moments for all of us are the times when someone new to the drop-in gets upset—maybe because they think a person at their table looked at them funny, or they're hungry and feel their wait for the food is too long. Staff can't be certain then which way things will blow. Sometimes they call me in from my office at the front to help out, but mostly they handle it themselves. Getting the police involved is a last resort—seeing uniformed officers in the space immediately changes everything.

But for all the Bobbys who come through The Stop, there are far more guys like Abdul, just trying to make it through the day. A refugee from Somalia, he was part of the large-scale immigration to North America from the war-torn country in the early 1990s. Abdul speaks at least four languages and lives near The Stop in a small apartment. He's fastidious about his appearance. I often see him walking alone along the street outside our office going from his apartment to the beer store down the street. I first began noticing him attending the breakfast drop-in. Then he was convinced to join an East African Men's Cooking Group in our new commercial kitchen.

After a long renovation, we finally finished the space. To accommodate all of our new programs—and the staff to facilitate them—we've moved into a larger office and program space, taking over the public health unit office when they moved to another location. I miss the public health nurses, with their lunches, tea and wise counsel, but we have more room for our growing programs, as well as direct access between the offices and the program area. The little kitchen in the drop-in was never going to be enough for our new food initiatives, so we've carved a large commercial-style kitchen from a former meeting area—the place, in fact, where I used to join the nurses for lunch. Though there were jaw-dropping mechanical costs to bring in a ventilation system for the gas stove, as well as the usual renovation delays and hiccups, the space is beautiful, efficient and functional. A big, green marble-topped island for food prep takes pride of place in the middle of the room, and tidy maple cabinets line one wall. But it's the six-burner gas stove and range hood, the industrial dishwasher, fridge and freezer, and massive dough mixer that I often go in to ogle. I spent hours touring the city's restaurant supply stores, talking shop with the owners and staff. I became a certified kitchen supply geek.

I can smell the food cooking before I walk into the kitchen—a pungent mix of cumin, cloves and onion. Rumana, an Eritrean woman with a linguistics background, is leading the ten participants in the East African Men's Cooking Group through a workshop on preparing a dish she calls *shiro wat*, a chickpea flour stew cooked with a berbere spice mixture. Abdul and several other men from Somalia and Eritrea are all standing around the marble island. They each wear hairnets, have a small plastic cutting board and onion in front of them and are chopping furiously. Some are casual, their shoulders relaxed; others look tense and squeeze their onion in one hand, foreheads pinched as if they've never held a kitchen knife in their lives.

It was after drop-in staff started noticing a large East African contingent coming in for meals that we had Rumana, who'd been working with our perinatal program, set up this group. She found participants by talking to people at public housing buildings in the neighbourhood, putting up posters at laundromats, even dropping by some of the bars on a nearby street. She tells me that the men were reluctant to get involved at first. In their cultures, women are usually the cooks. But most of the men in the group are single like Abdul, alone in a foreign city with no one but themselves to rely on. A number of them are also dealing with addiction issues and alcoholism, as well as other fallout from the trauma of war. In the beginning, Rumana says, they were more like helpers than cooks. But after a few weeks they loosened up and began sharing stories about how the simple African dishes they prepare are different in each of their countries. The men get along well, despite language and cultural differences.

I stand beside Abdul to see how he's doing with his onion. He chops haltingly while listening to a couple of men across the island talk to each other in rapid-fire Somali. Abdul translates for me, explaining that the one man is telling the other a story about his childhood. They get so animated, everyone is listening. Then they all begin to laugh.

We've planned this kitchen to accommodate just such a program. It will also be used, of course, by our part-time chef and volunteers to produce breakfast and lunch for the growing numbers at our drop-in. I love that The Stop is becoming a place that people come to for so many different reasons. Men like Abdul may come for the free meal but stay for the community kitchen. Others, like Glenn, need an emergency food hamper but find a new lease on life as a volunteer. And there are many people like Tania and Rosa who have built a community here. Creating programs that feed from each other and benefit participants through mutual support is a key part of the idea behind the Community Food Centre.

The ability to offer a variety of food programs under one roof is also resonating with our funders. When we started raising money for the kitchen renovation last year, we were nearly bowled over by the donations that began coming in right away. The stove was donated by the manufacturer, the massive slab of marble was provided by a friend of mine in the stone business, and anonymous donors, the city, and a family foundation pitched in for the rest of the $115,000 price tag. We used to have people call us up and say, "We have an old fridge, do you want it?" Quite often it would turn up without a door handle, or the freezer would be broken. With this fully outfitted new kitchen, we don't need to accept those anymore. And we plan to hire a full-time chef as soon as we can find the money.

Rumana offers me an apron and I readily accept. She divides us up into stations. One pair is instructed to get the plates and cutlery ready, another to tend to the bubbling stew on the stovetop. Abdul and I are sent off to clean some of the mixing bowls. We quickly get into a rhythm, loading up the dishwasher rack, and washing and drying the bowls by hand. We don't speak. We don't have to. By the time we're done, the smell of the chickpea stew is so thick in the air I can almost taste it.

WHEN I'M TALKING TO PEOPLE about my work at The Stop I often say poverty affects us all. What I mean is that I believe we have a shared obligation to support people who are struggling. Sometimes it's as neighbours, friends or family, but our obligation extends beyond our small circles and I think it needs to be expressed collectively. We are connected to each other in an essential way—by our shared humanity—and when thousands or millions of people are living in poverty, in poor health, hungry and poorly housed or homeless, our society as a whole is lesser for it. I think that anyone who's ever walked by a homeless person lying over a warm grate and felt powerless in the face of their misery, or watched someone dig through a garbage can for food, knows what it is to be diminished on a moral level by such inequality.

I'm not talking about feeling a blush of guilt because your toddler has fresh fruit while someone else is eating from a dumpster; instead, this is a deeper, more profound recognition that we are only as strong as our weakest link. That other's suffering is also our own. This connection is why we need to work together to create the spaces, public institutions, laws, policies and regulations that will ensure that everyone can participate freely, actively and meaningfully in our society.

From this belief also arises the understanding that there are systemic reasons for poverty: racism, inadequate minimum wages, social exclusion of the mentally ill, lack of childcare, to name a few. And the biggest determinant of where you end up in life—rich or poor or in between—is who you were born to, the great big lottery of life. There are exceptions, of course, but while they capture our imagination—everyone loves a Horatio Alger tale of the child born in the slums who goes on to become a billionaire—they remain rare.

Formed by my experience working in low-income communities, this belief in our profound connection to each other is self-evident to me. But it's a world view that has lost favour over my lifetime, as the cult of the individual has become the dominant narrative. That people operate best on their own and that it's natural, right and inescapable for the fittest to come out on top has become the story of our culture. Accordingly, anyone who's poor is simply lazy, their circumstances the result of their own failures, even a "lifestyle choice."

It's the kind of thinking that spawned such pernicious developments as welfare snitch lines for vindictive people to tattle on neighbours they think are cheating the system. It is also the ethos that has driven massive cuts to entitlements and the welfare system across North America and many other parts of the world over the last three decades. Not long before I arrived at The Stop, one cost-cutting local politician helpfully created a shopping list for those trying to live on reduced social assistance benefits. According to his calculations, a frugal single adult could live on a food budget of only a few dollars a day. Welfare recipients were encouraged to eat pasta with no sauce and haggle with supermarket cashiers over tins of tuna fish.

When people started to investigate the numbers, it was revealed that not only was the food budget he proposed far below the local public health unit's recommended minimum daily food allowance, his suggested diet was less nutritious than the one provided in our prisons. But in his view, poverty and hunger were merely the result of poor household budgeting—or even a character flaw.

This theory about the cause of poverty has become so widely accepted that the poor and marginalized themselves sometimes echo the line. At The Stop, we used to receive complaints from tenants in Symington Place claiming that the people using our services were causing trouble, loitering in front of the town-houses at the back, leaving garbage or dealing drugs. At residents' meetings, lots of accusations were flung around, and our city councillor was forced to get involved in negotiations, almost always taking the side of the people who wanted us out.

But when we began to dig down into the neighbourhood, doing annual surveys and getting to know the community better, we discovered that many of the people who use The Stop actually live in Symington Place. We aren't bringing in outsiders, we're supporting those living in deep poverty in the community itself. Certainly there are drug addicts who use our services, but they are just as likely to either live in the neighbourhood or be visiting residents as they are to come to The Stop on their own accord. The complaints have dissipated as our staff have ensured that they, not the local city councillor, are the first port of call when something goes awry, and that tenants' concerns about noise or drugs are dealt with swiftly.

If someone is outside the food bank near the townhouses

making noise, we'll ask them to move along or at the very least to respect the neighbours. We provide containers for cigarette butts and have tried to beautify the space with flowers, planter boxes and a colourful sign welcoming people to The Stop. We also make an effort to communicate with Symington Place residents about events being held on the weekend or renovations that might affect them. Most people in the complex would now agree that we actually help keep the area safe because there are more people around, more eyes on the street and more sense of community. Still, it's an indication of how deeply this villainizing of the poor has infiltrated our culture when even the most disadvantaged look down on those who are more vulnerable than they are.

This notion of poverty as a character flaw also sets the stage for the withdrawal of government supports for low-income people. When you believe that the poor deserve their poverty and should bloody well get on with pulling themselves up by their bootstraps, it's easy to justify cuts to public housing and social services. But the result of these kinds of punitive policy decisions is not the pulling up of bootstraps, it's the growing gap between haves and have-nots. Davenport West is not the only place affected, of course. The Organization for Economic Co-operation and Development (OECD) reports that income disparity in industrialized nations has reached a thirty-year high. In Canada, the top 10 percent of earners make ten times the amount of the bottom 10 percent, a figure slightly worse than the OECD average. Meanwhile, the United States is edged out only by Mexico, Chile and Turkey for the highest poverty and inequality rate in the OECD. The top 10 percent of American income earners make fifteen times more than those in the bottom 10 percent.

This income gap is part of the impetus behind the international Occupy movement that began in 2011 to take over streets and parks and minds all over the world, as the wealth of the richest and the deprivation of the poorest began to seem increasingly unconscionable. But people in Davenport West have been on the front lines of this schism for years. One of the last holdouts of working-class downtown Toronto, our neighbourhood and its residents have long struggled to find footing in a divided city.

The challenges our community members face, of course, are not theirs alone—a sentiment of solidarity that Occupy has begun to popularize with its rallying cry about the 99 percent standing up together against the wealthiest 1 percent. But there is more to this common cause than shared disgust at the insanely high compensation of certain corporate CEOs or the heavy environmental impact of a one-percenter. We need to look at the impact poverty has on all of us not only on a moral or ethical level, but also on an economic one—in lost productivity, unrealized potential, crime and unsafe neighbourhoods, ballooning health care budgets and a shortage of skilled workers.

The World Health Organization itself calls poverty "the single largest determinant of health." According to "Poverty Is Making Us Sick" from the Wellesley Institute, an urban health think tank, the poorest one-fifth of Canadians—like many of those who use The Stop and other food banks—have a "sixty percent greater rate of two or more chronic health conditions; more than three times the rate of bronchitis" and "nearly double the rate of arthritis or rheumatism." This same cohort has a "358% higher rate of disability" as well as "128% more mental and behavioural disorders; 95% more ulcers; 63% more chronic conditions; and 33% more circulatory conditions."

The impacts of poverty on the health care system and on productivity are enormous. And these are only some of the costs; there's also the money spent on income supports and welfare payments, the criminal justice system, education supports associated with early childhood and high school completion, and the cost of lost opportunity. In Canada, according to the National Council of Welfare, the total cost of poverty to the public purse is about $25 billion a year—a figure based, the council explains, on a "cautious estimate." Other research suggests it could be more than three times that number—a loss to the economy of somewhere between $72 billion and $84 billion a year. In the United Kingdom, the Joseph Rowntree Foundation estimates child poverty alone costs the country 25 billion pounds (about $40 billion) annually. In the United States, the Center for American Progress estimates child poverty costs the nation at least $500 billion a year.

The National Council of Welfare explains that spending only half the $25 billion on such things as adequate social assistance, accessible childcare and higher education, and support for immigrants would significantly raise the standard of living for those below the poverty line. Quite simply, it costs less to eliminate poverty than to allow it to persist. So why don't we work upstream on this—and save those babies before they fall in the water? Why not invest in prevention?

There are plenty of examples, especially in Scandinavian countries, of governments that have made poverty reduction a priority. Not piecemeal programs or money thrown hither and thither, but a comprehensive policy response that involves such things as sustained investment of the tax base in public housing, childcare, increased minimum wages, accessible food, health care and education. The result is a more egalitarian society, a stronger economy, more social mobility, greater cohesion, less violence, better health and that incredibly hard-to-quantify thing: more happiness.

In their award-winning book *The Spirit Level: Why Greater Equality Makes Societies Stronger*, British academics Richard Wilkinson and Kate Pickett used every measurement possible—from mental health to teenage pregnancy rates, suicide to prison stats—to prove that greater equality benefits everyone (the poor, admittedly, see their prospects improve the most). Examining worldwide data, they showed that health and social problems are less severe in more-equal nations; mental health problems and homicide rates are lower; teen births are fewer and rates of imprisonment are less. People in more-equal countries even report that they trust each other more than those in nations where disparity is greater.

Wilkinson and Pickett explain that if inequality were sliced in half in the United Kingdom, murder rates would also be halved, 80 percent fewer people would be imprisoned, and levels of mutual trust would grow by 85 percent. They also note that obesity levels would nosedive, with rates dropping by 50 percent. All over the world, they found, higher rates of obesity are connected to inequality. Even within the United States, the states with the largest gap between rich and poor (for instance, Texas, Louisiana and Mississippi) have the highest number of obese adults. Increasingly, in developed nations, obesity is seen as a disease of the poor. At The Stop, many of our participants struggle with being obese or overweight and the accompanying health problems. A report by the Trust for America's Health and Robert Wood Johnson Foundation estimates the medical cost of adult obesity in the U.S. is $147 to $210 billion per year.

Naturally, the kinds of interventions that promote greater equality (with direct benefits in reduced obesity, homicide and teen births and greater social mobility) cost money up front that must be generated by public policy change and taxes. Despite the growing evidence that nations will actually save money and build a better life for their citizens if they invest in such preventative policies, it's an ongoing struggle to convince some politicians and voters of the wisdom of the expenditure. The political will to stand up and fight for real, substantive changes to our increasingly unequal society is in short supply.

As Wilkinson and Pickett point out in *The Spirit Level*, "The task is now to develop a politics based on a recognition of the kind of society we need to create and committed to making use of the institutional and technological opportunities to realize it."

I couldn't agree more. In fact, I see The Stop as helping make the case for this new kind of society every day. By establishing a respectful, dignified place where low-income people have access to healthy food and opportunities to learn new skills, as well as take advantage of resources that will help them build a better life for themselves, we are creating an organization that reflects the kind of world we'd like to see.

MARCH 2004. From the sky, São Paulo, Brazil, seems to go on forever. Tiny houses all jumbled together give way to skyscrapers and then more skyscrapers like towering white dominoes. A rambling metropolis of nearly twenty million souls, the Greater São Paulo region is the largest city in South America, one of the biggest on the planet.

Even though I'm groggy after a long flight from Toronto,

the sight of the city below energizes me. When we step off the plane, I offer to negotiate with the rental car outlet in my pidgin Portuguese and drive us to our hotel. My travelling companions, Debbie Field from FoodShare and Wayne Roberts, head of the Toronto Food Policy Council, agree gladly. But as soon as we pull out of the massive airport into a phalanx of oncoming traffic, I regret my enthusiasm. We manage to get onto the ring road in our economy Fiat; forty-five minutes later I realize we're nearly back to where we started. First we circled São Paulo in the air, now we're circling it on land.

Despite this minor-league complication—and the fact that Andrea is back in Toronto nearly ready to give birth to our second child—I can't help but feel excited about the Brazilian hunger and nutrition conference we've been invited to attend as delegates. At this moment, the vast, complicated, fascinating country is to food politics what Graceland is to Elvis aficionados. The recently elected president, Luiz Inácio Lula da Silva, known by everyone as Lula, made ending hunger a key plank in his election platform. His rousing speeches and ambitious promises have galvanized the vast ranks of the Brazilian poor as well as people all over the world who care about social justice.

Using an innovative mix of programs—including cash transfers to low-income mothers (according to the number of children they have in school), universal school meals, community kitchens and support for small farmers—Brazil is at the forefront of new thinking about how to deal with hunger. It couldn't have happened soon enough for many of the country's citizens. Brazil has long been one of the most unequal countries in the world, with tens of millions of people—more than the entire population of Canada—living on less than a dollar a day.

A former labour leader who grew up in deep poverty, drinking water from ditches and working as a shoeshine boy, Lula has built an almost messianic following. His promises to end hunger in the country entirely, raise the minimum wage and reduce disparity have found welcome ears.

There's no doubt such a wholesale transformation of Brazilian society will encounter some major obstacles, but there's much to be learned from the example. We're all looking forward to seeing the programs and people—on scheduled tours and in workshops—when we head to the northeast coast where the conference is being held and Lula will give the keynote address.

Toronto, I've learned from Debbie and Wayne, has long had links to Brazil. One of Brazil's intellectual heroes, community organizer Herbert de Souza, known affectionately as Betinho, landed in the city during the 1970s following his exile from Brazil's military dictatorship. There, he inspired many social justice groups with his analysis of democracy and Latin American politics. In turn, he was inspired by the power and influence of civil society organizations in Canada and brought this influence back to Brazil, creating his own nongovernmental organization aimed at promoting community control, democracy and food security. Though he died in 1997, Betinho's campaign against hunger helped spawn the current food movement in Brazil.

Cecilia Rocha, a Brazilian-born economist who now lives and works in Toronto, is another important link between the two countries and food policy. She's one of the reasons we were invited to Brazil in the first place. Cecilia's going to the conference, too, and will meet up with us after visiting her family. She's spent a number of years documenting the innovative food programs piloted out of the Brazilian city of Belo Horizonte. An entire municipal department there is devoted to food access, and it has developed programs like government-run popular restaurants and open-air markets offering local produce at a fair price. The impact has been dramatic: falling infant mortality and malnutrition rates, increased consumption of fruits and vegetables (while other Brazilian cities report a decrease), money in the pockets of local small farmers, and more equitable access to healthy food.

Cecilia sees Belo Horizonte's new food system as instructive for other cities around the world, particularly in the way that it emerged directly from government intervention, rather than from purely entrepreneurial, market-based initiatives. She's also interested in how the nationwide creation of social councils (made up of both politicians and members of civil society) that monitor and control the food access programs has led to more citizen engagement in the political system.

Despite—or perhaps because of—its profound inequalities, Brazil has a rich history of citizen-led democracy. Early thinkers in the Catholic liberation theology movement, who considered it their role as Christians to fight poverty and social injustice (including hunger), were active here. Brazil is also the birthplace of Paulo Freire, who wrote so compellingly about the political potential of education. More recently, I've been following the participatory budget-making process in the city of Porto Alegre (where Lula's workers' party, Partido dos Trabalhadores, is in charge). Since 1989, thousands of citizen delegates have been involved in an annual process of identifying priorities and voting on how to spend public funds.

But the thing that makes Brazil especially fascinating to me is the way that these policies and ideas around food access, poverty and citizen participation are integrated, all working together toward building a more equitable society. The government, for instance, mandates that at least 30 percent of the fresh food for its school meal program is sourced locally—helping hungry kids enjoy a healthy meal at the same time as building the local economy and promoting environmental sustainability. The subsidized markets and popular restaurants are also built on this model—feeding the hungry and supporting local farmers. The emphasis on citizen engagement through the social councils is another part of this approach; food access policy is seen as a way to both feed people and involve them in governance.

In many ways, I see the food programs and projects in Brazil, which are guided by a community development ethos and the belief that real social change happens when everyone has a place at the table, as a model—writ large—for us at The Stop. It's one of the reasons I'm so excited to be here and see it first-hand. Looking at food as a tool for change is a far cry from the food bank approach we've had for so long in North America. In fact, Brazil's holistic take on food access couldn't be more different from the response to hunger we've developed in Canada and the United States.

As The Stop forges ahead, reimagining itself along these lines, the differences between our approach and the traditional food bank model are continuing to cause tensions. Not long before I left for Brazil, Cliff had an unfortunate exchange with a food bank staffer from another organization in which she accused him—at a picnic for volunteers—of lacking compassion. She had sent someone to The Stop, but Cliff had to turn him away because he'd been given a hamper previously, and our policy is that people can use our food bank just once a month. He told the man about our regular breakfast and lunch drop-in and encouraged him to use another local resource, but the staffer was angry when she heard and asked Cliff if he just didn't care that people were going hungry. Quite rightly, he felt personally attacked, when he was adhering to The Stop's stated policy, one that we've consciously instituted to create space, time and funding for other programs that we believe are more effective.

I also read an interview with Sue Cox in which she told the journalist that community gardens and their ilk might be nice but "we delude ourselves if we think they're going to end hunger." Such programs, she suggested, are window dressing on the real issue of low incomes.

It wasn't the first time I'd heard this argument, and Sue is right that our gardens aren't going to end hunger. But they are so much more than window dressing. Our garden isn't just a pretty place for our community to go and see flowers or touch the herbs; it's a zone of engagement for children and adults that is both political and personal. Our community kitchens aren't just warm and homey-smelling spots; they're ground zero for connecting isolated people with their food, their health and each other. We aren't just digging in the garden waiting and hoping for government to change. Instead, by creating programs where participants can find their voice and learn new skills, we're creating opportunities for people in our neighbourhood to articulate their needs and begin to fight for their rights.

Many food bank advocates see their everyday work supporting hungry people as distinct from their (often considerable) efforts at fighting for social change through lobbying government and public awareness campaigns. At The Stop we don't think they should be distinct at all. We provide a place to meet immediate needs—usually hunger, always poverty—but we also see our programs as so much more. This isn't one-off advocacy or simply about handing people a placard and sending them to wave it about; it's more subtle, time-consuming and, we believe, effective. Through our programs, The Stop builds relationships and establishes hope and trust, laying the essential groundwork so that people can express themselves—with placards, maybe, but most importantly with their own voices and actions.

Here in Brazil, this grassroots approach seems far less controversial than it sometimes does at home. After exploring the buzzing maze of traffic congestion and skyscrapers that is São Paulo, we head to the oceanside city of Recife near the conference site. Early in the morning, we're whisked off to see a former sugar plantation recently taken over by its workers and supported by government-funded staff whose aim is "community empowerment." The plantation also has an aquaculture component, with ponds where workers grow carp to add more protein to their diets. On our tour, a worker tells us they've adapted the well-known proverb about self-sufficiency to "Give a person a fish and they'll eat for a day; teach a person to *breed* fish, and they'll eat every day."

The conference itself is in Olinda, a historic city north of Recife with beautifully preserved colonial buildings. Held in a vast convention hall named for Herbert de Souza, the conference is more than a thousand people strong, two-thirds of them elected delegates from Brazil's twenty-six states. These are not politicians, but average people chosen by their peers to tell the rest of the country about how their communities are tackling hunger and poverty. Each state has a booth outside the main lecture theatre describing the interesting projects they've created—from popular restaurants to procurement strategies that increase local foods in hospitals, schools and other government-funded facilities.

It's hard not to be struck by the fact that in Toronto it's hard to get a meeting with the mayor to talk about hunger and food issues, whereas here every federal minister in the country is attending a conference to talk about how they're working on

Lula's Fome Zero (zero hunger) program. Brazil even has a federal minister of food security with a mandate to ensure that no one in the country goes hungry.

While we're inspecting the booths and talking to other delegates, we hear a big commotion outside. It's a demonstration by the Landless Rural Workers' Movement (MST), a group of farm workers fighting for social justice, local control and land reform. Part of the international peasant movement La Via Campesina, the MST faithful have resisted aligning themselves with Lula and his party despite promises of "so much land you will not know what to do with it." Some MST leaders have repeatedly turned down offers of top government jobs.

We watch the demonstration from the sidewalk outside the convention hall. Here in the middle of what feels like a Lula lovefest, it's hard to imagine why they don't want to be involved. But one of the Brazilians I've met tells me that Lula's government is struggling to meet not just its own promises but also high public hopes and expectations for rapid change. Having inherited a massive foreign debt, Lula is under tremendous pressure from the World Bank and the International Monetary Fund, as well as currency speculators who sent a chill through the currency market because of Lula's Marxist background. In fact, partly because of concessions made to these international bodies, unemployment remains high, workers' wages have actually gone down, and interest rates are some of the highest in the world. Agrarian reform is unlikely to happen as swiftly as some in the MST would like.

Word goes through the conference crowd that the president will be speaking soon, so we head inside to our seats in the big auditorium. But I feel slightly chastened. I hate to think these successful food access initiatives will be derailed by the international banking system or other pressures from outside the country. It's another reminder to me of how important political will is to advancing an issue like fighting hunger and poverty. We need engaged citizens and progressive organizations who will put politicians' feet to the fire and make it impossible to ignore the needs of low-income people, and also strong-minded and committed politicians and bureaucrats willing to work with civil society to effect real sustainable change. And even then, it's tough.

Three hours after he's scheduled to speak, Lula finally arrives. Despite the demonstration and the long wait in the sweltering conference hall, when his entrance music begins, the excitement is infectious. People sing and dance in the aisles for a good ten minutes before they settle into their seats.

Considered by some to be one of the most popular leaders in the world, the gravelly voiced president with the trademark thick, grey beard has the room in the palm of his hand as soon as he starts speaking. He cracks a joke about how the conference is wrestling with how to achieve zero hunger; his problem is zero sleep. Speaking without notes, he responds to his detractors with a call for patience, saying that the kind of platform of change he and his party were elected on will take time.

Lula knows the power of his story. He tells the crowd about the hunger he experienced as a child and how he was so ashamed he'd try to hide it from his friends. It makes me think about all the people with their heads down, eyes averted, in food bank lineups back home, and about all the people who need the services of a food bank but don't use it because of the shame of having to ask for a handout. Lula reminds us that no one should have to feel that way. People living in poverty and experiencing hunger need to speak up so the problem doesn't get swept aside, he says. Fighting hunger, he tells the assembled group, is a "sacred" task. His words build to a climax. "We can't have some eating five times a day while others don't eat for five days!" he bellows.

People are clapping and shouting. I'm on my feet, as well. Looking around at the flushed faces and passionate cheering, I'm already trying to think about how we can capture some of this energy and bring it home. Seeing the Brazilians' efforts to end hunger—at farms and schools, in markets and city halls—the citizen participation and the political backing for it has my wheels turning. People are stomping their feet now. I can feel the thunder of their enthusiasm reverberate in my body.

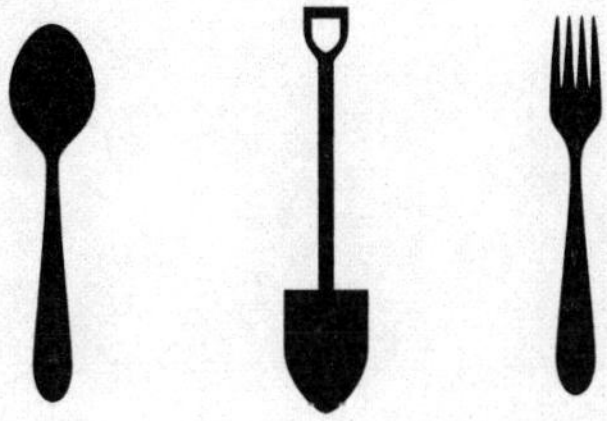

FIVE

CHANGE HAPPENS BECAUSE PEOPLE FIGHT FOR IT

MAY 2004. Theora Spooner is sitting at a table surrounded by six other women. They're in a corner of the community space between the small stage and the windows that reach to the floor. Multicoloured balls of yarn and knitting needles are strewn on the table in front of them. Several of the women hold the needles expertly in their hands, the clickety-clack of plastic against plastic a conversation all its own.

Theora's in her late sixties. She's from Barbados, and has an easygoing charm that draws people to her. She first came to The Stop for the food bank, but then she started dropping in on other programs like the community breakfasts and lunch, and began to volunteer. But it was when one of our staff offered baking and cake-icing classes that Theora became a true regular. Recently, she agreed to help form this knitting group and share her knowledge; with her mellow presence, it's proving popular.

Theora and her knitting club are a good antidote to the frustration and anger that can hit The Stop like a flash of lightning. We had another incident recently that shook us all. It began when an ex-offender volunteering as part of a training program was asked to leave. Cliff had caught him stealing food twice and the man was furious. He made threats, denying his guilt despite the evidence. Soon afterward, gasoline was thrown around the front entrance, the containers left at the door. A few days later, Cliff received an anonymous voice message saying there was a bomb in the building. Police cruisers, fire trucks and the Emergency Task Force arrived at the front and back entrance within minutes. The building had to be evacuated and searched. It turned out to be a hoax, but it frightened everyone. Police traced the call to a phone booth not far from the volunteer's apartment.

I load up some of the melamine lunch dishes at a table near Theora's knitting club and take them to the kitchen, grabbing a damp cloth to wipe down the surface. I like to come by here and talk to people. Working in an office away from the program space, I sometimes miss the day-to-day buzz of community work, the in-the-trenches rewards of building relationships and getting to know people and their lives. It's not easy work, of course, but there is tremendous satisfaction in doing something that can make someone's life better—even in a small way.

When I've finished cleaning the table, I sit down and ask Theora about her family, her church and her health. "I'm alright," Theora drawls with a gentle smile. The other women are so busy—hands flying, mouths moving—they barely notice me. Theora's like a calm mother hen with a brood of chattering chicks. Some more women come by to join the knitting group and I get up so there's space at the table. The breakfast drop-in was busy, too. Once school lets out, we'll start to see more and more children coming in with their parents. Without even the meagre patchwork of school food programs available in this country, many low-income families find the summer the hardest time of all to keep their kids healthy and fed. Before I leave, another woman asks shyly if she can join the group. It's starting to get squishy at the knitting table, but Theora is imperturbable. She gives up her own seat.

I try to take some of Theora's calm with me when I head toward the food bank. I'm a generally even-keel sort of person, but there's a lot going on these days and I have to work at it more than usual. In addition to all the programs and activity at Symington Place, we're continuing to move forward with the sustainable food and education project at the old industrial space that we proposed when Rhonda first started at The Stop. We're calling it the Green Barn and for me, the entire endeavour has been an education in patience and the challenges of community building.

I didn't understand it fully when we first put in our proposal, but the redevelopment of the five former streetcar maintenance barns several kilometres east of Symington Place, closer to downtown, was the topic of heated neighbourhood debate long before we arrived on the scene. Built on a 4.3-acre site between 1913 and 1921 and considered to be some of the city's most important historical structures, the five attached "barns" had been mostly vacant after the Toronto Transit Commission (TTC) stopped actively using them for streetcar repair in the mid-1980s. Long, wide brick structures, they were outfitted with large wooden doors at either end. In the site's heyday, the yard outside was filled with streetcars waiting for service. But by the mid-1990s, the buildings were unused and boarded up, the lot weedy and overgrown. The city began looking to redevelop the prime location with high-density housing. The relatively affluent community nearby rallied against it, managing to convince City Hall to save at least some of the historical structures for community use and to make the site into a park. But determining what constitutes a park in a contemporary urban setting turned out to be very contested terrain.

I've been involved in neighbourhood organizing long enough to know that trying to gather and incorporate community feedback is never a seamless process. There are invariably many different motives at work. Meetings can become angry and difficult in less time than it takes to yawn at the agenda. But even knowing this, the intensity of discussions about the redevelopment of these derelict barns surprised me.

Once our proposal was accepted by the lead developer, Artscape—a nonprofit urban development group with a track record of converting old buildings into live/work spaces for artists—the debate about the community's definition of a park began in earnest. There were those who just wanted green space—a baseball diamond, a few trees—and those who wanted green space as well as repurposed buildings for artists and community use. I spent hours and hours in meetings, watching a group of neighbourhood moms knit enough scarves to warm the entire city in winter, arriving home bleary-eyed at two and three in the morning with nothing resolved. I listened to people scream and argue and point fingers, discussing the merits of this or that style of park, throwing around accusations about the promises allegedly kept or broken by local politicians. I even saw children paraded to the front of meeting rooms to parrot their parents' views on the matter—in the hope, I suppose, that the kids' words would tug at the community's heart strings. The process has been long and fractious, and even now, several years in, there are days when it's hard to believe that it's actually going to happen. Keeping The Stop's board on side and trying to figure out how we'll fund our portion of the redevelopment is turning into a whole other job, in addition to my role at Symington Place.

To make things more challenging for me personally, Andrea and I have a new baby at home. Another preemie, though little Quinn had a few more weeks in utero than his early-bird brother, and had to be hospitalized for only two weeks. He was still small, and it was frightening at the beginning, but it was less stressful than our first time in the neonatal intensive care unit.

Between what's happening at home and at work, I'm running on fumes. I breathe deeply and walk into the food bank. It's like being hit by a blast of wind when you step outside through a revolving door. The place is a zoo. A delivery has just come in from Daily Bread. Giant pallets are covered with sky-high stacks of unopened boxes; milk crates and garbage cans dot the space. A big load of veggies that we bought is waiting to be bagged. Volunteers are rushing around.

Still, it's far better organized than it used to be. A front desk volunteer extends a welcome, and bulletin boards are strategically placed to offer information and resources. A new walk-in fridge and freezer—a major capital investment that cost nearly $25,000—helps keep things organized. It also means we can buy more perishable items to offer at the food bank. About 80 percent of the food we hand out in the hampers is still donated, but more and more we try to supplement it by buying fresh food that we choose.

On busy days like this, it's all hands on deck; even our fundraiser comes into the back to bag green beans or unload pallets of canned goods. Sometimes I go into the food bank just to clean. I get down on the floor, underneath the fridges, behind the shelves. We fight a constant battle against cockroaches and mice, and I don't feel I can ask others to do something I'm not willing to do myself. Cliff confessed recently that he and others in the food bank call my occasional cleaning frenzies a "Nick-fit." Today I have extra cause to go into my act. We're expecting visitors from Brazil for a tour, some of whom I met when I was there.

Cliff leaves the new walk-in fridge, a big box of broccoli in his arms. "Only ninety-two more sleeps until the Ex!" he says. The Canadian National Exhibition, or the Ex, is the annual end-of-summer fair on Toronto's waterfront. It's Cliff's favourite time of the year. He puts down the box for a minute so we can discuss the plan for the Brazilian delegation. They're in Toronto to explore the idea of introducing food banks to their country. Cliff and I agree we won't mince words: we'll tell them not to do it.

It's times like this that I realize what a complicated position Cliff is in. He's rightly proud of his work in the food bank. He's helped make it a much better place. And he and his team support thousands of people who need this food. They bring dignity, humility and humanity to what can be a demeaning process. And he's always trying to figure out how to make sure the system is more efficient and transparent, the food healthier and more representative of the cultures in our neighbourhood. But he also understands the limitations.

Recently, he's been studying food security part-time at university and taking Spanish lessons so he can communicate with our many Spanish-speaking community members. Cliff's willingness to learn and change, to never be defensive when we talk about the unhealthy food in the hampers or discuss the problem of food banks in general at staff meetings, is a tribute to his big spirit and inquiring mind. If we're going to make changes to the food banking system, we all need to be open to new approaches and solutions.

Cliff pulls some fresh Swiss chard and several different kinds of greens out of the fridge. We've come a long way from the days when we offered members wilted iceberg lettuce. The Stop is brimming with people and ideas: we have kitchens and the garden, drop-in meals, Healthy Beginnings, as well as a bake oven we built behind the health centre next door for making pizza and bread. We're also beginning to share what we've learned about building a healthy community with other neighbourhoods through the Community Food Animator Project, a collaboration between FoodShare and other food groups. Each organization contributes staff members and their expertise in a particular area (community markets, kitchens, gardens, emergency food). These Community Food Animators work in public housing developments across the city, supporting the under-resourced neighbourhoods to create shared gardens and community kitchens and host fresh food markets in an effort to get better-quality food to low-income people.

The city has changed, too. A new mayor was elected who is more receptive than his predecessor to community-driven planning. Homelessness hasn't disappeared and people in our neighbourhood continue to struggle, but there's a hopeful air, a sense of possibility here. Torontonians, often loath to celebrate their city, are beginning to embrace its potential.

I'm working hard to capture some of this excitement as I fundraise for the Green Barn. Sandy Houston and the Metcalf Foundation were the first to see the project's city-building potential, making a $500,000 contribution to kick-start the development—part of it for the initial planning, the rest intended as capital for the building stage. Sandy is working at the foundation full-time now, and, since the family patriarch left a major contribution to the organization in his will, has more funding at his disposal. He's also carried through on the plans he had when I met him the first time, hiring staff who look after different portfolios (the arts, the community sector and the environment) and professionalizing their funding strategy. We've become friends as our organizations have grown up alongside each other, and I rely on him for wise counsel and insight into managing all the competing demands. Under his guidance, the Metcalf Foundation has truly become a galvanizing force in the city—a funder with a social purpose that is stepping into areas where government used to play a larger role.

Metcalf's contribution gave the Green Barn project much-needed momentum. And because the grant was awarded to The Stop, but was used to mobilize the entire Barns project, it helped cement our position as a partner to Artscape and an anchor tenant in the redevelopment efforts. There's still a lot of uncertainty and the costs keep going up, but we can begin to imagine the Green Barn as a new platform for our Community Food Centre model.

A few years ago it may have been wishful thinking on my part, but today The Stop is truly a place where people come to cook, grow, eat, learn about and advocate for good food. The distance we've travelled really hit home for me when we received a letter saying that our long-time food bank volunteer Richard had died. I knew he'd been sick, though we felt his presence still in the many volunteers he'd referred to us over the years. He remained slightly cool with me until the end, but I'm pretty sure we won him over to our new approach. In his will, Richard left The Stop a significant bequest.

◆━

BRAZIL WASN'T THE ONLY COUNTRY that began looking at food banking as a response to growing hunger around this time. In fact, it was just as The Stop began to solidify its new direction and programs, reimagining emergency food in our neighbourhood, that food banks began to expand their reach outside of North America. Colombia started opening food banks in the early 2000s; Argentina created a food bank network in 2004. And by 2006, a global network of food banks had developed, with Mexico, Canada, the United States and Argentina as founding members. Today, that organization, The Global FoodBanking Network (GFN), has expanded into more than twenty-five countries, including developing nations such as India and Guatemala. European food banks have their own twenty-one-country-strong organization called Fédération Européenne des Banques Alimentaires.

Based in Chicago, the Global FoodBanking Network's mission is to alleviate world hunger. It supports existing food bank operations so they can become more efficient and better serve their communities, and encourages new food banking systems to form. In its promotional materials, GFN suggests food banking is one of the key solutions to alleviating hunger and improving food security globally, and emphasizes the link between people without enough to eat and the vast amounts of food waste in the world.

The message that the end of hunger is possible if we just figure out better systems to collect and distribute excess food continues to prove a powerful one. According to the Food and

Agriculture Organization of the United Nations (FAO), one billion people in the world go hungry while more than a billion tonnes of food goes to waste every year—because of failure to harvest, postharvest loss or product disposal, which is the result of overproduction, expiration dates, damage or a failure on the marketing side. People in the world's wealthiest countries, FAO reports, throw away 222 million tonnes of food every year—nearly the same amount as the entire net food production in sub-Saharan Africa. It seems unconscionable that such food waste and hunger should coexist.

Food corporations have also jumped on the global food bank bandwagon, just as they did in North America. The food and beverage industry is one of the largest and most influential on earth—valued at nearly six trillion dollars and rising. The companies that dominate the international food system are vast and powerful. Nestlé, the biggest packaged food company in the world—which makes everything from dairy products and coffee to chocolate bars and pet food—has profits of upwards of $32 billion a year and employs a small city's worth of people around the world. In the United States, ten large companies control more than half of all food sales.

As these companies rapidly expand their reach and market share in the developing world, it makes economic sense that they would ally themselves with food banking as it puts down roots in more nations. Some of the largest companies in the industry—including Cargill, General Mills, Kellogg's, Walmart, Nestlé, Kraft Foods, Unilever, PepsiCo and Sodexo—are partners with GFN. The network also hosts an annual leadership institute sponsored by these companies where food bank leaders from around the world gather in San Antonio, Texas, to share knowledge and establish international connections.

In fact, wherever they turn up, food companies and food

banks are deeply intertwined. From the food banks' point of view, these relationships ensure a consistent supply of food for hungry people. For the food companies, it means a ready outlet for their surplus, unsold and failed products—avoiding the costs associated with disposal of the food. They also connect themselves with "good works" and build brand loyalty—in some cases with new consumers in the developing world, an essential market as the middle class expands globally.

The problem with these cozy relationships is that they make it difficult for food bank leaders (if they are so inclined) to ask tough questions about the nutritional value, production, labour practices or environmental impact of the products donated to them—and eaten by the hungry people they serve. To do so would jeopardize their supply of food.

So food banks by and large end up treating food in the same way their corporate partners do: as strictly a commodity, an item bought or donated, divorced from culture, health, community and the environment. To probe more deeply would open up questions that could threaten the whole house of cards. Food banks would have to ask how these multinational food companies and their highly processed foods are contributing to the move away from healthy traditional foods and to accelerating levels of obesity, diabetes and cardiovascular disease all over the world. They would be forced to ask if the fossil-fuel-intensive, corporate-controlled, industrial agriculture–based system represented by the big food companies is part of the problem in the first place.

Certainly, there are examples of real emergencies, such as the devastating Japanese earthquake and tsunami of 2011, in which existing food bank networks became essential to survival. Following the disaster, Second Harvest Japan had the vehicles and food sources needed to get food to hungry, isolated people.

However, emergency responses to hunger should not be confused with everyday reality. After a flood or hurricane wipes out other options, any food truly is better than nothing. But day in and day out, it's not good enough. The shame and humiliation food bank users report feeling and the disproportionate number of diet-related health problems they face are clear evidence of the inadequacy of such an approach. Plus, as we've seen over decades in North America, it's simply wrong-headed to think food banks and the redistribution of edible foodstuffs will meet the vast, consistent need for healthy food—let alone end hunger. Food banks are notoriously underfunded; they run out of food and are forced to ration hampers. There is consistently more demand than food donations—and that's not including the millions of people who report not seeking food bank help despite living in households that lack consistent access to healthy food.

The bottom line is: food banking hasn't worked here and it won't solve the problem of hunger elsewhere. Poverty and hunger—whether in Toronto, Buenos Aires or Hong Kong—aren't simply the result of food going to waste unnecessarily. Systemic poverty and malnourishment are caused by war, corruption, greed and/or a nation's failure to ensure an adequate social safety net—in other words, by political and policy decisions. Charitable handouts in Mexico, Bulgaria, England or any place in between won't change this system. Only sustained, thoughtful, prevention-focused social and economic policy will build a more equitable society.

When the Brazilian delegation came to speak to us, Cliff and I said all of this. Having just returned from the conference in Olinda, I was surprised that a country that seemed to be on the cutting edge of thinking about equitable access to food was interested in a model that so clearly doesn't work. The group explained to us that the focus of their "food bank" would be on reclaiming excess edible food from stores, restaurants and other places and turning it into meals and prepared foods suitable for distribution to institutional settings like daycares and community centres.

Preparing the food and channelling it through these community gathering places distinguishes this strategy from the usual emergency handout approach. Still, we'd tried a similar set-up and found that relying solely on leftovers for our drop-in meal programs had made it a real challenge to serve healthy, dignified food.

But getting into granular-level detail about how The Stop works wasn't the point of the tour. The message we wanted to convey to the Brazilians, and to others who visit us to talk about food banks, is that simply handing out donated food to the hungry and sending them on their way isn't an answer in and of itself. Anyone working on the front lines with people experiencing hunger and poverty must also work upstream, trying to change the social and political environment that makes such deprivation possible. In Brazil, of course, forces were already mobilizing at all levels of society and in government, and this influence was clear when we talked to the delegates. We have much further to go in Canada—and elsewhere around the world—to embed such thinking into our national debates.

At The Stop we've tried from the beginning to make the link between our individual programs and the larger social change our community wants and needs to see. Through advisory committees, town hall meetings, surveys and programs, we encourage people to express their views. We support those who want to make deputations to municipal politicians on issues they care about, we host political debates in our community space and we make connections with antipoverty groups. But it was when we hired dedicated staff to focus specifically on civic engagement that we really began to see the potential for bringing our community into the conversation.

THE DAY THAT EVERYTHING CHANGED for her, Nicole Mitchell says, she was in The Stop's kitchen, leaning on the island, pouring out her frustration to our new full-time chef. A twenty-five-year-old single mother from St. Lucia, Nicole had a difficult story to tell. She grew up moving between city and country, and fled the Caribbean when she was twenty-two to escape the jealous, violent father of her two eldest kids. Upon arriving in Toronto, she started working and trying to upgrade her education, finding poorly paid jobs as a telemarketer, housekeeper (for two hundred dollars a week, she was handed a toothbrush and told to use it to clean the entire bathroom) and caregiver for the elderly. She was on and off social assistance, trying to make ends meet and feed her kids. Her little family ate a lot of cheap packaged ramen noodles, she recalls, until she met Winston, a fellow St. Lucian, a country boy with a good job who paid the rent on an apartment in Davenport West. He made her feel more secure in a cold and foreign country.

But over time, Winston became more and more controlling. Then he stopped buying groceries and coming around altogether. Nicole heard he was seeing another woman. When Nicole learned she was expecting a child with Winston, she was nearly at the end of her rope.

Someone told her about The Stop's Healthy Beginnings program for pregnant women, and one Wednesday she came up to see what it was all about. At first she stood on the sidelines, observing the workshops and the other women, too shy to join in. Still, she was glad to get a food hamper and small grocery store voucher as part of her participation, and after the first week she began to sit down with the others.

But then things got worse at home. Nicole was eight months pregnant the day she came into Healthy Beginnings and started crying so hard she couldn't stop. She couldn't hold it together anymore. The Winston situation was unbearable, she had no money to feed her kids and she needed help. A counsellor who works in the program listened to her story and set her up with a crisis worker. The counsellor found Nicole a spot in a women's shelter far from Davenport West, where she could stay until she got her life back together. After years of scraping by, making do with what little support she could find, Nicole was shocked to learn that she actually had options. She had figured she would either have to go back to St. Lucia or stick with Winston, despite everything.

Nicole stayed at the shelter until baby Tinecia was born. Then, thanks to the work of the crisis team, she and her family were offered a spot in a public housing community in Toronto's north end. But the apartment was far from the neighbourhood where she'd finally found a support system. Alone with a new baby and the older boys in a community she didn't know, she was lonely and scared. She fell into deep postpartum depression and seriously contemplated suicide.

When a man was murdered and a woman sexually assaulted in a stairwell in her housing complex, Nicole called Winston and told him he needed to look after her and the kids. Things went wrong immediately. He came to visit and he beat her up, leaving her with a blood clot in one eye, welts all over her arms, bruises and scratches everywhere. Terrified, she didn't say a word about what had happened, but as soon as she walked into the hospital, the nursing staff called the police and Winston was arrested.

It wasn't long after that day that Nicole found herself with our chef in the kitchen at The Stop. "It feels like I've fallen into a big black hole," Nicole told her. "I've got housing, but with three little kids and no other supports it's a deep hole you disappear inside. I feel like I'm drowning."

Jonah Schein, a new Stop staffer, happened to walk by and overheard her lament. He told her that she should come and talk with the newly formed Civic Engagement group. Her story of this gap in the system would no doubt be one that others share. Maybe they could try to figure out how the government and community can support people in similar situations and ensure they don't drown, too.

Nicole agreed to attend and over time discovered a kind of support she didn't realize she needed. Each week, Jonah opened the meeting with a simple question, "How are we doing today?" and the stories would just start flowing. There were a lot of tears. Then, slowly, with Jonah's careful prodding and the accumulated evidence of shared experience, people started moving beyond the catharsis of sharing their stories toward talking about how their story fit into the bigger political picture.

"It all began to make sense," Nicole recalls as she looks back on those days. "I hadn't really been able to talk about my personal problems at the parenting group. But, for whatever reason, I could at Civic Engagement. I found out that I wasn't the only one who was struggling, wanting to die. Realizing that I was part of a bigger system, that my poverty and struggles weren't all just my fault, made a big difference to how I saw myself.

"I also felt for the first time that I belonged to something. What I said was valued. We talked a lot about how we can use our experience, our stories, to help others, to bring about change. It was the first time I felt I wasn't alone."

This knowledge altered Nicole. She ended up training at The Stop to work as a community advocate, helping others in similar situations navigate the labyrinthine and often demoralizing social service system. She even got a student loan and went back to school for a social work program at a local community college. The structure and support of the Civic Engagement program, she says, made a huge difference to her sense of her own potential. She graduated from her college program with honours.

"This is me," Nicole says, tapping her dangling silver butterfly earrings. "I'm a butterfly. I've been battered. I've been through so much. But now I can take that experience and turn it into something positive."

JONAH SCHEIN IS A SHY GUY. Strongly built, with dark hair and eyebrows, he's self-effacing, too, the kind of person who always gives credit to others first. But behind this, he's a fierce advocate for low-income people who never backs down from a fight. He landed at The Stop in his early thirties when he was doing a student placement for his master's in social work, and he was surprised, he says, by the relative calmness of the space. He'd worked at men's shelters before and found that the mix of children, men and women at The Stop made the atmosphere different from the drop-ins he was accustomed to. "It's like the extended living room of Symington Place," he says. "Food makes a difference, too. But to me, the most important thing is the community feel of the place."

Jonah carried this feeling into the Civic Engagement program when he was hired permanently, and his sensitivity and compassionate leadership helped the program find its legs. With funding once again from the Metcalf Foundation, the program started out with lofty goals: to increase minimum wage and social assistance rates. But there was a lot of learning to do—on the part of both The Stop and the community members involved in the project. The first meetings of what we called the Income Security Council were, as Nicole remembered, charged affairs, with tears flowing and emotions running high. People discovered a welcoming public space to share their stories of poverty and they ran with it. There were people struggling with mental health issues, some living outside or in shelters, and others with difficult lives.

"Some people would come just for the food and the transit tickets," Jonah recalls. "It was pretty raucous sometimes. I'll never forget the woman who stood up and said, 'My name is Jane, and I'm a drain on the system.' We had to really unpack that one. After years of people telling you you're no good, that's how it sometimes feels."

Many people weren't used to sitting in meetings for long periods of time listening to others speak. To make it even more complicated, each week new people would show up, and the whole process would have to start again.

"I did a huge amount of just supporting people on a personal level," Jonah says. "I had to. People in the group needed it. Hearing their stories and worrying about them kept me up at night for a long time. They were often in terrible situations—dealing with abuse, getting kicked out of their homes. Sometimes it seemed insane to me to be talking about social change when people needed just to pay their bills."

Kathryn Scharf, the FoodShare colleague who'd joined our board not long after I arrived at The Stop, had become staff by then. As program director—in charge of everything from the food bank to drop-ins, community kitchens, garden, Healthy Beginnings and education initiatives—she worked with Jonah to shape the project. Both Kathryn and Jonah realized that it would be easy for it to become simply a self-help support group—something people clearly needed. But the program was designed to foster democratic engagement, and they needed to figure out how to translate those cathartic moments into organizing for change. They also wanted to reach out to a larger segment of our community. They put the whole project under the microscope, combining Jonah's deep knowledge of community members and Kathryn's talent for getting to the heart of a matter, asking tough questions about what was working and what wasn't. They talked about how to keep their eyes on the larger goals of social change without shortchanging the essential work of relationship building. There aren't many front-line community-based organizations doing this kind of work, and they had to make it up as they went along.

Eventually, they decided to switch things up. The Stop continued to hold regular social justice events that were open to everyone—movie nights or guest speakers invited to talk about topics ranging from the plight of undocumented workers to the history of globalization. More than a hundred people turned up one night to talk about how to move the provincial government to increase minimum wage. The Income Security Council was reinvented as two groups: one that would organize and mobilize for antipoverty events, and the Speakers' Bureau, a series of adult education and training workshops that could help participants prepare for public speaking opportunities and other ways of spreading the group's message to a wider audience. Every Tuesday a small coterie of interested folks—including Glenn

Kitchener—would meet for a meal and a workshop on things like race, culture and diversity training, political economy, media analysis and public speaking.

We asked journalists to come and talk to participants about how they might present themselves to interviewers, how to remain authentic—and true to themselves—without sharing so much that they end up feeling violated by the exposure. We had a labour leader talk about political theory, the changing workforce and the influence of international trade and policy on jobs. For some people, it was the first time they'd heard or thought about these topics. Glenn says it was his first experience learning about the theory behind politics and he began to see everything differently. He started to think that he might have a say in shaping his world.

After all, change happens when people fight for it. People in the middle class have no trouble advocating for themselves. You want to oppose a housing development on your street, you call up your city councillor, ask your neighbour who works as a lawyer to write a stern letter, gather other interested stakeholders. But for low-income people—isolated and stigmatized, disenfranchised by a political system that often doesn't benefit them—it's not so straightforward. Without privileges, access and connections, simply being heard on an issue can feel like a nearly insurmountable challenge.

As Glenn, Nicole and the other participants developed a more sophisticated analysis of poverty—the way it is created and lived, the way the poor are represented in popular culture—they were energized and inspired. They no longer saw themselves as passive recipients of food or services, but as citizens with common concerns and problems.

Eventually, the Speakers' Bureau members took this newfound

knowledge and hope outside The Stop, speaking to newspaper and TV reporters, to church groups, in classrooms and at City Hall about the reality of living on social assistance and food bank handouts, and about policies that need to be implemented to improve their lives and the life of their community. Nicole appeared on the front page of the *Toronto Star*, articulating her fear about raising her children on welfare. "It's scary for me because I have boys. I'm worried, not having the money to put them into [after-school] programs that will help develop their minds properly, what will happen to them," she told the reporter. "You can never move ahead if you're stuck on social assistance. . . . [I]t's not something I'd wish on anybody."

Seeing the lucidity and sense of purpose of participants like Nicole and many others brought a new vitality to The Stop as well. Staff would chat with Speakers' Bureau participants in the office as they were using the photocopier, and everyone would be invited to join in during their education workshops. I'd see the group promoting events they'd organized, talking them up with other community members, and we'd all make a point of attending. For me, it felt like an injection of passion into the organization. The Stop was finally fulfilling its promise and my hopes for our work—combining hands-on programs and food access with smart, strategic efforts to put low-income people in charge of their own lives.

I was spending more and more of my time away from Symington Place, talking to funders and other supporters in an effort to raise money to build the Green Barn, and the very existence of the Civic Engagement group helped feed my enthusiasm for our work. The Stop had helped create a solid core of people who—with training and organizing opportunities—had become advocates for themselves and others.

Building hope and knowledge among participants was as important—especially in the early going—as any political goals, but the Civic Engagement group also managed to have real influence, collaborating with other antipoverty groups to push elected officials and citizens to pay attention to low-income people. During one election campaign, they organized and hosted a debate focused entirely on poverty issues, and held voter education events to provide other community members with information about the candidates. They collaborated with the head of the city's public health department to expose the direct causal links between poverty and ill health, garnering a front-page story as well as an op-ed about the health impacts of poverty.

Of course, policy revisions that genuinely change people's lives—such as an increased minimum wage or more generous welfare benefits that would make it possible to live in dignity— can take a long, long time. Wins are elusive, and they can also be dismantled when an election changes the government or the political pendulum swings. In the face of such challenges, it's not easy for anyone to maintain enthusiasm, but for low-income activists living the reality of poverty every day—returning to rooming houses and empty fridges—change simply can't happen fast enough.

"We ask a lot of people," says Jonah. "We ask them to put their stories on the line, their privacy. Just asking them to keep the faith that what they are doing matters is a lot when your life is precarious—dealing with health crises, financial crises, family crises. Middle-class people with comfortable lives often don't get involved in working toward greater equality, and here we are asking people with huge barriers to get out there and fight."

Recognizing these challenges but not wanting to lose the momentum or the cadre of articulate new activists, we soon added a Community Advocacy Project. It gives graduates of its training program an opportunity to apply their knowledge and skills to support their neighbours. We pay the advocates a small stipend for their work, and they help people who come to The Stop one-on-one with landlord issues or difficulties accessing health care, getting into a shelter or getting out of an abusive relationship. The advocates feel powerful realizing that with a few phone calls and referrals, they can begin to make things happen for other people.

Nicole, who was one of the first trained advocates, says people come up to her regularly in the drop-in or food bank and introduce her to friends saying, "This is your girl. She can get things done."

Considering the transformative impact the project had on The Stop, it might be surprising so few social service organizations support low-income people with civic engagement opportunities. But, dependent as they are on private and government funders, many of these organizations worry that raising issues about poverty or entitlements will make them appear partisan, potentially alienating donors. One women's shelter I know offers beds and a meal, as well as emotional support and referrals for women seeking an escape from abusive relationships, poverty or the street, but management refuses to allow its staff to make public deputations at City Hall calling for better supports for women living in poverty or to attend antipoverty demonstrations as representatives of the organization. The shelter's leaders, staff have told me confidentially, are terrified about getting cut off by funders who don't agree with a particular stance or, worse, worry about being deregistered as a charitable organization for being in defiance of government regulations.

In most countries, governments place strict limits on charitable organizations. In Canada, the U.S. and the U.K., for instance, partisanship is entirely restricted. Charities may engage in certain political activities, but only if they are not directly or indirectly supporting or opposing a political candidate or party. Failure to adhere to the policy can mean losing your charitable status.

The problem is, it can be difficult for organizations to parse the law and sort through what sort of nonpartisan political activities and how much is, in fact, allowable. In Canada, there is a 10 per cent cap on resources allocated to such political initiatives. But what is considered to be within that 10 per cent is not always easy to discern. The same issues arise in Britain and the U.S.

As a result, the rules—and some highly publicized cases of nonprofits being chastened by crackdowns on their activities—have some boards and nonprofit leaders so worried about crossing the line that they fear doing any advocacy at all, no matter how deeply linked it is to their work and how important fighting for such change is to their community. But what I'm arguing for, and the kind of work we're doing with our Civic Engagement program, is nonpartisan. It's not about supporting any political party or platform; instead, it's about building democracy and strengthening our community. It's about empowering people to speak for themselves. When we talk about or advocate with our community against specific policies that so negatively affect the life of our neighbourhood (say, cuts to social housing or welfare benefits), or join with the advocates to call for policies they believe will help (say, an adequate minimum wage or welfare rates that allow low-income people to eat healthily), it is not partisanship. It's doing our job.

SEPTEMBER 2OO7. People started gathering early near the weedy, hard-packed flower beds at the back of the building. By the time I arrive, about fifty community members—drop-in regulars, Speakers' Bureau participants—are milling about. They have noisemakers—drums made out of plastic margarine and olive tubs strung around their necks, a megaphone, pots and pans to clang together—and hand-painted signs they've been working on for the last week. "PAY NOW OR PAY LATER. ENDING POVERTY MAKES ENE," reads one placard painted bright yellow. Rhonda, always up for street theatre, is wearing a carrot costume with a fuzzy orange body and a huge, green feathered wig. People shuffle their feet and chat, everyone excited or nervous.

I see Glenn and shake his hand. He's been proving himself invaluable around the organization. He's still involved in the Speakers' Bureau as a volunteer, but we've also hired him as a part-time janitor and he picks up shifts assisting in the kitchen or wherever else we need extra help. He likes to joke that he's done everyone's job by now except mine. He doesn't know it yet, but we're planning to recognize him at the annual general meeting as our volunteer of the year.

For Glenn and for others, today's big antipoverty protest will be their first demonstration. With a provincial election coming up, groups across the city and the province are hoping to have their voices heard and make sure poverty is an issue in the debate. But before we head to the government buildings downtown, we're going to stop by our local politician's office down the road. A long-serving elected official, he's managed to maintain a hold on power in the area despite doing little to improve the lot of this struggling neighbourhood. The Civic Engagement group has visited his office before. Jonah remembers one woman, with her ten-year-old in tow, bursting into tears as she told him, "I can't afford to feed my daughter breakfast." The politician offered her a chocolate bar from a stash in his office.

This time, the noisemakers and signs will do the talking. When we set off down Davenport Road toward the office, I can feel the small group's confidence swell. The noise and chanting of a demonstration can sometimes feel forced or put on, but here, taking over the street in our neighbourhood, marching with people for whom the issues have grave personal importance, it's like a shot of adrenalin.

We pass the giant billboard on top of a deserted smoke-stained factory featuring a handsome biracial couple drinking cappuccinos in their gleaming kitchen. "Townhomes from $300,000!" It's hard to reconcile these happy, sunbathed pictures with our band of community members shouting and singing out their grievances. The Symington Place apartment building, its narrow balconies stuffed with bicycles and old furniture, garbage bags and the detritus of people jammed into too-small spaces, bears little resemblance to the shiny homes of those billboard couples.

As we approach the small storefront office, children at a school perched on a hill above run to the fence. Energized by the audience, our group bangs and chants even louder. The children shake the chain-link fence.

The politician has heard us coming and he's already outside when we arrive, wearing his signature red tie, white shirt and blue polyester pants, topped off with a white golf cap. Jonah and some others set up the PA system they've carted over in a baby carriage, as members of the group shout out that politicians are ignoring the issues of the poor. The schoolkids are going crazy.

But the politician can't take it anymore. "Bull! That's bull!" he calls to the protesters as the children watch. "I want to speak!" he shouts.

This time, Jonah tells him, it's the community's turn. Glenn takes the mic. "Glenn! Glenn! Glenn!" the group chants. But they're silent as he begins to talk, his voice scratchy and uncertain. He takes off his sunglasses and looks down at the ground. I wonder if he's going to fold under the pressure. Maybe this is too much. Maybe we *are* asking too much of people already under so much stress. But Glenn clears his throat and his voice grows steadier and louder as he tells his story of losing his business and having to go on welfare, the way he felt disrespected and treated like crap everywhere he went. He talks about being hungry and how hard it is to cope on an empty stomach. He looks at people one by one, piercing us with his quiet strength.

The crowd is rapt as Glenn builds to a crescendo. "I was hungry yesterday and I am hungry today. And the way this province treats us, I'm going to be hungry tomorrow!"

He lowers the bullhorn, lets it dangle at his side. The crowd cheers. Glenn catches his breath, his chest heaving in and out.

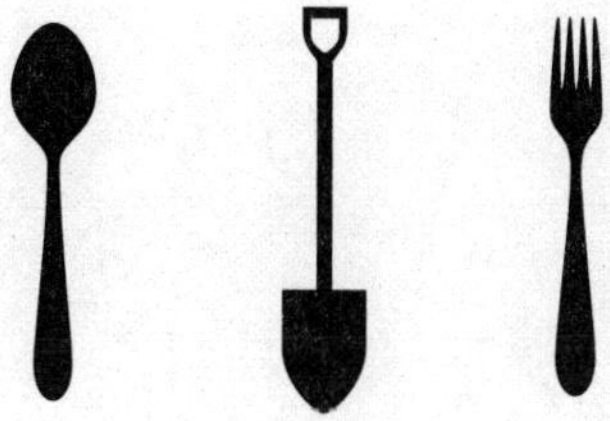

SIX

BUILD A BIG TENT

OCTOBER 2007. The tiny courtyard in front of St. Michael and All Angels Church is thronged with activity. White pop-up tents shade tables laden with squash and tomatoes, apples and onions. Milk crates and coolers, a knapsack or two and cardboard boxes stuffed with produce are stacked on the ground underneath. A few vendors selling dried herbs and tinctures have set up a table in the sun. Kids are running around, there are balloons and a banjo player is settling in. I see a woman I recognize from the many Wychwood Barns redevelopment meetings handing out flyers for a fundraising event.

My two boys are tugging impatiently on the leg of my jeans, but I really want to buy some chard from one of the farmers. He's a wiry guy with a red face and a bush of white, curly hair, a fourth-generation vegetable farmer and an organic pioneer in the region. He was one of the first to sign on with our new farmers' market, and we were thrilled when he agreed to come.

We're calling it a pilot project, but this market is intended to be one of the bedrock programs at the Green Barn just two blocks south of here. It's been nearly seven years of talking and planning and raising money for the project, and I can hardly believe it's almost finished. Once the new site officially opens—with twenty-six live/work units for artists, studios, offices for community groups and environmental organizations, public spaces and a big park with a playground, splash pad, volleyball court and room for a homemade skating rink, not to mention the Green Barn itself—we'll move the market down there, making it one of the largest year-round farmers' markets in the city.

Only ten minutes by streetcar from Symington Place, this area couldn't be more different from our low-income neighbourhood. Skimming the edge of one of the city's wealthiest enclaves, it takes its character from the main street, St. Clair Avenue. Sitting on top of one of the city's hills, St. Clair is a mixed bag of ethnicity and income. The stretch closer to The Stop is known as the landing place of the second wave of Italian immigrants. Banners in red, green and white, and street signs—as well as a smattering of Italian restaurants, stores selling Italian goods and one of the best gelato shops in the city—proclaim it Corso Italia. Closer to this church and the Green Barn, it's more of a cultural hodge-podge: boutiques selling expensive knick-knacks or pretty dresses rub shoulders with Vietnamese nail salons and a Portuguese chicken restaurant. There are a number of new restaurants and specialty food shops, as well as several thrift stores, a Jamaican patty joint and several payday loan stores.

The streets north of St. Clair are treelined and almost entirely residential, with modest but well-tended single-family homes of the solidly middle and upper-middle class. Below St. Clair there are more middle-class families as well as pockets of wealth. Several social housing apartment buildings, rental homes and seniors' residences complete this very urban mosaic. Still, the economic divide between this neighbourhood and Davenport West is substantial, with average incomes here more than twice those of the area around Symington Place.

It's also a neighbourhood with a history of deep engagement in community affairs. When McDonald's proposed adding a drive-through to a location just west of here a few years ago, the community fought back with a vengeance. "A live-in community— not a drive-through!" they proclaimed at weekly pickets and regular rallies, at fundraisers and on a website. They eventually won the fight and McDonald's pulled the plug on its plans. More recently, the building of a dedicated streetcar lane along St. Clair consumed the community's energy as businesses struggled with the disruption of construction, and costs and timelines ballooned. But as I've seen, there was still plenty of passion left over to get into a heated and occasionally ugly debate about the transformation of the old streetcar maintenance buildings where our Green Barn and the farmers' market will be.

For a time, it seemed as if the battle would tear the neighbourhood apart. The divisions ran deep. The group calling themselves Friends of a New Park—those advocating for both green space and community use—saw the city block–sized site as having the potential to become the centre of their neighbourhood. Their vision for the site bumped up against Neighbours for 100% Park, a mostly anonymous group that claimed a traditional park with grass, flowers, trees and kids' activities would be better for the area. Neighbours argued that artists living and working in the space would bring drug use and illicit behaviour to the area, and that The Stop would import food bank users and other undesirables. They wanted nothing to do with the historical structures (hence the 100 percent park) and suggested that it was the aim of Artscape, the developer, to build an "entertainment megaplex" on the site that would bring people from out of the neighbourhood, maybe even out of town. Those well-meaning locals who were combatting a drive-through at the McDonald's were urged by the Neighbours group to fight Artscape's own "drive-through."

One of the great ironies was that a particularly vociferous member of Neighbours, casting aspersions on artists and the poor, was a resident of nearby Wychwood Park, a beautiful self-contained cluster of Arts and Crafts–style houses, ravine, pond and old trees that began in the 1870s as an artist colony. She was also a one-time Stop donor who, when she realized we were part of the project, pressured us to pull out. She dangled the possibility of future financial contributions if we agreed to withdraw and the spectre of mobilizing protest against us if we didn't. One of the national newspapers interviewed her about her objections to the plans for the site—with its park and community spaces— and she explained her stance with the baldest sort of NIMBYism: "What if my friend . . . wants to have a dinner party? Where are her guests going to park?"

The good thing about such blatant self-interest is that when it asserts itself, it makes everyone else realize not just what they're against, but what they're for. While the early debates about the site were draining and difficult for everyone, in hindsight I think those tensions were actually good for the project as a whole. Every good idea needs a naysayer. They galvanize people to take action. Friends of a New Park eventually had thousands of people signed up on their email lists and petitions—many who'd never been involved in community organizing before but didn't want the naysayers speaking for them. As more and more people grew excited about what became known as the Wychwood Barns, the Neighbours group realized they didn't have community support and backed off. That's when we were able to get down to the fun part: planning a new park and multipurpose site with a committed, enthusiastic community. There were many more long meetings and difficult questions about things like parking, programming and noise issues, but with everyone working toward similar goals, and goodwill on the table, the process moved ahead steadily.

In fact, the community consultation began to seem almost straightforward compared to the process of realizing our ambitious vision. The plan for the site was designed by architect Joe Lobko, with a gold Leadership in Energy and Environmental Design (LEED) designation in mind: a geothermal heating, ventilation and air conditioning system with ground-source heat pumps; a stormwater harvesting and reuse system; energy-efficient lighting and appliances; and water-conserving plumbing fixtures. It was an inspiring design, but converting an old, long-abandoned building into a modern, energy-efficient space was not straightforward. The old bricks and concrete were crumbling and needed to be carefully restored. The rotting wooden roofs were a massive challenge for heritage restoration, and some needed to be entirely replaced. The charmingly patinated paint on the brick walls was full of toxic lead. The geothermal system cost far more than originally expected. Add to that two significant labour strikes in the construction industry, and everything cost more than we expected and seemed to take twice as long.

In the beginning, our fundraising goal was $3 million to develop the eight-thousand-square-foot space assigned to us—with a year-round greenhouse, bake oven, sheltered garden protected from the elements for a longer growing season, compost demonstration area, community kitchen and classroom. Later, as costs ballooned, it grew to $5 million for the Green Barn alone (the entire project would eventually cost $22 million, more than tripling the early estimate of $8 million). Half of the money we raised was intended for bricks and mortar, including building and outfitting the greenhouse; the other half would sustain the Green Barn and our programs over the first three years. For The Stop, an organization with a total budget just pushing $1 million in the early days of our involvement, it was a huge amount of money. Thinking back, it was probably crazy for us to take it on. Though we had big dreams of building a Community Food Centre, we were still a small neighbourhood-based organization supporting a very vulnerable population. We were lucky the whole process—community consultation, raising money, design, construction—took so long, because we had time to grow up in the interim.

There was one day deep in the planning and development process that the entire project nearly ground to a halt. Rhonda and I had been called to Joe Lobko's offices for what I understood as a "gut check meeting"—an opportunity to hash out where things stood with Artscape and the rest of the development team. Joe is a tall man with a shock of curly hair, bushy eyebrows and black-rimmed glasses. He loves his work and despite playing a leadership role in many of the city's most interesting design projects, he has no ego. I knew him and the rest of the development group well by then and, thankfully, they got to the point quickly. Joe and the folks from Artscape told us that the costs for the whole project were escalating, and we all needed to find ways to cut back. The barn we'd been allocated—Barn #4 of the five being developed—was divided into twelve smaller bays, each about as wide as a school bus is long and sixteen feet front to back. They told us that in order to reduce costs, they wanted to cut our portion of the space down to six bays and put the greenhouse on the second floor. They'd even done drawings to show us what it would look like.

I was gobsmacked. This dream we'd been working on, discussing and imagining, fighting for in design meetings and committee rooms for years suddenly didn't seem so interesting anymore. It was like the difference between having your own house and your own room. We'd have to seriously scale back our programming and our presence at the site. I wasn't even sure I'd be able to find new funders who'd be interested in this truncated version of the project.

We pushed back, reminding the group about the passion we'd all shared for the original vision, how we'd come together around this idea of a space that celebrates art, food, the environment and social justice. We hadn't come this far to see the vision downsized. We urged the group to stay the course. There had to be another way. We said that we would find our part of the money.

I think, in some ways, our response to this smaller, less inspiring version of the space was what the others in the development team needed to hear at that moment. Everyone was nervous about the costs (for good reason, as it turns out) and needed a reminder about what we'd all been working toward. Artscape agreed to crunch the numbers and look at the design again. There was a lot more nail-biting to come, but we were able to keep our twelve bays and our dream.

Much of that nail-biting would involve fundraising. It's always hard to find the first person to dance, whether it's at middle-school graduation or funding a new project like the

Green Barn. No one wants to take the chance. The Metcalf Foundation's early grant helped mobilize the project, but there was $4.5 million more to raise. I needed to find more people with both deep pockets and a deep commitment to our work.

It's hard to overestimate the impact of early adopters like Michael MacMillan, former executive chairman and CEO of broadcaster Alliance Atlantis (operator of, among other things, Food Network Canada), and his wife, lawyer Cathy Spoel. I'd first met Michael in 1999 when, brand new to The Stop, I saw an article about him in a business magazine discussing both his work and his passion for food. I wrote him a letter and suggested, considering our shared interest in food, we get together to talk about The Stop. Since he's a generous, down-to-earth guy, he agreed and I went to meet him at his downtown offices.

I explained what we did—at the time The Stop was still largely a food bank, though I described my dream of a Community Food Centre—and when he asked what I wanted from him, I served up the first amount that came to me: a million dollars.

He didn't answer right away. It was a bit forward, I suppose. Plus, Michael was in his mid-forties with three young daughters and a company that he and his partners were building from scratch. Still, he was kind about it when he sent me on my way. After that meeting, every once in a while I'd write a note to Michael's assistant and send over our newsletters and annual reports, but nothing came of it.

Nothing, that is, until the Green Barn. By late 2007, I was seriously pounding the pavement looking for money to fund construction. We'd created a powerful case for support—a key document illustrating our vision and our record using food to build community—that we used as the cornerstone of the fundraising campaign, and we'd created a roster of supporters including the then-mayor, an influential public radio host, food writers and business people. By then, Michael and his partners had sold Alliance Atlantis and he was in the initial stage of creating Samara, a charitable organization aimed at strengthening democracy and citizen engagement. And not only did I have a plan, but The Stop had a vision for a beautiful multipurpose site that would marry social justice and good food—two issues that Michael and Cathy care about deeply.

The day was sunny and crisp when I took them for a tour of the construction site. I was going there so often, I kept my muddy rubber boots in the trunk of our family car. I'd taken Michael through before, but he wanted to show Cathy around this time. There was muck everywhere, piles of dirt and debris, construction bins and vehicles packed into the western portion of the land that would one day be a playground. The barn buildings themselves had been gutted, the walls inside exposed to the elements. We all donned white hard hats and steel-toed rubber boots to wade through the gigantic puddles outside.

The barns were grand and evocative that day in a decaying-industrial-wasteland sort of way. They had soaring ceilings and vast holes torn in the walls where windows would go. In the floor, you could see the tracks where streetcars would once have trundled in for maintenance. Michael, Cathy and I finished up outside the Barns in one of those white vinyl-sided mobile homes construction companies drag on site, and I showed them the plans for the entire project. Though the drawings and our tour of the buildings certainly suggested the project's potential, it still took a lot of imagination to see what it might become.

When Michael and Cathy thanked me and left that day, I figured I'd done everything I could. We'd talked about their love for sharing good food, their interest in the environment and democratic engagement, and the way food connects people. I'd told them about our many programs and about our hopes for this new site. I went back to Symington Place and was just settling into my desk when the phone rang. It was Michael. He said, "Cathy and I would like to give you a million dollars." I sputtered thank you and hung up, though not before he told me that he wouldn't just give us the money, he'd help us raise more.

For The Stop's board and staff, including me, it was a major boost of confidence, though it would still take another two years of talking to people and raising funds before we had enough money to meet our goal. I trooped through that muddy construction site many more times in my hard hat and rubber boots, describing The Stop's vision and explaining our story of community transformation to anyone who would listen. True to his promise, Michael often joined me and helped get others on board by conveying his passion for the project and The Stop's mission. He even started to volunteer in the kitchen at our main site, working with our chef on the drop-in lunch once a week.

Many of the other people who fought for this project are also at the farmers' market in front of the church today. Joe Mihevc, the local city councillor whose fierce championing of the Wychwood Barns won him both admirers and detractors, is here. And so are some of the neighbours active in the Friends group. We even hired one of the tireless community activists who endured those endless meetings. She'll organize and coordinate the farmers' market here and at the Green Barn, once we move. I can see her rushing around trying to make sure the farmers are satisfied with their tents and the tiny space we can offer them in front of the church. I can only imagine what will happen when we move into more spacious digs at the Green

Barn. After all the late nights and difficult conversations, the meetings and challenges both big and small, seeing the permanent market and the Barn finally open will be sweet reward.

But there's no time for such contemplation now—my boys have joined forces to lobby for a cinnamon bun from one of the vendors. They consider it their levy for putting up with me talking to everyone here. They steer me away from the farmer and his leafy greens. Their campaign is short and brutish, and I cave quickly. The baker hands me the sweets with a wink.

IT'S IMPOSSIBLE TO OPEN A NEWSPAPER, go to a bookstore or turn on your TV or computer without reading or hearing about food. Where farmers' markets were once rare in urban centres, they've become popular gathering spots for everyone from families and downtown hipsters to retirees and tourists.

When food first started to claim its place in the zeitgeist, chefs and diners, farmers and gardeners were inspired by books like *Fast Food Nation* by Eric Schlosser and *The Omnivore's Dilemma* by journalist Michael Pollan, reissues of *Diet for a Small Planet* by Frances Moore Lappé as well as the movie that transformed thousands into vegetarians, Morgan Spurlock's *Super Size Me*. Now there are too many gurus to namecheck, and there's so much written on the topic that food gets its own (non-cookbook) category in bookstores. Every aspect of the food system—from safety to diet-related illness, from school meals to school gardens, from the impact of food production on the environment to the impact of fast-food culture on the family—has been researched, dissected and discussed.

In fact, food stars like Jamie Oliver have transcended their celebrity and now play a public role, pushing governments and communities to change the way they think, act and create policy around food. And many other chefs—both famous and otherwise—have followed suit, recognizing that their livelihoods depend on it. Indeed, average people, not just food activists, have begun to understand that the food they eat is part of a vast, interconnected system and that what they eat matters. It matters to the environment, it matters to our health and it matters to the economic well-being of farmers, to relationships between nations, to the future of the planet. Michael Pollan's much-quoted mantra that you can "vote with your fork" three times a day has resonated around the industrialized world, and now appears on everything from T-shirts to bumper stickers.

While The Stop has benefited mightily from this interest in food and food politics—through exposure in the media, funding from new sources and relationships we've forged with chefs and farmers who share our interests—I also feel strongly that this consumer model for change has significant limitations. The vote-with-your-fork approach posits that changing what you eat or the kind of producer you buy it from will lead to societal change. It's a compelling notion that makes people feel they are in charge—and makes doing something about the vast problems in the food system as relatively easy as choosing the right tomato in the grocery store.

Of course, it's not that easy. Changing what we buy is part of the solution—those choices push producers, packagers, marketers and others in the food system to offer more sustainable, healthy products. But it's not the whole package. We are more than just consumers. Our "voting" shouldn't just occur at the store or even at the table, but at the ballot box, in the leaders we elect, the social, economic and political policies we create, and in the civil society we build together.

That's why I think we need to forge a larger food movement that includes consumer power but also goes far beyond it to assert our rights and responsibilities as citizens. Without this sort of big-picture political and social framework, voting with your fork means the change can stop at the checkout counter. It also means leaving out a very significant population: low-income people.

For the most part, poor people have had no voice in the growing conversation about creating a healthier food system. When change is all about throwing around your individual economic power—the ability to deny or award a company, store or individual your business according to how they operate—people on low incomes get left in the dust. They are, more often than not, forced to choose food that is the cheapest and most accessible, rather than the tastiest, healthiest and most sustainably or ethically produced. And what makes changing this situation even more urgent is that low-income people are more profoundly affected by the ill effects of the industrial food system than anyone else. As food activist Mark Winne explains in his book *Closing the Food Gap: Resetting the Table in the Land of Plenty*, the rich get local and organic, the poor get diabetes. All over the world, this scenario plays out, as the rising cost of food affects low-income people more immediately and forcefully than it affects those with a financial cushion.

One of our key jobs at The Stop is to ensure that our community participates and has a say in the issues that affect them. But I also think—especially as we stake a claim in a new community with the Green Barn—that we can have a role tapping into the largely middle-class enthusiasm about food we're seeing and connecting the dots between the poor and everyone else.

After all, entrenching a two-tiered food system that benefits the middle class while fostering greater suffering for the poor is hardly a just or desirable long-term goal. The costs of such inequality in exploding rates of diet-related illness and health care expenditures are already clear. And unless the changes to farming practices, production, processing and distribution that the middle class is increasingly demanding are systemic—unless everyone has access to sustainably grown food—none of it will be effective. When a river is poisoned, after all, everyone gets toxic water. Advocates for reimagining the food system simply can't afford to leave low-income people out. There's no way to build a genuine, far-reaching alternative without them.

From the beginning, we saw the Green Barn as the perfect site for illustrating the connections between all the players in the food system. Set in a more stable and affluent community than we'd been engaged with before, it seemed an ideal place to find common ground. As the gap between rich and poor grows everywhere, there are fewer and fewer places where people come together across income and class lines. I often field phone calls and email from exasperated friends and educators who want their adolescent children to volunteer in Stop programs. They say their middle-class kids have no idea about their own privilege because they never see anyone living any other way. Their kids are isolated in a bubble of entitlement. These well-meaning people want their children to see how others live so that they will appreciate all that they have.

Of course, we're not equipped as a rehab centre for over-privileged children. The Stop has a stringent application process and a waiting list for volunteers, not to mention thousands of people in our centre who need our attention, so we don't usually comply with such requests. But to me, it speaks volumes about the class divide that is growing ever larger in our society. That people see The Stop as a place to break down these barriers also reflects an intuitive sense about the potential of food—growing it, cooking it, sharing it, advocating for it—as a great equalizer. We built the Green Barn, in part, to test this intuition, to see how a public space focused on good food for everyone can begin to bring together our divided society.

One evening a week or so before the "soft" opening of the Green Barn in November 2008 (the official launch wouldn't happen until the following spring), I took Andrea to see the nearly finished space. She'd lived through the whole thing with me, and as a writer helped us craft much of the material we used to tell donors and other supporters about the Green Barn. She'd waited up for me when I was out late at meetings, talking through every twist and turn of the long saga. Over the years, The Stop has become the family business.

It was dusk when we arrived, and the lights were on in the greenhouse. From the street outside, the building seemed to have an otherworldly glow. We walked in, past the protected garden that Rhonda and her crew would soon plant with herbs and sunflowers, through the covered courtyard by the space where the bake oven would one day be. Inside, the double-height ceilings and big windows made the empty open-concept education room seem much bigger than it is. I could see how well Joe Lobko's intelligent design had come together, retaining the industrial feel of the old maintenance barns but introducing a contemporary edge. He'd kept the exposed steel beams, but used modern, efficient windows so that light floods the space. As a wayfinding technique and an aesthetic tie-in to the other spaces, an enormous number 4 was painted on the original Douglas fir wooden doors that close off one end of our Barn from the new children's playground. They'd also ensured the sign at the top of the barns with the year of construction—1921 in the case of the Green Barn—was showcased.

We wandered around, and I showed Andrea the small but efficient kitchen with all-new equipment—another opportunity to show off my kitchen supply geekery—and a window looking out at the sheltered garden. We poked our heads into the hallway where kids will be able to hang their coats, and the still-empty office space with windows into the greenhouse on one side and the teaching area on the other.

I knew all the things that had gone as planned, the compromises we'd made, the things that hadn't turned out exactly as expected, but seeing it that night, it felt just right. The Green Barn is the tangible realization of all that we've worked toward at The Stop for close to a decade. A physical manifestation of our mission to link the fight for equity with sustainable food; a reimagining of how we think about poverty and hunger. A place where low-income people and the rest of the city can find common cause in building a better food system for everyone.

We went into the greenhouse last. Opening up the door, we were hit with a gush of warmth, the powerful smell of growing things. Seedlings had already been started in bright yellow and orange-brown trays; little yellow labels poked out announcing the name of the plant. The green of the new shoots looked electric against the brown soil. Pipes and hoses and lights hung from the ceiling. Looking around at the beautiful glowing structure, it felt like a whole new beginning for all of us.

⟞⟝

THE FIRST TIME ELEVEN-YEAR-OLD Ariana Rogel visited the After School Program at the Green Barn, her heart was beating really fast. Light poured in through the tall windows onto the kids sitting at the big, rough-hewn wooden tables and benches. There were boys and girls she'd never seen, and everyone was talking really fast. It seemed like they all knew each other.

The slight, dark-haired little girl had learned English quickly after she and her family arrived from El Salvador a few years before, but she was still shy. She didn't look at the other children, just dropped her knapsack and grabbed a seat, her eyes glued firmly to the table. But the program leader and her battalion of students and interns quickly made sure Ariana and the other fourteen kids were comfortable as they launched into icebreaker games.

By the end of the first session, after making pizza together—rolling out the dough and choosing the toppings, including herbs from the greenhouse—Ariana had made several friends. It was so much fun, in fact, that she continued to come back three times a week. She joined in the Summer Food Camp and March Break Camp, too. When that was over, she became part of the Graduate Program, coming on Thursdays after school to meet up with her friends. She learned how to cook and grow vegetables and herbs in the greenhouse and sheltered garden; she took yoga classes and learned hip-hop dance moves. Every week there's a food literacy exercise, like learning about how to read food labels or playing the Game of Real Life, a role-playing game designed by Stop staff to help kids learn about food justice and the difficult choices people living on social assistance have to make.

Ariana's favourite was the week when they went to a market in Chinatown for a scavenger hunt. She's become quite a chef, too, able to negotiate many different kinds of food with a knife and cutting board. At home, she's instituted a weekly lunch plan for school and helps her parents prepare other meals, as well. "I talk to my parents about the menu and figure out what we can make. On Mondays, for example," she says in a teacherly tone, "I make sandwiches with tomato, lettuce, cheese and ham."

Ariana's parents, Delmy and Gilberto, nod happily listening to their daughter. They're proud of their smart child who's found her way around a new country and new language with such ease. But as we're talking Ariana starts to get squirmy, and Delmy tells her to go to the playground in the park surrounding the Green Barn while we continue to talk.

Delmy is a small woman with a round face and bright eyes that narrow when she smiles. Gilberto sits beside her and they often look to each other, as if for confirmation of what they've said. Delmy tells me she heard about The Stop's free After School Program when she saw a poster on a pole near Ariana's school.

Stop staff try to place information about the After School Program in spots where kids who will benefit most from the program live. In a mixed neighbourhood like the one around the Green Barn, poverty is much more hidden than in Davenport West. And yet it is still there—people living in social housing buildings and small apartments, some with multiple families in one unit, lots of new immigrants. We talk to teachers and community workers, and go to drop-ins and community centres, trying to make sure the program is accessed by the families and kids who need it.

Delmy Rogel didn't need any prompting. She called the Green Barn right away. She knew about The Stop because she'd been to our main site before. In fact, it was during one of their first weeks in Canada that the Rogels—then just Ariana, Delmy and Gilberto; now they have two little boys, as well— discovered The Stop. Arriving from El Salvador with no friends and little English, the family was directed to the Community Action Resource Centre at the front of Symington Place for help translating the many documents they'd been given when they landed in Canada. When they were finished, someone suggested they head around the back to The Stop for something to eat.

There were people everywhere, Gilberto remembers. Flags from nearly every nation hung from the ceiling. A Mexican man greeted them. "'Welcome,' he said to us. 'Take a seat and we'll bring you some food.' We sat down, but Delmy and I were looking at each other. *What kind of place is this?*"

"We thought it was a restaurant," Delmy laughs, rocking back on her seat, her eyes flashing.

"We were in shock. Out of the blue, no one knows me, but they serve me food. Good food. It was incredible," Gilberto remembers. "We don't have anything like that in El Salvador."

"They don't know you, but there you are equal. I wanted to cry," says Delmy. "We were not rich in El Salvador but we had a house, jobs. And in our work, Gilberto and I both helped people. Here, we are poor. Here, other people help me. But when they gave me that plate of food, I didn't feel like a poor person."

It was a good way to begin what would prove a sometimes difficult journey. At first, the Rogels didn't actually intend to stay in Canada. They'd left El Salvador when Gilberto's work as a public relations and communications director with a high-profile nonprofit in San Salvador caused him to fear for his safety and that of his family. His work involved lobbying on behalf of the public against a major corporate power in the country, and he found himself a target, with people following him and making threatening calls to his home phone. It got so bad the Rogels were forced to move house in the middle of the night. When they were offered temporary jobs in Canada, they figured they'd go for a short time, wait out the danger, and return home.

But once they arrived and began to settle in, they realized that going back to El Salvador wasn't an option. They couldn't risk their daughter's life or their own safety. And despite the cold, Canada offered a whole new set of possibilities. Ariana, especially, was thriving. They began to imagine another life for her.

Still, there were big hurdles to overcome. Gilberto had taught political communications and journalism at Don Bosco University in San Salvador, and both he and Delmy had experience as journalists. But without stronger English skills, they found it impossible to find work in those fields. Gilberto tried his hand as a cleaner, then did some painting for a short time. ("I told Delmy that perhaps I have many skills," he laughs. "I've taught university, I've done PR, I've worked at a radio station. But painting is *not* one of my skills.") Anyway, he knew he'd be stuck in what the two call "survival jobs" forever if they didn't improve their English and train for jobs in Canada.

"Education is the key," the couple repeat like a mantra, turning to each other as they do. Ariana, too, has picked up on the sentiment. Every time she finds a coin on the ground, they tell me, she puts it into a jar to pay for university.

Gilberto and Delmy signed up for ESL classes and prepared to go back to school. Delmy also connected with The Stop's Healthy Beginnings program when she was pregnant with their first son. She continued with her second boy. "It was my opportunity to socialize," she says. "And the information was so good. I learned that in Canada you can have your husband in the room with you when you labour; in El Salvador you have to pay extra for that. I met some good friends at The Stop." Later, Delmy began volunteering at Sabor Latino, the Spanish-language community kitchen group, doing intake with newcomers and making people feel comfortable, as others had done for her.

After the Rogels had been in Toronto for a few months, they applied for and eventually received refugee status, then permanent residence in 2008. Gilberto completed a social work diploma at a private college, and Delmy decided to take the community worker program at another local college. These days they're living on student loans, carefully monitoring their finances, signing the kids up for swimming lessons and dance at the local community centre, exploring their new home by walking the streets and taking advantage of free family events around the city. They're hoping for the best.

The Rogels' immigration story is a common one at The Stop. There are people from some forty different countries in our programs. More than half of our food bank members were born outside of Canada. All of them are trying to find support and connection in their new home. Recognizing both the diversity and this longing for community was one of the reasons we started the Global Roots garden project at the Green Barn. With seven small fenced-in plots running alongside the wide walkway outside the greenhouse, the project pairs seniors and youth from a range of ethnic communities that have large populations in the city (Chinese, South Asian, Somalian, Italian, Latin American, Polish and Filipino). They share the planting and tending, harvesting and cooking. We're also using the small plots, which are set up in a very public space, to show visitors the potential for small space gardening and for growing crops like okra and bitter melon that are familiar to the diverse communities in the city.

I stopped by one evening and met an Indian woman in the South Asian garden working with a Chinese high school student to weed among the cardamom, methi and chilies they are growing. The older woman, wearing white gloves and dressed in a brilliant blue sari, a scarf covering the back of her hair, was crouched down low picking at errant plants while the teenager watered with a watering can. The older woman smiled when she got sprinkled by mistake and teased the girl that she was going to drown her *and* the plants. A small, grey-haired Chinese woman was working her plot alone, her young partner missing for the moment. She looked shy when I asked her what she was growing, and pointed to a cabbage. She patted her chest. "Favourite," she said.

The garden gives the older participants—many of whom grew up farming but haven't been able to grow anything since leaving their homeland and moving into city apartments—a chance to share their wealth of knowledge about agriculture. Their younger partners have a chance to learn from them and hear their stories.

Like the Rogel family, these gardeners are looking to connect with other people and contribute to the city. It's a sentiment I hear from people in our neighbourhood all the time—whether they are new immigrants or not. People want to volunteer; they want to share their skills and help others. No one wants to be poor or marginalized. Given the chance, everyone would like to be a contributing member of their community. Of course, many people aren't given the chance. It's one of the things that makes The Stop such an important place for people in our neighbourhood—it can act as a springboard back into life.

Ariana comes in from the playground and plops herself down beside her mom. She's thirsty after running around in the park and digs around in her knapsack for her water bottle. Delmy smiles at her daughter. "I'm just ready to move forward with my life," she explains. "I'm not going to be a journalist here. I want to work with the community now. It's one of the reasons I decided to go to college and do the community worker program. So many good people helped me. Now, I want to do the same for others."

AUGUST 2009. The bake oven behind Symington Place has been heating up for nearly two hours, and there's the toasty, soothing scent of woodsmoke in the air. With a colourful hand-crafted mosaic of flames, flowers and even a Mickey Mouse character embedded in its surface, the bake oven is the hearth around which our community gathers on Tuesday afternoons.

It's early still, but people are already starting to arrive for the fresh food market and free bake oven pizza. The grass in the small courtyard has been trampled into submission, no more than a few hardy patches of green left here and there. There are two raised garden beds with herbs that people can cut and sprinkle on their pizzas, and beside them, a little playground area where children are jumping and shouting. It's a small space—the entire court-yard no bigger than a high school gymnasium—but it's packed with action. People in wheelchairs and elderly folks, young moms with toddlers, a few homeless guys. I recognize a couple of Mexican men sitting on the benches. They're regulars at the drop-in, part of a fairly large contingent of Central and South Americans using The Stop these days, who feel more comfortable here thanks to our many Spanish-speaking staff.

Abdul, the Somali man who was involved in the East African Men's Cooking Group many years ago, is here, too. He's sitting on another bench by himself. I still see him regularly making the trek to the beer store, but he's been looking worse and worse lately. His tweed jacket now hangs off his tall frame as if it were made for a much larger man. His face is thin and, though he always waves gamely to me when he passes my office window, I can see that he's drunk. Rumana, who's gone on to work for the city, tells me he's estranged from the East African community, too. It's hard to see him this way. But the reality is, there are people who slip through our network of support. The path out of poverty and, in his case, addiction is rarely linear. There are many in our community who lead complicated and extraordinarily difficult lives. I see our role as being always available, making sure people know we'll be responsive and nonjudgmental when they turn to us.

I spot Gordon Bowes with his trademark baseball cap and an apron emblazoned with The Stop's logo standing guard near the oven, and go over to say hello. Gord has been around The Stop for as long as I can remember. He's sixtyish now, an average-sized man with small, blue eyes and a patch of hair on his chin. The cane that he uses to get around since a car accident a few years ago is resting against the mosaic-covered table in front of the bake oven. Gord shakes my hand but goes right back to his work. He takes his volunteer job stoking and tending the fire very seriously. It's something of an art to get the oven hot and keep it there, but not so hot that the pizza chars.

I think of Gord as one of our community elders. He moved away from the area when he got a spot in a seniors' building across the city, but he still comes back each Tuesday to tend the bake oven and on many other days, as well. Gord tells me he first heard about The Stop a few years before I arrived. He was living in that notorious apartment building the public health nurses used to tell me about. It was a place where you could buy crack and the services of prostitutes in the hallways and elevators any hour of the day or night. ("Hey there, wanna get lucky?" they would ask him several times a day.) It was a cockroach-infested place of last resort. Gord had recently lost his job at the railway as a coach cleaner and was going through a difficult time.

Tough times were nothing new for Gord. He grew up near The Stop but left home for good at fifteen, fleeing a father who beat him up when he was drinking, something he did every day. Gord lived on the street for nearly fifteen years, sleeping in laneways, abandoned buildings, garages and shelters. Most of the time, he didn't know where his next meal would come from. Like his father, he too learned to "drink like a trooper," he says. But by the time he was thirty, Gord was tired and spent. "I was sick of it. The stress of having people steal stuff from you, of being hungry, not knowing where I'd sleep—I wanted a steady roof over my head," he says.

He began looking for casual labour, taking on cleaning jobs, security work, even cooking, and found cheap rooming houses where he could lay his head. Eventually he managed to quit both drinking and smoking, and though he was diagnosed with diabetes in his late forties and told he needed a triple bypass in his fifties, he had a more stable life by then.

When he first turned up at The Stop's food bank in one of our old locations, Gord was embarrassed. After everything he'd been through to get his life in shape, he hated to ask for a handout. But he quickly realized that he could also volunteer, and that made a big difference to how he felt about it. He took on tasks at the reception desk, greeting and interviewing people, driving the truck and handing out food. He was even asked to join the board of directors. Inspired by his volunteer work, Gord enrolled in the same community worker program at a local college that Cliff and later Nicole and Delmy would attend. He even did a work-study placement in our food bank.

The Stop became Gord's second home. He'd come to all of our events and help Cliff in the food bank. When we dug the first fence post holes for the community garden at Earlscourt, Gord was there. When Herman served up callaloo, Gord was there. When Rhonda set up strawberry-picking or corn-picking trips, Gord was always on the bus.

"I wouldn't have finished my college degree if it weren't for The Stop. It took me six years—I had that car accident in the middle of it—but I got it. My father always said I never finished anything. Well, look," he says, pretending to dangle a piece of paper in the air. "Here's my college degree!"

Gord leans over the bake oven and checks inside. The heat is steady. It's ready to go. I can see people starting to get antsy waiting for the pizza-making to begin.

On the western edge of the courtyard, the Good Food Market staff and volunteers have set up three long tables laid with rustic-looking burlap. They're unloading vegetables from the mishmash of carts and wagons they use to transport them from a meeting room at The Stop to the courtyard. There are zucchini and mushrooms, bananas and strawberries, peppers and lettuce, okra and eggplant. The volunteers display them nicely in baskets and artful piles, producing handwritten signs just like those at the farmers' market we host at the Green Barn.

This market is one of several Good Food Markets in the city—part of the Community Food Animator Project we've been involved with for years—and is supported by our old friends at FoodShare. They buy fresh produce at the Ontario Food Terminal—a vast depot where farmers and wholesalers bring their wares—and offer it to communities like ours at close to cost. That means we can offer a head of lettuce for as little as fifty cents, a bag of apples for a dollar. FoodShare tries to buy what's in season and support local farmers wherever possible, but the focus is on getting healthy, reasonably priced food to low-income communities.

Produce sells out fast every Tuesday. We have lots of regulars, people who show up early with their own shopping bags. They chat with staff and volunteers, and share cooking tips and recipes. Everyone is glad not to have to trek on the bus to No Frills or Price Chopper to get fresh food. And the prices can't be beat.

Rosa Lamanna, another of our community elders, is behind the market table. She volunteers here every week. She calls herself the bag lady because she arrives early and helps separate and clean bunches of produce before they're stored in plastic bags. Her son, Tony, is hunched over in the corner by the door into the health centre working on an upside-down bike. His head is down, concentrating, his thick black hair flopping over his glasses. Tony is a vital part of the Davenport West bike repair team—a perfect job for a guy who's loved to play with bikes since he was little. The team is busy all the time, helping oil chains and adjust brakes and cables. People drop off their bikes while they shop for produce at the market, and Tony and the other volunteers fix them up for free.

In the warmer months, the Good Food Market makes Tuesdays the highlight of the week at The Stop. Staff, students and volunteers have managed to create a bustling, festive gathering place for the neighbourhood. In fact, the Good Food Market doesn't feel so different from the Green Barn farmers' market down the street, which has been thriving since we opened the new facility. During the winter, the market is held in Barn #2, in the area known as the indoor street, a long, open space where huge blown-up historical images of the area and the barns line the brick walls. In the summer, the market is moved outside, winding around the west and south sides under pop-up tents. There's organic coffee and artisanal bread, gourmet cheese, pickled turnips, organic greens, jams and jellies. Mennonite farmers offer both fresh and frozen meat and fishers supply freshly caught whitefish from the Great Lakes. Chefs provide tastings. There's hot chocolate in winter and ice cream in the summer. A thousand people a week come out to chat with the farmers and chefs, listen to live music and visit with their neighbours.

It's everything we hoped for—and the Wychwood community has embraced it. In fact, real estate agents have begun to promote properties in the area with phrases like "minutes from the Wychwood Barns" or "in the prestigious Wychwood Barns neighbourhood." I've even seen a few of the people who once fought the redevelopment of the Barns site chatting happily while they buy foraged mushrooms and leeks from a guy who brings them down from Northern Ontario.

The major difference between our two markets, of course, is the price of the food. At the Green Barn, we're catering to the kind of affluent consumers who seek out local farmers and heirloom vegetables. They don't mind paying the cost of organic produce, either simply because they can or because they believe it's important to support local production and pay farmers a fair price. At The Stop's Good Food Market, the costs are low and the price is subsidized by our fundraising and volunteer labour. Many of our customers are also food bank users, people who don't always know where their next meal is coming from. Cost is most important, and even if they'd like to buy organic, most of them cannot.

When we cut a long, green vine to officially open the Green Barn in the spring, one of our community advocates from Davenport West spoke about the two markets. She told the assembled dignitaries and friends, people who'd been fighting for this project for years, that she'd found her voice and a home at The Stop. She said that while she was glad the Green Barn was there (and she anticipated being able to cook and grow and learn in our beautiful new space), there was no way she could afford to buy anything at the Green Barn market. She said she was a cancer survivor and had been told that organic produce was important to her health, but living on welfare, food like that simply wasn't an option. It was a poignant moment, a bit difficult considering the celebratory nature of the event, but an essential reminder of the reality of our two-tiered food system and the real people whose lives it affects.

That's why we continue to try to find ways to use the Green Barn and the connections it makes with both communities to build bridges across economic lines. One initiative is YIMBY (Yes in My Back Yard), a new backyard-sharing project that connects people who want to garden but have no space—because they live in apartment buildings or rooming houses—with those who have yards but no time. The Stop helps set up garden-sharing matches and provides a tool-lending library, free gardening workshops, some free seedlings, a seed exchange, and opportunities to meet and learn from other gardeners.

We also have a table at the farmers' market staffed by community advocates who promote their educational events like film nights and raise awareness about our advocacy campaigns. We're even trying to create a social justice group in the Green Barn neighbourhood. We don't want people in this community to feel that the only thing they can do to support our work and promote alliances is to write a cheque to The Stop. We want them to ask themselves, if local and organic is good for the middle class and good for the planet, why shouldn't low-income people be eating this food, too? We want them to ask themselves how we're all going to ensure that they can.

The crowd at the Good Food Market behind Symington Place is growing restless. Gord lets the kitchen staff back at The Stop know that the oven is ready to go. A volunteer comes out from the kitchen carrying the pizza dough, individual portions all lined up on a cookie tray that's covered with several tea towels. Other volunteers trail her with tomato sauce and grated cheese, some basil from the garden and a few other toppings. I can feel the surge of excitement in the crowd when they see the parade of food. A lineup begins to form and it's soon twisting through the courtyard.

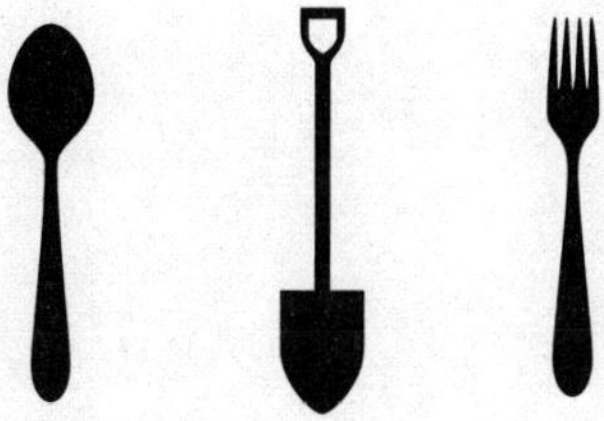

SEVEN

EAT THE
MATH

▷━━▶

APRIL 2010. A long table has been set up in the food bank near a wall painted a vibrant tomato red. Chairs line it on one side and there are a few microphones in the middle. The media are starting to gather in front. Photographers, reporters from the major networks and newspapers, and bloggers with notebooks and recorders are crowded into the small, warm space.

Cliff and the food bank volunteers are ready to go. Jonah and the staff who organized this press conference to launch our Eat the Math campaign are fussing around, getting everything ready. We've just received word that Naomi Klein—the author, activist and global phenom—is going to be a bit late.

A full complement of other participants is already here. City councillor Joe Mihevc stands behind me with his eleven-year-old daughter, along with the head of the city's public health department and Stop supporter Michael MacMillan. A few of the participants sit at the table beside me; the others line up along the wall. It's a curious mix of actors, musicians and foodies—all willing guinea pigs in our food bank challenge. The cameras start flashing before I even open my mouth to introduce everyone.

We've been working on this project for more than a year. It's the second part in a civic engagement campaign that we call Do the Math, created by our staff and community members to bring attention to the abysmal state of social assistance rates. With 77 percent of Stop members living on some form of government assistance, it's an issue that's close to home for us.

Last spring, we launched a web-based project that asks people to calculate the real cost of living and compare it to the basic $580 per month that a single person on social assistance receives from the provincial government in order to survive. People who come to the website are guided through an online survey and asked to plug in the amount they think a frugal single person would need to spend every month to meet basic needs (food, housing, transportation, toiletries). The site adds it all up and, on average, people figure it requires about $1,500 for a single person to get by.

It's a shock for most of the website users who Do the Math when they are informed that social assistance offers about a third of that amount. Most people are further bewildered when they learn that the $580 per month is completely arbitrary—not based on the real cost of living, but simply on successive governments' manoeuvring for popularity and votes.

To make matters worse, the right hand doesn't seem to know what the left hand is doing. Every year the government mandates public health departments across the province to create a report on the cost of a "nutritious food basket" in each city or region. These reports are intended to show the real cost of healthy eating, and the information is used to promote policies that ensure people have access to nutritious food.

But such policies haven't been forthcoming. According to our city's public health department, it costs a man in his forties approximately $240 per month to eat healthily. But with housing using up most of a person's cheque (an average bachelor apartment in downtown Toronto rents for more than $800 a month) and other fixed costs like phone, hydro, water and heat, people on welfare have little or nothing left for food.

For those who Do the Math, the utter inadequacy of social assistance and the impossible choices forced on people who must survive on it—pay the rent *or* feed the kids, skip meals so you can take public transit to look for work, live in a cockroach-infested apartment in order to have enough to eat—become obvious very quickly. At The Stop, we see these choices play out every day. Our members tell us that they spend 58 percent of their income on housing; two-thirds of them say they sometimes don't eat because they don't have enough money. And with the downturn in the global economy, the number of people needing the food bank has increased dramatically. People who never thought they'd need food handouts are taking a number and accepting our hampers. With this kind of economic shakeup, the line between being okay and being unable to feed your family is thin and capricious.

Our hope for the Do the Math project is to put pressure on the government and citizens so politicians can't help but pay attention to poverty and inequality issues. We're asking people who Do the Math to register their concerns with their political representatives and urge them to take action. We suggest making calls, meeting with politicians or sending postcards asking them to advocate for benefit levels that reflect the real cost of living. As a down payment on a transparent, adequate social welfare system, we'd like to see a hundred-dollar healthy food supplement added immediately to cheques.

I photocopied one of the postcards someone in our neighbourhood sent to her local politician, and put it up on the bulletin board in my office. She'd written: "Sick. No hope." That postcard reminds me every day what we're fighting for.

We also teamed up with the Social Planning Network of Ontario on their Put Food in the Budget (PFIB) campaign, offering the tools and strategies of Do the Math to other community groups around the province.

Nicole Mitchell, with a newly minted college degree in community work and a passion for advocacy, has recently been hired part-time to do relief work at The Stop's drop-in and food bank. She was also asked to be one of the community spokespeople for the provincial rollout of the Do the Math campaign. She and the PFIB group met with more than forty politicians and had them Do the Math, too. On average, these representatives from across the political spectrum figured $1,314 was enough to pay for the necessities of life—less than the average person who did the survey, but over seven hundred dollars more than a single person actually receives on social assistance.

The PFIB group also approached the government minister in charge of Community and Social Services. The minister wouldn't do the survey, but told the team proudly that it was a family tradition of hers to go with her kids to the grocery store and have them choose things to donate to the food bank. Nicole was not impressed. "There is no dignity in giving *my* children what *your* children want to eat," she told the startled politician. "We want real change to this system, not handouts."

The Civic Engagement program held a town hall meeting in the sanctuary of the church next door to The Stop. The minister of Children and Youth Services (and chair of a government committee on poverty reduction) was invited, and told the audience that there was no money in the budget for an increase to social assistance rates. When one community member asked if the minister could explain how the government came up with the specific amount it provides to welfare recipients, there was a long silence. "I don't know," she finally told the assembled crowd.

The Eat the Math press conference today launches the next step in this project: drawing attention to the issue by having a group of well-known Torontonians try to stretch a food hamper from our food bank—like so many social assistance recipients must do—as long as possible. These "celebrities" will write, blog and talk to the media about their experience. It will culminate in a town hall meeting at the Wychwood Barns. The exercise is not intended to be a criticism of food banks, but rather an indictment of the social assistance system that forces so many of our fellow citizens to rely on charitable handouts just to get through the month. Admittedly it's a stunt, but this stunt has a purpose. The campaign was created in close collaboration with our community members, especially the activists in the Civic Engagement program, who've recently renamed themselves Bread & Bricks Davenport West Social Justice Group. It's essential that the entire project be grounded in lived experience and guided by community members if it's to be more than an elaborate piece of performance art.

Bread & Bricks laid out the strict ground rules based on their own lives. In order to replicate the isolation and limited choices of people living in poverty, participants may not eat anything outside the hamper unless it's at a free drop-in program (not even at work meetings or other people's homes). Participants may use five items they already have in their pantries, and they must use public transit, walk or bike to get around.

Members of Bread & Bricks explained all of this at a dinner we held in the Green Barn greenhouse. Each advocate was paired with a celebrity challenger and given the task of conveying the rules, explaining to their partner the reality of life on social assistance. It was a tough meal, even a bit uncomfortable for those participants who were forced to confront their own privilege and the unfairness of inequality face to face. But I think it made everyone recognize the gravity of the issue, and the way the Eat the Math challenge is profoundly connected to the realities of living in poverty. By arming participants with information and the stories of real people, it also made them better spokespeople for the cause.

I open the press conference with a short introduction. I'm always a bit nervous just before I speak publicly, but today I feel emboldened by this group of people from so many different worlds standing behind and around me. "Food bank handouts are not the answer to the crisis that so many low-income people are facing," I say. "What we need is real political will, and people to come together like we are today—faith groups, labour, business, citizen groups, artists and activists—to demand change to our welfare system.

"In private, I know a lot of politicians figure dealing with welfare is a vote detractor—and it probably is. But today we're saying we must work together as citizens to create momentum. There must be a political price to pay for failing to support low-income people to live a dignified life."

When the talking part is over, Eat the Math participants head to pick up their food hampers. The head of public health, whose responsibilities include creating the annual nutritious food basket costing for government, is one of the first up. He picks up his starch-heavy hamper: three kinds of pasta and potatoes, no meat or bread. Then Joe Mihevc and his family choose their wieners and beans, cans of tuna and a few pears.

Frankly, seeing the food on offer this morning, I feel a bit demoralized. Even though I've been at The Stop for more than a decade, worked in the food bank, have an office fifty feet away and see it every day, looking at what is available today—under the glare of the lights and attention—drives home once again how wrong it is that people have to survive on this. It's not good enough for anyone.

I know, objectively, that the food at The Stop is much better than it used to be. It's better than any other food bank I've seen. Our Healthy Food Fund, to which people can contribute to support nutritious food purchases for Stop hampers, has made it possible to have milk, eggs and fruit today. But some weeks are better than others. And there are still a lot of cheap calories. Processed stuff. Canned pork and beans, canned spaghetti. And while we say our hampers are intended to last two or three days, many, many people who use the food bank are forced to stretch them for much longer.

Naomi Klein, who arrived during the press conference, reaches the front but there's little she can take. She's on a restricted diet because of allergies—no wheat, no eggs, no dairy and low sugar. She says she feels like a pill to be so demanding, but her experience is not unlike that of many people in our community with health issues. They also have dietary requirements that the food bank usually can't accommodate. As he does with all of our members, Cliff tries to help Naomi, offering her rice instead of pasta and extra beans instead of eggs, but it's not going to be easy for her to live on what we can provide.

Cliff moves around behind the counter, taking it all in stride. He's his usual easygoing self, directing traffic, joking with

volunteers, calmly accepting the chaos of cameras and microphones everywhere. But he's been sick lately, and he's had to take
some time off. It started out when he noticed one fingernail
turning black, and we were all shocked to discover that it was
cancerous. He had his finger amputated, and things seemed to
be going as well as could be expected. But he's learned recently
that the cancer has spread up his arm.

Seeing him there in his familiar spot behind the counter,
I can't help thinking how The Stop has changed so much over
the last twelve years. We started out with two full-time staff
and now have upwards of thirty (plus part-time people), as well
as three managers—Kathryn, Rhonda, who now manages the
Green Barn, and Cheryl Roddick, who leads our fundraising
team organizing events, donor appeals, social enterprise and
grant writing, helping to raise our four-million-dollar annual
budget. We have more programs, more members, more space
and two sites that we move between.

Through all these exciting changes and sometimes overwhelming new directions, Cliff has remained at the heart of
The Stop. His rootedness in the community and his willingness
to welcome new and challenging ideas are at the core of what we
are as an organization. His cancer has been devastating to him
personally—he's still a young man and has recently fallen in love—
and it's also hit our close-knit staff and neighbourhood hard.

But there's little time to slow down with The Stop busier
than ever. The Green Barn has garnered a lot of attention in the
media, and we've had to devote a fair amount of effort to fielding
phone calls, email and tour requests from around the country,
even the world. There are many nonprofits, food organizations,
graduate students, university professors and community activists
who want to talk about our approach and how they can do

similar work in their own communities. It's exhilarating to have people interested, but the requests are time-consuming and we've been joking at staff meetings about offering "Stop in a Box"—a how-to guide for creating a Community Food Centre. Eventually, we began to take the idea more seriously, thinking carefully and strategically about how we've built the organization and why it matters. With a small grant, we started to write it down. It wasn't easy to codify the essence of The Stop's vision and growth—something I've often described as building a plane in the air—but it was a useful exercise and it got us thinking about how we might bring the model to other cities and towns and help them create their own Community Food Centres.

When it's my turn, I pick up a hamper for Andrea and me. We're going to Eat the Math at home, too, though we're leaving the kids out of it. The cameras are still going and people are milling about when I survey the offerings and choose our food. Looking at our hamper, I can see it's going to be a difficult week.

◆━

MARY E. MILNE IS A GRANDMOTHER in her early seventies. She's always been politically and socially engaged, unafraid to stand up for herself and others. So it wasn't a huge leap to become one of the members of the Bread & Bricks cadre who helped shape the Do the Math campaign. She was involved in helping set the ground rules for Eat the Math—ensuring the experience of the challengers was as close as possible to the reality of trying to survive on a food bank hamper—and was part of the team that strategized how to get the word out about problems with the welfare system.

Mary understands intimately the challenges of getting by on social assistance. She owns her own home close to Symington

Place, but she's been struggling since 2003 when an injury forced her to leave her job. With no money coming in, she was unable to afford to heat the house. Then the pipes burst, and she couldn't even close her bedroom door for the giant column of ice blocking it. Mary reluctantly applied for welfare and turned to The Stop's food bank to get through the month. She's been coming back ever since.

With her signature homemade jewellery and big glasses that make her look like a wise owl, Mary quickly became a welcome presence at Symington Place. She's generous with her considerable artistic talents (her colourful signs and drawings are often featured on The Stop's walls), and she has a gift for connecting with people—rich, poor or in-between. There are some, perhaps, who are born that way, but this chameleon quality is surely also the result of leading an interesting, varied life. A published poet and artist who's hosted a weekly open mic night at a local union hall for the last sixteen years, Mary grew up the youngest of three in a middle-class family of artists—"a simmering cauldron of creativity," as she wrote in one of her poems. Though she loved words and devoured a book and a half every day, she did poorly on tests and struggled in school.

When Mary was seventeen, her mother became seriously ill and her father asked her to drop out of school to help out at home. The caregiver role wasn't a great fit, though, and Mary became so severely depressed she attempted suicide that year. Two years later, still trying to escape, she got pregnant and married the baby's father. She stayed with her husband—an abusive alcoholic—for thirteen years and thirteen days (significant numbers in Mary's eyes), and they had two children together. When she finally left, he offered almost no child support. But Mary hunkered down and continued to work, holding down jobs as a bank teller, bartender, waitress, factory worker and cleaner—usually taking on both a full-time and a part-time position—in addition to renting rooms out to boarders in her home.

For ten years before she first arrived at The Stop, Mary had a solid position as a bartender and wine steward at an exclusive golf and country club. She was knowledgeable about wine and enjoyed her job, often working overtime to make extra money. One day at the club, while carrying a tray with wineglasses on it, she slipped on the wet stone patio and fell on the broken glass. One knee took the impact of her fall, and the other was deeply cut. The injuries took a long time to heal, and though she tried to go back to her job, Mary soon realized that she couldn't work on her feet for long hours anymore and left the club.

She was in her early fifties, then, out of work and out of money. It took numerous hearings and six years, but eventually, she received workers' compensation for her injury. She hoped to retrain as a social worker or life skills counsellor, but as part of her compensation package she was placed in a computer course. It felt like high school all over again. She took the course, but it was a struggle and, not surprisingly, she wasn't able to find work. "I got lots of nice rejection letters. The truth is, nobody wants a computer novice in her fifties," Mary says.

That's when her heat was cut off, and she wound up at The Stop. Mary soon began volunteering at the front desk in the food bank, picking up a hamper for herself once a month. She took on the role with her usual determination; recognizing that the food bank needed a better filing system for members, she created one. Later, she helped out in the kitchens and at the Good Food Market, eventually joining the Speakers' Bureau. By the time we rolled out the first stages of the Do the Math campaign, she had become one of The Stop's most accomplished public speakers.

Mary's a natural in front of a crowd. When she stood up to speak at our annual general meeting one year, the big, busy, noisy room—its tables and chairs packed with volunteers, neighbours and donors—went silent. People couldn't take their eyes off her. "You don't realize until you're there how close we all are to the edge," she said. "I never thought I'd be up here talking about going on welfare." She told her story, gathering steam as she explained: "Poverty hurts everybody. It's not how things should be." By the end there wasn't a dry eye in the room.

As media attention built during Do the Math, Mary appeared on the most popular public radio shows and was invited to speak at workshops and events, from a talk hosted by a Sikh service organization to one held at an elite private girls' school. One day during the campaign, she spoke to more than six hundred people. Her difficult story of being a senior living in poverty—buying nearly expired meat from the discount section of the grocery store, looking for the cheapest, most calorie-dense food rather than the most nutritious and living with the unhealthy consequences—was not one that people had heard before. It shocked everyone to see such a well-put-together, articulate older woman with her lipstick and carefully chosen thrift store clothes standing in front of them telling this harrowing story.

Mary thrived in the spotlight. She continued to volunteer at the Good Food Market and pitch in as a paid community advocate. Like so many others in our neighbourhood, she says it makes her feel good to help other people. "The Stop restores my soul," she explains.

People come in all the time, she says, with problems that seem insurmountable to them, and they leave with supports in place. "I helped a Spanish-speaking man with a knee injury recently. He didn't have a doctor and didn't speak English very well. We looked up doctors who are taking new patients and got him an appointment. He didn't know the name or number of his welfare worker, but I called up the office, found the person and we faxed her his medical forms. He was so happy. He'd found hope."

Not every problem has such a straightforward solution. Mary still can't afford to maintain her house, and it's falling apart around her. She doesn't often invite her grandchildren or friends home anymore because the ceiling is caving in. She tries to remain positive. Making art helps a lot. Sometimes she makes enough money selling poster art, sketches and homemade jewellery to cover incidentals like laundry and public transit, but healthy food continues to be hard to come by. Mary continues to drop in for meals at The Stop three or four days a week, and relies regularly on food bank hampers like the one I took home. For her, eating food from a hamper is no experiment.

APRIL 2010. When we get home after the press conference, Andrea and I lay our food out on the kitchen table. We take inventory: one box of cereal, two one-litre containers of 2-percent milk, five carrots, three tomatoes, four pears, two limes, eight eggs, one box of microwave popcorn, some potatoes and onions, a bag of rice, a bag of pasta noodles, one can of pasta sauce, one single-serving SpagghetiOs, a box of tea, a chocolate bar, two single-serving yogurts, three cans of soup, two cans of vegetables, two tins of tuna, two cans of pork and beans, something called "apple crisps" (which look like dried, sugary apple peelings), two lunch-size macaroni and cheese, one jar of peanut butter.

Spread out like this, it actually doesn't look too bad—though Andrea is skeptical about the canned spaghetti and vegetables. As a family, we like to eat, and we spend a good portion of our weekly budget on food. Lots of fresh vegetables and whole grains. We sit down together for dinner most nights—though it's rarely the relaxed family meal Andrea and I are hoping for (more like racing to get the food on the table, then racing to get out the door to the next school or sports event). People assume because I run an organization that's all about good food that I'm some sort of puritan, but I'm not. My own guilty pleasure is a roast chicken with extra sauce from Swiss Chalet. And I don't turn up my nose at making the occasional boxed mac and cheese for my kids—my own father deemed it "magic dinner" when I was a kid, forever embedding it in my mind as the easiest solution for a busy night.

Still, I appreciate good, fresh food and we make most of our meals from scratch. Since Ben, our older son, declared himself a vegetarian at eight years old, we rarely eat meat. The food bank hamper is nothing like what we would choose for ourselves. We're hoping we'll be able stretch it with some creative cookery. For our five home pantry items, we choose salt, flour, olive oil, soy sauce and coffee. Andrea's planning to make unleavened bread with flour and water as a vehicle for the peanut butter.

We start off with canned chicken noodle soup for dinner with a carrot on the side, plus apple crisps for dessert. But by the time I get home late from coaching Ben's basketball team, I'm famished and sneak two eggs, half a Kit Kat bar, a bag of microwave popcorn and a glass of milk. Andrea isn't thrilled that I've binged like that, and she threatens to hide her portion of the food, but we're both still feeling good-natured about it all.

That changes by day two. We each go to bed with a headache after arguing about something stupid. We ate breakfast, lunch and dinner, so we're not starving, but there's not quite enough to feel full and already the lack of variety and fresh produce is nagging at us.

I'm one of those people with a fast metabolism, so I need to eat at regular intervals or my blood sugar dives. My family knows to not even bother talking to me when I'm hungry because I'm impatient and unreasonable. Living on this diet over the long term, I'm sure I'd lose it on a regular basis.

The headaches and irritability make me think how much mental health can be compromised by a lack of good food. I think about the tensions in our drop-in, or how difficult it must be for hungry children to concentrate on their schoolwork, or what someone looking for work must go through trying to put on a positive face when their stomach is empty.

By day three, living on this diet has become monotonous, difficult and frustrating. We're not starving and we have enough calories to survive, but it's a lot of carbohydrates and not a lot of protein or other nutrients. There's also tons of salt and fat in the processed canned goods. Neither of us has the energy to argue anymore, but there's a low-grade tension in our house. I'm glad we decided not to include the kids in this experiment.

Adding to the tension is the fact that at midday, I enjoyed a delicious meal at The Stop lunch drop-in—and emailed a picture of it to Andrea. I wasn't gloating, exactly, but the cheese and potato kugel, lentils with broccoli and cauliflower, and salad greens from the greenhouse made Andrea's SpaghettiOs eaten out of a plastic tub seem much, much worse.

We're keeping track of the other participants on blog posts for The Stop's website and in interviews they're giving to local papers. Joe Mihevc and his family have reported becoming obsessed with food—thinking about it, talking about it and constantly planning their next meal. "We all ate a lot less," the city councillor told a reporter who renamed the project *Survivor: Ontario Welfare Edition*. "[We got] tired more quickly, and your engine just isn't firing on all cylinders." One of the other participants, a hardcore punk rock singer, also reports feeling the impact on his mental health. "In a real way you feel kind of defeated," he told the same reporter. "It's hard to feel happy when you're miserable about your most basic sustenance." By day four, Naomi Klein is struggling to find food in the hamper that she can eat with her diet restrictions. She reports that she's had to reach into her own cupboard for brown rice pasta.

That same day, Andrea and I run out of milk, and we divvy up the last of our eggs and canned vegetables. Tuna from a tin seems like a rare, exotic delicacy after having so little protein all week. On day five, with not much more than a can of soup and some peanut butter left—plus a major basketball tournament that Ben's playing in, I'm coaching and we're all attending—Andrea and I stop our welfare diet. We are too headachy, tired and hungry to continue. We both feel ashamed.

Being able to stop the experiment so easily, and being able to choose not to include our children, are stark reminders of how far apart we are from those we are attempting to show solidarity with. People on social assistance can't just pack it in because they're tired and bored of the same old soup or have a tough weekend ahead of them. They have no choice. I've been careful when I talk to people not to overdramatize my experience. I know Do the Math was an experiment and not some magic wand that gives me deep insight into what it's like to live on social assistance week after week, month after month. But I do feel I have a more emotional understanding of some of the challenges that I've spent my working life trying to combat.

Losing the ability to make choices about what and how we eat, how we socialize and where we go was by turns depressing, disheartening and isolating. It's not just about having reduced choices as a consumer (although that, of course, is one of the first things lost by someone living in poverty). It goes much deeper. Partly, it's because food isn't like other consumer goods—you can do without a TV or nail polish, whereas food is a basic need—and not having a say in what you eat feels like being stripped of something essential. The experience made me feel enervated and trapped.

It also made me understand even more viscerally the deep reserves of strength and dignity required by people like Mary and Glenn and the other community advocates who, despite living in extremely difficult circumstances themselves, speak up and fight back. People ask me all the time about how I personally manage to remain hopeful for change working in a low-income community where poverty can be unrelenting and the victories few and far between. It's an honest question, but I guess I'm not really sure what the alternative is: pack it in? That's certainly not an option for Mary or the other participants in Bread & Bricks, or for the rest of the people who use our community resources.

My own response has often been that I am encouraged by the people I meet and the stories I hear. I see how our work is making a difference in their lives every day—the community members who find housing or a job with help from The Stop, those who access disability supports with assistance from our staff, the people who volunteer in our programs and feel more connected to their neighbours. I was riding my bike home the other day and a guy biking in the opposite direction called out to me, "Are you from The Stop?" When I yelled back that I was, he said, "Saved my life." Before I could ask him his story, he sped away.

Obviously, we don't always save people's lives. There are too many stories like that of Abdul, who continues to struggle, or Marie, a well-liked community member and antipoverty activist who died of diet-related health issues before we began the Do the Math campaign. For many people, all of our programs and efforts to provide healthy food and connections just aren't enough. The experience of Eat the Math made the urgency for change come home to me in a new way, leaving me profoundly—and, I think, constructively—angry about our society's collective response to poverty and hunger. Over and over I found myself trying to explain to people that the food bank hamper isn't just a supplement to an already stocked fridge, it is the *only* thing many people have to eat after paying rent. And despite the best efforts of food banks, it's inadequate to boot. It's not just wrong that so many people are hungry, isolated, depressed and unhealthy, it's not just bad for the economy, it's immoral.

WE ARRIVE EARLY for the culminating Eat the Math town hall meeting, but the Wychwood Barns are already alive with people. Risers are set up toward one end of the high-ceilinged Barn #2. Chairs are lined up nearly to the other end of the Barn, an aisle carved down the middle where microphones will be placed for the question and answer period. Stop staffers have tables where they're handing out literature and postcards to send to politicians registering the need for a hundred-dollar healthy food allowance. There are film cameras, too.

I'm nervous. Jonah and the Bread & Bricks crew have done an incredible job organizing and promoting the whole project. There's been coverage on every news station, online and in every major newspaper. Our participants have blogged and tweeted and told their stories everywhere. But who knows what will happen when there's a big crowd in this huge space. The project has been risky. While our focus was on the failure of social assistance to meet basic needs, the experiment has once again highlighted the inadequacy of our charitable response to hunger in general and of food banks in particular. And as I've learned over and over in my years at The Stop, raising questions about food banks gets people's backs up.

I've been accused of not caring about the poor and hungry because I don't think food banks are the answer. The Stop has been called hypocritical because we still offer emergency handouts. How can we be slamming food banks, we're asked, when we hand out thousands of pounds of food every year? I always explain that our food bank is different—healthier, more dignified—but more importantly, I say that it's only one of a complete roster of food programs, all aimed at meeting people where they're at and also working toward larger political and social change. This marriage of advocacy with community-driven programs makes us very different.

There are other possible challenges tonight, too. All the Do the Math participants have heard claims that what we're doing is a form of "limousine liberalism," "champagne socialism" or a self-promoting media stunt. There could be people in the crowd who consider our efforts self-aggrandizing and want to publicly question our motives. Indeed, there are those in the antipoverty movement (and they could easily be here tonight) who object in general to this kind of headline-grabbing project. By highlighting privileged people speaking out about poverty, they say, we deny the voices of those with real experience. I've heard this argument many times, especially from activists who've lived in poverty themselves and feel they were treated badly by community workers and agencies who speak *for* them, instead of *with* them.

But the entire Do the Math project has been shaped and defined by our community members. It's intended not to replace opportunities for low-income people to speak but to supplement those opportunities we've worked so hard to create. Eat the Math is an act of solidarity. And though trying to find common ground can sometimes be messy, I think it's essential. When you cut out middle-class (or other) voices from the mix of those calling for change, it's a recipe for marginalization. Low-income people must have the chance to tell their stories and advocate for themselves and their neighbours, but we are stronger when voices from all different walks of life push for the changes we want to see. I think of my own parents and their many fellow activists around the world who worked in solidarity with South Africans in the anti-apartheid movement. It's not one or the other, but both low-income people and those in solidarity with them who will move us closer to our collective goals.

Scanning the crowd, nearly four hundred strong, I can see that the Eat the Math project has drawn in people from all sorts of communities. There are retirees and young people in their twenties, some I recognize from this neighbourhood and Symington Place but lots of unfamiliar faces, too. There are even children in the audience.

Some of the musicians who did the Eat the Math challenge start us off with funky beats to draw attention to the riser where participants and Bread & Bricks community advocates are lined up in chairs. I introduce everyone and then, one by one, presenters share their stories and experiences. Later, we open up the floor to questions. There are lots of serious, thoughtful people who want to speak and share their personal and political outrage about the existence of hunger and poverty in our midst and the government's inadequate responses to these issues. All my fears were for nothing. It's one of those nights when you realize that even though it sometimes seems like we—The Stop, other anti-poverty groups and those living in poverty—are in the wilderness demanding a better life for low-income people, we're not alone. Not at all. People care and they want to do something about it. With so much of our political system mired in partisanship, red tape and citizen lassitude, many simply don't know what to do— or don't have a community and space to share their views.

Even still, when I call for breakout groups in the audience to discuss possible solutions and ways to move forward, I figure that the room will clear out. People have been sitting for more than an hour and with the noise and movement, many are sure to take the opportunity to slip out the door. But as Jonah and staff circulate a list of questions, the crowd digs in. Almost everyone stays. In groups of ten, they brainstorm how to bring attention to the inadequacy of social assistance rates. When the time is up, a representative from each group approaches the microphone to offer up their ideas to the larger crowd. Some suggest creating community action groups to push politicians on poverty issues; others recommend bringing social assistance recipients into classrooms to break down prejudice and preconceived notions about welfare. Still others advocate spreading the Do the Math campaign across the country. We'll be meeting again in two weeks to develop the ideas further with anyone who wants to continue talking.

When the formal part of the evening is over, it still seems like no one wants to leave. They've had a taste of what it feels like to be part of something positive, a group of people working toward a common goal. I know I, for one, don't want it to be over.

EIGHT

THE POWER
OF FOOD

▷━━▶

SEPTEMBER 2010. The sun is starting to go down, and we've been down every bumpy country road in a two-kilometre radius when we finally pull up to The New Farm, a family-run organic acreage near Creemore, Ontario, about two hours north of Toronto. Brent Preston and Gillian Flies have cleared a patch of their hundred acres so people can park close to the barn for the festivities. The field is muddy and already packed with vehicles. People from the area—farmers, teachers and artists— as well as a large contingent from the city have come out for a concert and outdoor dinner fundraiser for The Stop.

Brent and Gillian have been farming for less than a decade, but they've already managed to attract a loyal following for their organic veggies. Brent was raised in the Toronto suburbs; Gillian hails from Vermont, where she grew up on a sheep farm. They met when they were both with international development agencies in Malawi in south central Africa. The two spent nearly a decade supporting democracy movements in Africa, South America and Indonesia. They worked closely with former U.S. president Jimmy Carter and other heads of state, helping newly democratic nations build sustainable institutions and civic organizations.

In 2000, the pair married and moved to Toronto. They lived in the city for a few years, Brent working as a TV producer, Gillian doing international development consulting, before they sold their house and headed up to Creemore with their two young children. Neither Brent nor Gillian had farmed vegetables before. According to Brent, if they knew how hard it would be, they'd never have done it. "There is no economic justification for this," he laughs. "At the beginning, our whole idea was to use as little capital as possible, because that's the trap conventional farmers fall into. No tractor, nothing. We worked ourselves into a state of total exhaustion."

Nearly a decade on, The New Farm continues to be hard physical labour, but Brent and Gillian now have more equipment (a small tractor and Rototiller), they're assisted by interns who receive room and board in return for learning first-hand how to farm, and they're smarter about how they work. They started out planting about a hundred different kinds of crops, for instance; now they plant half that and sell all of it. And they're working toward making their small farm a closed system— producing their own compost from chickens, ducks and pigs, letting half their land lie fallow on a rotating system, and using cover crops to build up the soil. They still say it's the hardest thing they've ever done.

But they've also won enough converts to their many varieties of heirloom veggies—including purple carrots, zebra tomatoes and candy cane beets—to make a go of it. Local and city restaurants, as well as people who come by their stall at the local farmers' market, are devoted to New Farm produce. It's partly because the food is excellent—lovingly grown, flavourful, and weirdly beautiful in colour and shape. But the farmers are also savvy marketers who are unequivocal about the importance of valuing low-impact, small-scale farming.

Gillian takes care of much of the business-development side of the farm. She's the kind of person whose easygoing, intelligent manner makes everything she says sound eminently sensible. She makes no apologies for the fact, for instance, that their "handmade" vegetables are more expensive than the usual grocery store fare. New Farm–style sustainable agriculture, she says, simply costs more in the current marketplace. But that's because large-scale conventional farms are heavily subsidized by governments, and the real costs—to the environment and to our health—are paid by the public later on down the road.

"Our society is addicted to cheap food," Brent adds. "Food is completely undervalued."

Making a case for the productive possibilities of small-scale family farms and the importance of acknowledging the real cost of food is The New Farm's modus operandi. They're part of a new generation of farmers who want to grow organically and with less mechanization. These growers are committed to this approach, and have the gumption and entrepreneurial chops to sell directly to consumers at farmers' markets and through alternative distribution systems such as community shared agriculture—in which farmers sell shares in their future harvest directly to consumers, who in turn receive regular dividends in the form of food from the farm.

But Brent and Gillian haven't forgotten their long-time work supporting people living in poverty. They realized quite quickly that selling their hard-won produce to the wealthy at farmers' markets and upscale restaurants wasn't enough. They love their customers—people who come by their stall every week to chat and buy carrots—but they never intended to go into farming to further a two-tiered food system in which only rich people are able to eat well.

That's where The Stop came in. I'd known Brent and Gillian a bit in Toronto, and a few years into farming they got in touch with me. They'd seen how The Stop was building connections between low-income people and others interested in food, and they wanted to talk about how we might forge a mutually beneficial relationship. They liked that we see the food system in a holistic way—making the links between health and the environment, access and equity, farmers and cities. So we began to think about creating an alternative arrangement of our own, bypassing the big conventional players and getting good, sustainably produced food to our community members directly. The result was Grow for The Stop, a project that began modestly enough. Brent and Gillian had met a lot of people while selling their produce at local farmers' markets who believed in and wanted to more directly support their work and vision for sustainability. With Grow for The Stop, these people could make a donation to The Stop that was specifically allocated to buying New Farm produce for use in our food programming. Donors would receive a tax receipt, our community would get the best local organic food available, and The New Farm would be properly paid for its work.

That simple arrangement expanded when we created a Grow for The Stop line of New Farm veggies that would be sold at independent grocery stores in Toronto. Ten percent of the proceeds go to The Stop. We, in turn, invest the money in more New Farm produce for our programs.

The first place we went with Grow for The Stop produce was Fiesta Farms, Toronto's largest independent grocery store. Owner Joe Virgona is one of the last of a dying breed of old-school grocers. A native of Salina, an idyllic island north of Sicily, he opened his west end store a few kilometres from Symington Place more than twenty years ago to focus on serving the local Italian and Portuguese communities. But about a decade ago, Joe began to see the neighbourhood changing and started to get requests from young families and single downtown types asking him to stock organic milk, heirloom tomatoes and local veggies. He didn't waste time. He welcomed his new customers, and as word got out about the low-key feel and great local products at Fiesta, customers started coming en masse. He also introduced all sorts of new local and organic products—olive oils, honey, cheese, bread, meat—and built relationships with Local Food Plus (LFP), a nonprofit organization that certifies producers and farmers for sustainable practices. When we produced a cookbook of recipes from The Stop's kitchens called *Good Food for All*, placement at the Fiesta Farms checkout lanes helped sell out the book's first printing. So we were pleased that Joe agreed to stock Grow for The Stop produce in his store, placing it on a high-traffic shelf. Sales were so good that The New Farm began to offer its produce at several other independent groceries.

Today, The Stop is The New Farm's single biggest customer. Grow for The Stop produce is still available at indie retailers, but the main source of our buying power is the big farm fundraisers—like the one today. Brent and Gillian kit up their barn with twinkle lights and hay bale seating. They bring in musicians and actors and get a local brewery to donate beer. Proceeds go to The Stop, so we can buy New Farm produce for our community. It's a win-win situation. Creating a direct relationship with farmers has strengthened our commitment to sustainable food production and providing the best-quality food at the centre. In one year, our community enjoyed $56,000 worth of fresh New Farm food.

The relationship between The New Farm and The Stop has also helped us build connections with the wider community of sustainable farmers who care deeply about the health of the land and the reinvention of the food system. As we've begun to see things through their eyes, we've discovered how much low-income communities and farmers actually have in common. In many countries, including Canada, in fact, a lot of farmers *are* low-income earners. Certainly some large-scale farmers do well. But many small producers barely break even, go heavily into debt, and are forced to take on second jobs to make ends meet. The United States Department of Agriculture's projected median farm income for 2012 was –$2,799, with most farmers earning all their income from off-farm sources.

All around the world, farmers are under extraordinary pressure. As the food system has become deeply interconnected on a global level, and monoculture farming (one crop grown on large tracts of land) has become ascendant, the people who produce our food are forced to "go big or go home." But instead of providing wealth and security, this drive to produce vast quantities, often for export, using chemicals and intensive mechanization has devastated many communities, forcing farmers into debt or ancillary wage labour. And the use of pesticides, fertilizers and monoculture methods has depleted the soil—in some cases even killed it.

La Via Campesina, the international peasant movement that partners with the Landless Rural Workers' Movement I encountered in Brazil, has long worked against this tide by supporting small-scale sustainable farmers to reclaim their land

and dignity, and by helping give them a voice on the international stage. But the demands of the global food industry are unrelenting, and the stories about small farmers around the world struggling to find their place in this new global order can be harrowing. In India, there's been a devastating surge of suicides among farmers, particularly among those trying to move away from subsistence farming into cash crops. The genetically modified seeds and pesticides they are encouraged to buy to increase yields often aren't suited to the soil and water conditions. Deep in debt and unable to pay their creditors, more than 200,000 farmers in rural India have killed themselves since 1997.

Though they're at different ends of the food chain, neither small-scale farmers nor low-income communities benefit from the food system as it has evolved over the last half century. It makes sense to come together to create alternative mechanisms that bring the interests of farmers and food access to the fore. In fact, we see Grow for The Stop as a model for a new network of relationships that prioritize sustainability and equity and put control back into the hands of producers. We think that this direct link between farmers and low-income communities is endlessly replicable elsewhere, and with public support could benefit far more people.

In Brazil, such connections are already being made. One way is the government-mandated 30 percent local procurement requirement for school lunch. It reduces hunger, fosters better health and supports small-scale local producers. With nearly a billion government dollars spent annually on food for school meals, the money in the hands of local economies and organizations is significant. The Brazilian government also has programs to purchase and distribute produce from small family farms to daycare centres, community associations and hospitals.

Between 2003 and 2008, the government bought more than a billion dollars' worth of agricultural products through this scheme and distributed two million tons of food. Nearly seventeen million people benefited from the produce in 2008 alone, and the program supports several key government strategies: reducing hunger through food access, promoting social inclusion of rural people, and improving small farmers' ability to meet demand.

Here at home, Local Food Plus is actively recruiting institutions like universities and hospitals to commit to such local procurement policies. Several University of Toronto food and dining services were the first to sign on. Their pledge to buy LFP-certified foods for their facilities is the biggest local sustainable food contract in North America. Local Food Plus encourages institutions to commit to sourcing local food and does all the legwork: investigating and certifying farmers and food producers using a system that evaluates production, labour, native habitat preservation, animal welfare, on-farm energy use and greenhouse gas emissions. Then buyers of all sizes—institutions, individuals and grocery stores—can look for the LFP label and know that the food has met those rigorous standards. Started in Ontario, LFP is now rolling out its certification system across the country.

The potential to transform our food system by creating relationships that prioritize sustainable agriculture and equitable access to healthy food is enormous. Grow for The Stop is only a small example, but it's made a huge difference in the health of our community and of The New Farm. We see the program as making a case for a new kind of food system.

The people gathered at the farm for the fundraiser tonight appreciate the hopeful, community-minded vibe Brent and

Gillian have created. I see a cluster of people I recognize who shop regularly at our Green Barn farmers' market, and a couple I know who have recently moved up here from the city. It's getting dark as Andrea and I approach the barn, its big doors open, lights strung from the rafters.

We spot Gillian talking to The Stop's chef Chris Brown, who's come up to cook the dinner. They all seem completely relaxed, like they're hosting a family dinner rather than a 250-person feast, concert and theatre performance rolled into one. Brent arrives, the couple's young son and daughter in tow. He's wearing a trucker's cap that makes him seem about a foot taller, and he's holding a beer.

Gillian welcomes us, but one of their interns, a young woman with pigtails and rubber boots, quickly whisks the family away. There's trouble with the sound system and the play is scheduled to begin. Chris goes back to check the food. He's been here all day and plans to sleep in his car in the field tonight. People are standing near the beer table under a white tent, others are by the bonfire, more are laying claim to hay bale seating in the barn. Andrea and I stay outside for a bit, soaking it all in.

There are chickens and a pig or two in pens to the south, and late-harvest veggies under plastic season-extension tunnels lined up in rows near the house. Even though I know how hard Brent and Gillian work and the challenges they face, even though I understand that tonight is a gussied-up version of farm life, with the golden light of dusk illuminating everything in its glow, the scene is inspiring. It's a real-life example of people putting their values to work. I've been so inspired, in fact—by Brent and Gillian, as well as by the urban agriculture projects The Stop has birthed—that this past summer Andrea, the boys and I decided to try our hand at growing food. We built a ten-by-ten-foot raised bed on our small city lawn and planted veggies—some from seed, others from seedlings we bought or were given. When the soil was delivered, a big mound of brown organic matter edging onto the sidewalk, our neighbours seemed to come out of the woodwork. It reminded me of the day we first dug the fence posts for the Earlscourt garden and just about everyone in the park offered an opinion about how best to place them, and about what to plant and where. Alfredo, a retired Italian man who lives down the street with his extended family, helped us shovel the soil into our little plot. Tony, the Portuguese neighbour with the huge garden and fruit trees across the street from us, leaned on the fence offering advice and some good-natured groans at our inexperience. Families from the neighbourhood stood and watched. It was like a community project.

We spent the summer weeding and fussing, chatting with passersby—people we knew and many we didn't—about our tomatoes and cucumbers, how to deter squirrels from eating everything, the strange spots on the zucchini leaves and the deliriously sweet peas. Tony said I was a lazy farmer—too much talking, not enough work—but I was enjoying myself. We had a slow, steady harvest and though we certainly couldn't live on the vegetables we grew, it was a revelation about the pleasures and possibilities of growing your own food.

I liked the whole experience so much, in fact, I keep suggesting to Andrea that we should find ourselves a patch of land in farm country—or maybe consider raising chickens or one of those backyard dairy cows bred to live in small spaces. She's not so sure. For my birthday, her parents gave me a book about moving to the country that I think was intended partly as a joke, partly a cautionary tale. It's called *Forty Acres and a Fool*.

But standing just outside the large, open barn on Brent and Gillian's land, the moon like a big, yellow egg yolk on the horizon, I'm not interested in a reality check. Anything seems possible. I start tapping my foot as music begins to play, light leaking out in narrow strips between the barn boards as stars pop out of the indigo sky.

I'VE COME A LONG WAY in my food education. When I started at The Stop, I knew exactly nothing about either the prevailing science of food—nutrients, micronutrients, preservatives, additives—or, more importantly, whole foods. I didn't know much about farming, soil, compost or anything else. Frankly, I wouldn't have known the food system if it hit me on the head. Now, though I'm still not an expert on agriculture or nutrients, I'm so deeply engaged in thinking about food issues, I see connections everywhere. Over those same years of my own education, public interest in food—whether it's health concerns, school gardens, food miles and the environment, urban agriculture, food safety or any of myriad other issues— has increased by leaps and bounds, and our organization has surfed the wave.

We've also worked hard to raise the profile of food issues and equity. Our staff and community members take part in food policy committees, urban agriculture groups and food access organizations across North America. We've all spoken at conferences, meetings and public debates. Our program director, Kathryn, was involved in helping start up Sustain Ontario: The Alliance for Healthy Food and Farming, an organization that champions food system change. Rhonda was awarded a Vital People grant for her years fostering urban agriculture in the city.

I was given the Jane Jacobs Prize—an honour named for the much-loved champion of urbanism, and the author of *The Death and Life of Great American Cities*—recognizing the Community Food Centre model as an innovative response to the seemingly intractable problems of hunger and poverty.

Today, we can confidently say that The Stop is an important part of a thriving global food movement. Indeed, as it has grown and become more sophisticated, harnessing the energy and momentum of young people who care about sustainability and justice, I think that the food movement has become one of the most exciting social projects of our time. When I started at The Stop in the late 1990s, no one was graduating from university with a specialization in food politics or community food security; now many of the best and brightest students are thinking about how to change the food system. We see loads of young people interning at The New Farm, doing student placements in our Symington Place and Green Barn programs, becoming volunteers and staff. The people who come to us are politicized and passionate, and their idealism and sense of fun help flavour everything we do.

In an article called "The Food Movement, Rising" written for the *New York Review of Books*, Michael Pollan explains that one of the movement's biggest strengths, and one of the reasons so many young people are attracted to it, is that it's not only about laws, policies and regulations but "also about community, identity, pleasure, and, most notably, about carving out a new social and economic space removed from the influence of big corporations on the one side and government on the other."

The launch of the Green Barn, especially, came at the perfect moment to capture this new spirit. People wanted to talk about it, tour the building and learn how they could create their own Community Food Centre. The building itself won architecture and environmental awards, the market was voted the best in the city, and The Stop was all over the media as a model for how to build communities. There was so much attention that among ourselves we jokingly began to call the Green Barn "the shiny new object," a kind of mental warning not to get too caught up in the hype. Still, all the interest in our work and the feeling of being engaged in something that inspired others was thrilling. So when a wealthy developer offered to donate a patch of land for our next great project—an urban farm at the top of the city—I started scheming right away about how we might pull it off.

The property was a rectangle of land near the 401—one of the busiest highways in North America—which slices through a neighbourhood outside our catchment area but close to several public housing communities. We imagined that we could produce food, do skills training, create a farm demonstration site, maybe work with kids. And unlike the decade-long Green Barn saga, we were dealing with a single, private individual and things promised to move fast. We hired a consultant to help us with a feasibility study, which highlighted some of the potential pitfalls and possibilities, and I got so excited I spilled the beans to a journalist friend, who included it in a local magazine package itemizing the Reasons to Love Toronto. "Number 30: we have an organic urban farm in the shadow of the 401."

Just after the story came out, we had a spring staff and board retreat at the new Green Barn facilities. It started early on a Saturday during a surprise hailstorm. When I arrived, chunks of ice the size of golf balls were pounding on the roof. Despite the ominous weather, things seemed to be going well through the morning, but as the day proceeded, I began to notice an undercurrent of grumbling from our usually enthusiastic staff. After lunch, with hail still drilling the roof, we talked about the possibility of the urban farm. The response was not at all what I expected. The room was actually quiet. All the passion and excitement I had come to expect from our close-knit staff team was missing in action. A few people piped up that they liked the sound of it, but others expressed worries about how we'd manage a new project when they were already overextended. I had the sense that if I'd pushed it, people would have gone along with the project, but I wasn't sure why I would. It quickly became obvious to me and the board that the organization needed to retrench and regroup. We had stretched ourselves to the limit building our shiny new object, expanding our staff team across two sites, and trying to create brand-new programming as well as respond to and engage with all the people and organizations wanting to replicate our experience. Keeping all of our current projects going was enough to keep us more than busy.

I didn't look forward to the phone call telling our angel investor that we had to refuse his generous offer, but the more I thought about it, the more sense it made. Not only was the site far outside Davenport West, it would require a whole new staff with a different set of agriculture skills. And the Green Barn—as well as the Symington Place site—required attention. Staff needed a break from all the activity of the previous year or two. Plus, there was no reason we couldn't use many of the ideas we'd begun to formulate for the urban farm at the Green Barn site itself.

It was a challenging moment for The Stop and for me, but saying no was also a powerful lesson. The urban farm was exciting, but not every good idea is the right idea—or the right idea at the right time. Turning down this opportunity helped put a finer point on The Stop's mission and focus. The staff's luke-warm response also made me realize how easy it is in an organization that feeds on the passion and idealism of its workers to forget that even such individuals have their limits.

This realization was underscored for me in Oakland, California, when Kathryn and I went to a Community Food Security Coalition conference. Called Food Justice: Honoring Our Roots, Growing the Movement, it was the organization's fifteenth anniversary, with delegates from nearly every state, many Canadian provinces and five continents. Oakland and the Bay Area have a long tradition of food justice work, including the Black Panthers' Free Breakfast for Children program in the late 1960s, which eventually grew to feed thousands of kids a hot meal every day in cities across the nation. Since then, the area has turned into a hotbed of activism on the food file.

Wanting to see as much of this work as possible, I joined a series of early morning bus tours. The first day was devoted to looking at school food projects, starting with an impressive garden at Cleveland Elementary School in Oakland, then on to the bucolic Edible Schoolyard in Berkeley started by chef Alice Waters. We arrived on an old, white school bus with red stripes, walking up through the concrete playground of Martin Luther King Jr. Middle School to the gentle slope where the garden stretches out over an acre. We saw the bake oven, the little red hens bathing in the dirt, a small greenhouse and a supply shed. We wandered amid rows of broccoli and saw the espaliered apple trees, their branches reaching out like arms. One of the staff talked to us about this amazing, transformative project that has inspired so many school gardens across the world—including one at my own sons' school in Toronto—while we sat under a leafy arbour in a teaching circle. She told us how they integrate gardening, cooking and food literacy, bringing the joy of food to children through hands-on activities in the soil and the kitchen.

Later, we headed down the bay to drop in at a farmers' market set up in front of the entrance to a West Oakland school that serves many low-income families. With people and produce everywhere, pop-up tents suggesting a festival, it made me think of our own bustling Good Food Market. We learned that there are numerous fresh food markets like the one we saw. SNAP benefits are accepted, and kids and parents have plentiful opportunities to become involved with the farmers, including helping to sell the food.

But even with these markets and other food projects, the neighbourhood of West Oakland remains a food desert with no local full-service grocery stores. There are more liquor stores, dollar stores and fast-food outlets than places to buy healthy food. It wasn't always this way. West Oakland, our guides told us, was once a thriving centre for arts and culture, a neighbourhood known for its small businesses and strong sense of community. A number of public works projects starting in the 1950s—including a freeway that sliced through the neighbourhood, destroying local businesses and dividing the area from the rest of the city, and the razing of dozens of blocks of homes in the cause of urban renewal—triggered the neighbourhood's decline. The economic and social fallout was swift. The many small mom-and-pop grocery stores and supermarkets, sources of both food and community, moved to the suburbs. West Oakland became a poor, racially segregated and markedly unhealthy neighbourhood. The result was the food desert environment that continues today, and health disparities that have led to disproportionate numbers of both diet-related illness and premature death.

According to a public health report, an African American born in West Oakland "can expect to die almost fifteen years earlier than a White person born in the [wealthier] Oakland Hills."

On the second day, we visited other local projects aimed at combatting the food desert problem, stopping by the historic California Hotel. In the 1950s, the California Hotel was *the* jazz hot spot of the West (Billie Holiday and James Brown both sang there). But by the 1970s, the hotel—and the area—had hit hard times. The California was abandoned for more than a decade before being turned into affordable housing by a nonprofit developer. But in 2007, it looked as if the historic site, by then in a state of disrepair, might be torn down. Eventually, after years of fundraising and legal battles, several organizations came together to rehabilitate it with more low-income housing units and other social services. A nonprofit called People's Grocery was invited to bring in food programming, using the parking lot and small outdoor space around the building. They've set up a market garden and greenhouse. They raise chickens, and also fish in an aquaponics initiative. The low-income participants learn gardening skills and earn money selling the produce they grow.

A bearded People's Grocery activist in an Oakland A's jacket, his black, curly hair poking out under a knit cap and a bright orange flower behind his ear, guided us through the site. He explained that the People's Grocery started in the early 2000s as an urban agriculture project that produced organic vegetables. They soon moved into food education and community outreach while continuing to grow and sell food through the Grub Box (a fresh, affordable produce delivery service) and the Mobile Market, a travelling produce store.

The organization has been working on the California Hotel project for a few years, collaborating with other groups in the area. In 2010, founder Brahm Ahmadi created a spinoff organization to raise capital to build a midsize grocery store called the People's Community Market (PCM) in the middle of West Oakland. Finding the money has not been easy, though the PCM was the first recipient of a grant from a public-private funding stream championed by First Lady Michelle Obama and aimed at increasing access to fresh food in under-serviced neighbourhoods.

We walked outside in the California sun, checking out the big painted mural depicting the history of the hotel, political statements by people like Cesar Chavez and Huey P. Newton hand-lettered on the side of the raised garden beds. There were chickens in a small enclosure with a handwritten sign that read, "EGGS ARE FREE. IF YOU'D LIKE SOME, PLEASE CALL . . ."

Later, we stopped by some urban gardens run by City Slicker Farms, including a farm on an abandoned lot squeezed between two houses and a noisy freeway. The many market gardens (all of them on underused or vacant lots) associated with City Slicker sell their food at a weekly farm stand where the produce is available on a pay-what-you-can basis. We closed the tour with a visit to Phat Beets, another urban agriculture initiative that calls itself a "food justice collective."

By then, the whole experience had become almost overwhelming—in a good way. Everywhere we went I was struck by the vibrancy of the people and ideas, the spunky DIY creativity and, especially, the belief in the power of good food to transform communities and create greater equality. Many of the organizations had logos of fists raised in the air; inspirational quotations and images of political radicals dotted walls, posters and signs. References to the legacy of the Black Panthers were everywhere.

In Canada, there are many people engaged in interesting, even groundbreaking, work around food issues, but the fight for justice rarely gets such play. Food banks, especially the large ones in our biggest cities, have dominated the conversation about food and poverty. And because food banks tend not to engage in questioning the industrial, corporate-driven food system that keeps their shelves stocked, the debate is seldom framed around radical change or even justice but rather around low individual incomes and the need for more private charity.

Of course, though many of the projects we saw in Oakland were exciting and innovative, they are also run on a shoestring. They have a handful of staff cobbling together funds, relying on donations, volunteers and interns to do front-line work in addition to fighting for justice. Even the beloved, internationally renowned Edible Schoolyard in Berkeley operates on a relatively modest US$600,000 a year and has fewer than ten employees, as well as a couple of members of AmeriCorps, a volunteer-based organization that functions as a domestic Peace Corps.

After years of working in community organizing and my experience with our staff's response to the urban farm, I know well how being under-resourced, overworked and overstretched can lead an organization and employees to burnout. Scraping by, just trying to make ends meet can also blinker even the most well-intentioned leaders, preventing them from looking beyond the day-to-day grind to fighting the conditions that cause poverty and hunger in the first place. I've begun to think, in fact, that relying on such small and ephemeral responses to the wide-reaching problems that plague our food system may prove to be a major obstacle to change. There's a whole lot of effort, great work and individual action, but not a lot of tangible systemic transformation. This is one of the big reasons we've continued to articulate The Stop's model of a stable, multi-dimensional organization that knits together food access and skills-building programs with advocacy. We're also working on finding ways to fund the creation of Community Food Centres elsewhere so that neighbourhoods in other towns and cities can begin to build adequately resourced organizations that move the food system toward greater sustainability and equity.

Funded by the Metcalf Foundation, Kathryn (along with Charles Levkoe, a former Stopper who worked in the urban agriculture program before heading to graduate school, and me) wrote a paper called "In Every Community a Place for Food: The Role of the Community Food Centre in Building a Local, Sustainable, and Just Food System." It gave us a chance to further research and reflect on the programs, experiences and core principles of the organization. In it, we suggest that with appropriate adjustments for a particular city, town or neighbourhood, the model we've created at The Stop could work anywhere.

The response, once the paper was released to the media and online, was like the Green Barn all over again. People began knocking down our door asking us to consider them as pilot sites for the Community Food Centre model. That's when Jamie Oliver came to visit, and tweeted to his millions of followers: "I've travelled all around the world and I've never seen anything like The Stop. Every city should have one." We were inundated with calls and email, requests for media interviews and people wanting to learn more about how they could become involved.

I thought a lot about this enthusiasm as we finished up the bus tours in Oakland and headed inside the conference hall for speeches and workshops. Kathryn and I were sitting at one of hundreds of round tables covered in black tablecloths, a thousand people around us all fuelled by a shared interest in food. Nutritionists and urban agriculture activists from Philadelphia and Salt Lake City, farmers from Texas and people working in schools and hospitals all over the continent, public health professionals and unionists, researchers and community organizers. Hank Herrera, whose work in Rochester inspired me so many years ago, was there, too. He now works in San Leandro, south of Oakland, managing another enterprise aimed at creating a sustainable local food economy.

When we told conference-goers about what we're doing at The Stop and our dream for Community Food Centres in other places, they were genuinely surprised at the breadth and size of our neighbourhood-based programming. More accustomed to small organizations like the ones we visited on our tour, they understood intuitively the potential of bringing the many passionate voices and food program possibilities under one well-resourced roof. It was exciting to hear their enthusiasm for the idea, and to feel part of something much bigger than our own organization.

At lunch on the last day, the conference organizers asked anyone who was interested to join a march in support of the Coalition of Immokalee Workers, farm workers from Florida fighting for fair wages and against notoriously exploitative working conditions (including sexual harassment in the fields and restrictions on access to water and shade). The march would end outside a nearby supermarket called Trader Joe's in an ongoing effort to persuade the chain, with its signature Hawaiian-shirt-wearing staff and folksy image, to sign a Fair Food Agreement. The agreement—aimed at raising workers' wages and ensuring such basic rights as clearly defined grievance procedures and safety education—had already been signed by fast-food giants including McDonald's and Burger King and some industrial food providers, in what the *New York Times'* Mark Bittman called "possibly the most successful labor action in the United States in twenty years."

We walked out into the street and joined a group of about three hundred people with signs, drums and noisemakers. The group began by taking over the middle of Oakland's main drag, waving placards painted to look like baskets of tomatoes reading "FAIR FOOD NOW!" and "RESPECT IN THE FIELDS." There were conference delegates from all over the continent, packs on their backs, families with kids in strollers, activists with bullhorns, people young and old. We stopped, finally, in front of the grocery store, a stucco structure with a Spanish colonial facade. Demonstrators were wearing handmade cardboard headgear designed to look like the Statue of Liberty, their pointed crowns painted yellow and orange, UNITY, RESPECT, and JUSTICE written across the front. The Oakland police were there, too, though the protest was peaceful and the group gathered in front of the store respected shoppers with their grocery carts and the cars trying to get through the lot. In fact, it felt more like a singalong than a protest.

We sang and chanted and banged the drums for a while, before a delegation went inside to speak with management. But the manager wasn't willing to offer any significant response to the protest or the demands. It wasn't the first he would have heard of it. The Immokalee Workers have been struggling to upgrade their working conditions for nearly two decades. And Trader Joe's itself had been the focus of several months of sustained campaigning to persuade its German owners to sign the agreement. Only a week before, hundreds of workers, activists and religious leaders had protested at the chain's headquarters outside Los Angeles, where they'd been met with locked doors and a refusal to even accept their letters.

I would watch as it took several more months of lobbying, protests and pressure from activists and consumers before Trader Joe's agreed to sign. Then, of course, there would be more food giants—including other major supermarkets and the United States Department of Agriculture, which purchases food for the National School Lunch Program—to persuade. The work is ongoing—and like all such struggles it takes vigilance, strategy and a lot of effort. That day in Oakland and many others before and since I think of something my father has said to me often over the years, whether we're talking about politics or a basketball game. "Don't forget," he likes to say with a playful grin and a pointed finger, "the other side is trying, too."

NINE

THE REVOLUTION
MUST BE
FUNDED

FEBRUARY 2011. The smell of onions and garlic wafts all the way to my desk at the front of The Stop. I imagine myself like a cartoon character drifting on the heavenly scent, out of my office, past the front door, down the hallway lined with photos and meeting room doors. I pause in the narrow passageway just outside the kitchen and watch the carefully orchestrated chaos inside.

Chris Brown is at the stove prepping for a big catering gig, his apron stained from a hard day's work. Scott MacNeil, our in-house chef responsible for the drop-in meals and other food for our programs, is nearby at the large island dressing an industrial-sized stainless-steel bowl full of salad. He's a big man, his arms covered in tattoos, a peaked hat pulled low over his dark hair. His T-shirt says: "I ♥ HUMMUS." Two other chefs whom Chris has called in to help with the catering job are working along the north side of the room at a prep station. Volunteers for the drop-in meal stand at the island, an assembly line of vegetable cutting and slicing. A half wall hides the dish pit from the door, but I can hear the clacking of bowls and utensils, the pressurized water beating down on dirty pots. Steam rises in a cloud from the dishwasher.

It's mesmerizing to watch, a kind of perpetual motion machine, each person an essential part, everyone working independently but also together. One volunteer reaches over to grab a pepper mill and another opens a cabinet door, narrowly missing the first volunteer's head. Music, talk and good-natured teasing mix with the pounding water, the hiss of the stovetop, the rhythmic chopping sounds.

It doesn't always work this well. In fact, Chris has been advocating for a while to find some dedicated space for the catering. Sharing the kitchen here at Symington Place and the much smaller facilities at the Green Barn is proving hard to schedule and coordinate. But today it's pretty close to beautiful.

I go over to the stove to ask about the catering job. "Stikeman Elliott," Chris says. "A client dinner tonight." The blue-chip law firm hires The Stop about a dozen times a year to do lunches, dinners and receptions. They've said they'd hire us more often if we had the capacity. Catering has become a big part of our fundraising work since Chris joined the staff. Funny and self-deprecating, with an apparently endless ability to work, Chris trained in Italy as well as at Toronto's George Brown College. Before coming to The Stop, he co-owned a celebrated restaurant called Perigee with his brother and father. It was the kind of high-end place where dinner is an event, the kitchen a glassed-in box in the centre of the room so diners feel as if they have ringside seats. When the economy tanked in 2009, the family was forced to close the restaurant. I'd met Chris many times as a member of Cross Town Kitchens, a group of young chefs who came together over the previous few years to offer a dinner series that they cooked collectively, rotating through their restaurants with proceeds going to The Stop. We happened to be looking for a new chef around the time that Perigee was closing, and when I asked if he had any ideas, Chris told me he might be interested himself. We hired him as soon as he was available.

Since then, Chris's easygoing attitude and widely respected skill has not only jump-started catering as a money-maker for The Stop, it's made our kitchen a draw for many of the city's best chefs. Chris has taken on this unique collaboration between high-end food and low-income people with passion and enthusiasm. His presence, in fact, has helped put us on the map with a lot of people who care deeply about food in the city. Chris's job title is food enterprise coordinator, and he's part of the fundraising team. The idea is that he and our fundraising staff take on food events that raise both funds and awareness about our work, while Scott holds down the fort cooking for the Symington Place community.

When we first started doing food enterprise, we tried a number of things, including cooking classes, but we found profit margins were small and it was difficult to consistently get people out to the events we organized. We decided to focus on catering—birthdays, weddings, corporate events, private parties and dinners. We also began monthly Food for Change dinners at tables set up under the stars in the Green Barn greenhouse. Diners can come and enjoy the five-course meal, or pay for a chance to join Chris and the other pros in the kitchen for the day. They're not just tourists, either, they're active participants in the preparation and cooking, working at the chefs' side to make a top-shelf meal for a discerning crowd.

As we've begun to see the potential for food-themed fund-raising, Cheryl and the fundraising staff have added other events. We have the Beer Garden, low-key Sunday afternoons at the Green Barn when we sell finger food like tacos or bake-oven pizza and beer from a different local craft brewery each week. There's also the Night Market, a two-night celebration of street food set up in a Toronto alleyway lit by fairy lights and paper lanterns. On Saturdays during the farmers' market, we also cook soups, sandwiches and desserts at what we call The Stop's Market Café.

But these food enterprise projects are different from programs some nonprofits run, where low-income people are trained to make and sell food or crafts in order to earn income for themselves. The People's Grocery, for example, calls itself a "health and wealth organization," and sees its mission as improving the health and economy of West Oakland by nurturing the local food system. Money raised from selling the produce grown at the California Hotel goes into the pockets of the handful of people who tend the gardens. Many of the food organizations we visited in Oakland were focused on skills training and creating economic opportunities, both jobs and more casual income.

We've decided to take another tack. Our goal is to raise money, pure and simple—money that is then funnelled back into our front-line food programs. While we sometimes hire community members with relevant professional experience to help out, it's not part of our specific mandate. My experience with the woodworking co-operative at the homeless shelter—where I discovered how hard it is for an organization to both support vulnerable community members and create a money-making venture—made me leery about trying to do too much at once. Certainly, creating wealth within one's community is a laudable goal, but it's not what we do. Instead, by building a professional, highly sought-after catering business, we've doubled the money raised from food enterprise each year since Chris arrived—money that goes directly into our programs. There are other ancillary benefits, too. People who might never have heard of The Stop find out about us through Food for Change dinners, the Beer Garden, the Night Market or the café. They come to Symington Place or the Green Barn, and fall in love with our story about the power of food. They wander back as regular donors. We think of it as a way to create allies as well as to raise money.

We first began to understand the fundraising possibilities of good food back in the fall of 2004 when we hosted our first annual fall event. Today a number of organizations run creative food fundraising events, but at the time, all you saw were sit-down rubber-chicken dinners with an auction and possibly entertainment. That year, we pulled together a group of young volunteers to host a casual evening at a new women's club, pairing wines with great food. The first event raised what seemed at the time like an astonishing amount: sixty thousand dollars. Since then, the annual event has grown enormously, and What's on the Table (woTT) draws more than five hundred people a year to a ticketed evening featuring top chefs, local wines and an array of auction items. Spearheaded by the fundraising team with an active volunteer committee, it's held in Barn #2, where the farmers' market runs on Saturday mornings. We set up the chefs at tables lining both sides of the long building. Many of the city's best restaurants provide bite-size taster dishes, while local wineries offer appropriately paired wines. There are auctions and an incredible feast that's become one of the city's fall highlights. Over the past five years, the event has raised $1.5 million for The Stop.

We've also added a second annual fundraiser called Big Night at the Green Barn. It's a family-friendly evening that celebrates immigrant contributions to growing food in the city, and it feels like a big Italian wedding. It's noisy and loud, with wine flowing and three generations of families at many of the tables: little kids with their parents and grandparents. The chefs each take a course: antipasto, primo, secondo, contorno and dolce. The food is served on large platters at the table where people can help themselves. Food Network star David Rocco hosted the first few years. It's been a huge success, exposing our philosophy and programs to a whole new network of people.

More than once, I've described what we do as entrepreneurial. It sounds counterintuitive to people who are more accustomed to social services being delivered in a conventional way, funded by government. But what I mean is that when it comes to raising money and building programs, we are creative and nimble, quick to respond to the needs of our community. Our mixed funding model—traditional sources such as individual donors and foundations, as well as money raised through food enterprise projects and events—makes this possible. Having access to funds that are not aligned with a specific stream (because of a particular government grant) means that we can put the money where we need it, prioritizing what requires support at any specific moment. When one of our staff notices an influx of a particular ethnic or cultural group into The Stop, for instance, we can create programming that meets the group's needs, as we did with the East African Men's Cooking Group or Sabor Latino. Instead of trying to find a government grant stream to twist ourselves into, we raise the money and start the program. When one of our staff saw a need in the Green Barn community for an after-school program for high school girls, we created the FLY Girls (Food

Leadership for Youth) program to focus on leadership, healthy eating, self-esteem and environmental sustainability.

This flexibility has been essential to our growth. It has allowed The Stop to be innovative and to take chances. It's also attracted interest in what we do from many quarters—from social investors and nonprofit leaders to traditional business people. But most importantly, it's made our neighbourhood feel that The Stop is not some monolithic organization that plods along and tells them what to do, but *their* community centre.

Chris offers me a taste of the sauce he's making at the stove. Sharon Francis, our drop-in coordinator, pushes through the heavy door from the community space. She grew up in this neighbourhood; her mother still lives in Symington Place. Sharon is the calm, competent centre around which the vortex of our drop-in revolves. "Lunch is ready," Scott tells her. He rests his hands on the edge of the counter and his shoulders relax a little. The perpetual motion machine pauses almost imperceptibly. Sharon takes the big salad bowl with her when she goes back to let the volunteers know they're on deck to start serving the meal. The door leading to the community space swings closed. The machine starts again.

●━━

IT SOUNDS EXCITING to be an entrepreneurial nonprofit, as if we've chosen to reinvent ourselves along new and modern lines. In fact, there's now a whole industry of people, books, lectures and university courses devoted to the often amazing efforts of social entrepreneurs or innovators—people who come at old social problems in new ways. We're glad to be considered in such august company, but on the financial side, one of the main reasons we spend so much time at The Stop seeking out partnerships, planning creative ways to tap into foodie culture, and finding alternative funding streams is because government has backed so far out of adequately supporting social services that we have little choice. Our entrepreneurship is, in many ways, born of necessity.

Much of our work entails what I have always thought should be the responsibility of democratically elected governments: ensuring the basic food needs of citizens are met, supporting low-income community members to live a decent life, advocating for people's access to the resources they need. But we rely on very little public funding. During my years at The Stop, the ratio has been consistent: 10 to 15 percent of our total revenue comes from government grants; the other 85 to 90 percent we raise privately through foundations, individuals, corporations, social enterprise and events. The only change has been the amount we raise. In 1998, our budget was $250,000 and we had four staff; today The Stop's budget pushes $4.5 million and we serve sixteen thousand people a year, have more than three hundred volunteers and employ forty people.

This emphasis on private fundraising is also partly the result of our history. When The Stop began, it was a church concern, supported by congregations, individual donations and volunteers. We still receive many donations from individuals, ranging from seniors contributing $10 a month, to people who give much larger sums. Later, as we grew and needed to seek out new funding sources, we struggled to break into the kinds of government granting streams that many large, long-established community centres rely upon. Today, we're still trying to refine the mix to find a balance between public and private money. Government grants are considered to be stabilizing—freeing leaders of non-profits to focus on the work of creating better programs and services for their communities. If we had more government money, for instance, we wouldn't have to spend time figuring out how to keep the lights on or to pay for the necessary but less appealing administrative parts of running an organization that supports thousands of people every year. (Not surprisingly, individuals prefer to donate to children or new moms—or even to purchase garden tools—rather than, say, buy a new photocopier or pay the salary of an administrator.)

But, as any organization that receives government money understands well, such funding also comes with strings attached—and lots of paperwork. The grants tend to be very prescriptive, representing the politics and direction of the party in power. And large bureaucracies inevitably move slowly, because of checks and balances embedded in the process. It means accountability for the taxpayer, but it also means that when a program isn't working well and needs adjustments, it's not always easy to shift gears or reassess.

I've also seen how overreliance on government money can result in a certain sleepiness in an organization. Why bother with websites and social media, newsletters and events if your funding is secure? It's easy to see these things as extras or distractions, unconnected to the real work of front-line community organizing. But at The Stop, we've discovered that connecting with the outside world and telling others about our work has contributed in no small way to the vibrancy of the organization. We've seen it with our many food-related events where we've met new supporters—financial and otherwise. And we've seen it with the Speakers' Bureau and Civic Engagement projects, where telling community stories has had a transformative effect on both the people who speak and those who listen, helping move the dial on the issues that matter to us.

There are also many tales of established nonprofit organizations that become overly reliant on one government funding source and are devastated when there is a policy change or a new party comes to power and the money is no longer so plentiful—or is taken away altogether. "Biodiversity" is as important in funding as it is in nature.

Of course, private money—whether it's donated by individuals or corporations, through events or foundations—can also be vulnerable. Cultivating donors is very demanding, and it's subject to the vagaries of the economy and human nature. (I think often of what might have happened if I'd succumbed to the donor who pressured us to abandon the Green Barn project.) It can also take up a lot of time. As the organization has expanded, our fundraising team at The Stop has grown from one person to five full-time employees. I also spend a much larger portion of my week talking to potential donors and funders. My colleagues used to say they knew I was going out to ask for money when I came to work in a pressed shirt. Nowadays, I do a lot more ironing.

Fortunately, I like talking to people and I never tire of telling them about The Stop. I see the kind of fundraising I do as somewhat similar to my efforts as a community worker. Both are about building relationships and listening to people. Andrea teases me that it's impossible to go anywhere in the city with me because I always end up talking to people about my work. When we're out for a rare quiet dinner together, she jokes that I'm not allowed to approach the chef or owner or wait staff about getting involved in our next event. Even my children frequently boycott a trip to the Green Barn farmers' market with me, because I usually end up in long conversations with the farmers and neighbours and friends.

Of course, raising money is not all hugging farmers and enjoying gourmet food. There are complex ethical issues to negotiate. The most obvious is what to do with funders whose values aren't in line with our own. This is particularly true when it comes to corporate dollars. Whether the question is companies with questionable labour practices, unhealthy food products or an environmentally unfriendly approach, it can be a veritable minefield.

Some nonprofit organizations will accept money from anyone that offers it, believing they'll do good work with it—and that it's better in their hands than those of the corporation. Some figure they won't ever affect change on the issues they care about if they exclude the big corporate players, however questionable their business practices. Others are committed to taking money only from companies whose work is aligned with their mission, arguing that such an approach forces companies to rethink what they are doing if they want to be associated with a particular cause.

Of course, food banks have been knee-deep in these issues from the beginning. Their relationships with big food corporations are nothing if not complicated. This interdependence was vividly highlighted for me when Campbell, the well-known soup company, came out with Nourish, a nutritious stew that offers a complete meal in a can—in vegetarian and meat versions—intended for low-income people. Consumers were encouraged to buy these cans (for approximately $2.50 each) at the grocery store, then donate them to food banks where hungry people would get a full serving of three food groups (veggies, grains and protein).

The product was conceived out of concern for the hungry. One year in the run-up to the annual Christmas food drive, Campbell staff took part in sorting food at a food bank and attended a food security conference. The idea for Nourish came out of that experience. When the product was launched, food bank spokespeople were quoted in the press saying they were "ecstatic." They were especially delighted that the company had asked them for advice about how to make the product meet food bank users' needs. The result was a can that doesn't require a can opener, and a stew that doesn't need water to be added. It can be eaten hot or cold, and it lasts for two years unopened. It's also high in fibre and low in fat.

Campbell promoted the product as a goodwill gesture, saying it could "put a serious dent in hunger" if its goal of 200,000 cans donated to food banks across Canada was reached. It started things off with a 100,000-can donation to Food Banks Canada.

The Put Food in the Budget people, whom we'd worked with before on Do the Math, were the first to raise concerns that Campbell's new product was less than it claimed to be. They argued that donating 200,000 cans of food was not going to put a "dent" in anything. With 900,000 Canadians going to food banks every month, PFIB explained in its public campaign, the donation wouldn't be enough for even one meal per person.

Even more, PFIB argued against the lack of dignity in the suggestion that a meal in a can is an appropriate substitute for fresh, whole food that a person chooses, or that low-income people should have special foods made for them. Such an offering, PFIB said, might make sense in a disaster, but it's hardly something people would want to eat or should eat every day. PFIB also questioned the "relative effectiveness of asking the public to pay for donations of Nourish in contrast with other strategies" to reduce hunger. They proposed a calculation showing that if taxpayers paid the same amount in taxes as they would spend on four cans of Nourish per month, the redistributed money would go a lot further toward supporting low-income people. Finally, PFIB made the point that Nourish contributes to the mistaken public impression that making donations to food banks will solve hunger. As The Stop and others have been saying for years, food banks exist because of poverty and lack of income, not a lack of food in the supply chain.

For three months before launching its campaign, PFIB asked for a meeting with the president of Campbell Canada. Their requests were ignored until just before the campaign was launched, and the company president was not happy. He reminded the leadership of PFIB that Campbell's intentions were good and that they had collaborated with food bank organizations to create the product. He also said that if Campbell was going to be criticized for the product, they might not continue with it—suggesting that it would be PFIB's fault.

Around the same time, I received a call from a senior staffer at a large food bank asking about The Stop's connection with PFIB. He asked me if I knew about the campaign and assured me that Campbell is a good corporate partner, providing products and significant dollars to support key staff positions within his organization.

It was a touchy and difficult moment that highlighted the complicated ties that bind the various players in the food system. The food bank organizations that had been ecstatic about the collaboration with Campbell were frustrated that the good intentions of their corporate partner had been questioned. They worried that being implicated in the PFIB campaign could make them lose significant funding. Campbell was concerned about its image. Nourish, after all, is a marketing tool.

In its social media promotion of the product, Campbell said it would donate a can every time someone clicks "like" on its Facebook page, comments on Campbell's wall, shares a video or tweets about the product.

PFIB, for its part, remained undaunted by the pressure from Campbell and the food bank sector, using the moment to publicly highlight the difference between charitable food handouts and real social justice. In fact, their campaign to pressure government to increase social assistance rates and "put food in the budget" continues. Meanwhile, Nourish is still available in stores, though the publicity campaign and the suggestion that the product will put a dent in hunger have been toned down.

To me, the situation drove home once again the divisions in the antihunger movement. There's no doubt that everyone involved wants to support people living in poverty. But there remains a wide gap between individuals and organizations that question the food bank model—and its interconnection with corporate food—and those who see food banks as the best available option. For those of us trying to build a new kind of holistic approach, the subservience food banks feel to the corporations that donate food is a serious obstacle to change. The donation system puts food banks between a rock and a hard place.

It's not easy, of course, for any organization to negotiate funding issues, The Stop included. There are some radical nonprofit groups, such as the authors of an essay collection called *The Revolution Will Not Be Funded*, that question any involvement, financial or otherwise, in what they call the "non-profit industrial complex." They see government funding as inherently corrupt, consider foundations to be nothing more than tax shelters for the wealthy, and argue that foundation funding is a form of social control.

We've taken a more pragmatic line. The Stop has grown at a relatively manageable pace over the last fifteen years, so we've been able to be careful about whom we ask for support and money. We've tried to stay away from large corporate food companies whose values run counter to our own. And instead of waiting for donors to come to us, we actively seek out organizations that we believe in.

Organic Meadow, a successful farmer-owned co-operative with over one hundred family farms producing a full line of organic milk, dairy products, eggs and grains, is just such an ally. The co-op started in 1989 when a group of grain farmers got together because they wanted to farm differently, rejecting synthetic chemicals, pesticides, herbicides and fungicides. The organic food business was new at the time and the farmers struggled to create an infrastructure to process, distribute and market their products. Eventually they joined forces with organic dairy farmers and they've managed to grow nationally, building an alternative system that values both the bottom line of small-scale farmers and the environment. We share so many values—and our stories of fighting the status quo—that Organic Meadow is a perfect funding fit for The Stop. It's still relatively small compared to the big food players, so its funding contributions as a donor of products to our programs and a sponsor of events are similarly modest. Still, we see this collaboration as something that can only grow over the years.

Once you get into larger sums of money and a national platform, there's a whole different dance. Will Allen, the good food guru from the Milwaukee organization Growing Power, MacArthur "genius grant" recipient and one of *TIME* magazine's one hundred most influential people in the world in 2010, knows this better than most. Allen is a former professional basketball player who has become a hero to many in the food movement. I've followed his food justice work for a long time and admired his tenacity and singularity of vision. With a mission "to grow food, to grow minds, and to grow community," Growing Power trains inner-city youth to cultivate food outdoors and in greenhouses. They have an apiary and an aquaponics system, as well as chickens, goats, ducks and turkeys. They also have satellite farms in Chicago (run by Allen's adult daughter) and Wisconsin, and training sites in numerous other states.

But in the fall of 2011, Allen and Growing Power made news for another reason. Growing Power had just accepted a one-million-dollar donation from Walmart in order to expand its urban agriculture work into new communities. People in the food justice world were shocked. Walmart has long been considered *persona non grata* by community organizations for its use of low-wage labour, vast market leverage and ability to demand lower prices from suppliers, as well as its reputation for driving smaller local businesses out of the market. Allen defended his move on the Growing Power blog, saying, "Walmart is the world's largest distributor of food—there is no one better positioned to bring high-quality, locally grown food into urban food deserts and fast-food swamps. We can no longer be so idealistic that we hurt the very people we're trying to help."

Others, like Andy Fisher, former head of the Community Food Security Coalition, disagreed, suggesting the contribution was Walmart's attempt to "co-opt opposition to their entry into cities," where they have not yet been able to make serious inroads. He maintained that despite Allen's claim, Walmart and Allen's "Good Food Revolution" do not share common goals, because "at the end of the day [Walmart] hurts communities more than it helps them."

Author and public health lawyer Michele Simon of the influential blog Appetite for Profit (as well as a book of the same name about the power of the food industry) was equally blunt with her claim that "by partnering with a group [Growing Power] that could otherwise be one of its staunchest critics, Walmart is taking a page right out of the Big Tobacco playbook: Buying silence."

Will Allen quickly stepped away from the fray after the initial flurry of attention, and the controversy petered out. He's continued to build Growing Power, launching a campaign to train more young farmers at regional training centres modelled on his home base. He's also cultivated a powerful ally in First Lady Michelle Obama, whose signature Let's Move! campaign to end childhood obesity within a generation is also collaborating with Walmart.

The reality is, the revolution is not easily funded. But in a world where corporations control so much wealth and have so much influence, nonprofit organizations must be cautious and vigilant, asking themselves from whom they accept money, and if by doing so they are undermining their own longer-term goals of social change. Fortunately, as we see consumers become better educated, not to mention louder and more effective at pushing companies toward better practices and supporting the ones that are already there, there are going to be more companies whose work we can all get behind. At The Stop, we often say that we can't allow the perfect to be the enemy of the good— but we also want to strive for something a lot better than okay.

As we've negotiated this tricky line, expanding our funding mix and building our capacity as an organization, a handful of progressive foundations like Metcalf have become important partners with The Stop. Recently, funding from the J.W.

McConnell Family Foundation—one of Canada's largest private foundations—has helped us develop a strategy for taking the Community Food Centre model into other neighbourhoods. It has also been instrumental in helping to ensure that we have a rigorous evaluation system as we roll it out.

These foundations have long seen the writing on the wall: as governments shrink and let go of their policy thinkers, someone has to step in to provide research, guidance and insight. Foundations like Metcalf and McConnell have begun to act as catalysts, research and development engines funding organizations like The Stop to quantify and communicate what they do and figure out how others might benefit. The holy grail for these funders is to seed an idea that will find its way into wider social or political policy.

Pathways to Education, a nonprofit that began its life supporting low-income kids in Toronto's Regent Park public housing community, is often held up as an example for social service organizations that want to scale up their model. Born out of the local community health centre in a largely immigrant downtown neighbourhood with low family incomes and a 56 percent high school dropout rate, Pathways was created to help kids stay in school. Using after-school tutoring, mentoring and advocacy, along with scholarships for students who pursue postsecondary education, they created an incredibly successful initiative. For kids in the program, the dropout rate was reduced by 70 percent and participation in postsecondary education was increased by 300 percent (more than 90 percent of these students were the first in their family to attend college or university).

With the help of The Boston Consulting Group, a large global management consulting firm, the organization was also able to quantify the social return on investment from its programs. The analysis showed huge economic benefits to society as a result of keeping kids in school—mainly through higher taxes paid (because of higher incomes earned) and fewer government transfer payments needed by the individuals and communities. Their most recent study suggested that for every one dollar invested in Pathways, there is a social return worth twenty-four dollars; each graduate offers society a cumulative lifetime benefit of $600,000.

Being able to quantify the economic benefits of the program made a huge difference for Pathways. Supported by these impressive figures and funding from several key foundations, the organization took its model on to a larger stage. Today it's creating sites for its successful program across the country. The Ontario government liked Pathways so much it's invested nearly fifty million dollars since 2007. In 2011, the federal government committed twenty million dollars over four years.

Not every social service organization has the resources or the ability to measure its success in economic terms. It's complicated, for instance, to measure The Stop's social return on investment. How do you quantify community-building, self-respect or a renewed sense of dignity in a monetary figure? We don't have a neat, readily measurable end goal like Pathways—get kids to graduate and attend postsecondary education. We try to communicate the wide-ranging benefits of our work through research emerging from surveys and questionnaires, as well as stories about the personal impact of our programs on members. We've found nearly 80 percent of people tried healthy new foods at The Stop, and almost half report their health is better since coming to our programs. Nearly 100 percent of moms in Healthy Beginnings give birth to healthy babies. Ninety-three percent of participants in the Civic Engagement group report that they feel more knowledgeable about the context of their poverty as a result of their involvement at The Stop. While not all of these stats translate easily into a single social return on investment figure, we're continuing to measure and evaluate, investigating ways to improve our evaluation toolbox so we can quantify the long-term economic benefits of our programs to society at large. There's no doubt such figures will help make our case for Community Food Centres in other towns and cities.

The Pathways example has been instructive. It shows how nonprofits can be creative and dynamic places where ideas grow, gaining traction and evidence of success and societal benefit. It also illustrates how private philanthropy can be important as an incubator and launching pad, providing the space for organizations to innovate and take the risks necessary to create something truly great. But as Pathways has seen as they expand nationally, philanthropy isn't likely to be enough on its own. In Canada, generous private individuals and groups (including foundations) donate $10.6 billion a year to non-profit organizations. Forty percent of that money goes to religious organizations, 15 percent to health organizations (excluding hospitals), and only 11 percent ($1.16 billion) to social service organizations. To put this in some perspective, the Canadian tax-payer funded health care system spends almost $13 billion—more than the total donations to nonprofits—just to treat diabetes.

It's clear that if we're going to expand The Stop's model to other places, we won't be able to rely solely on private money. To create a network of robust, stable Community Food Centres, public dollars need to be a major part of the mix. Of course, governments are already paying the costs of poverty downstream—in health care, crime and unrealized potential. It reminds me once again of that parable about the babies in the river. We can spend all our public energy trying to rescue babies as they float down the river, or figure out collectively how to stop them from getting into the water in the first place.

JUNE 2011. Wind is whipping the flag at the top of the white-stone town hall, sending hanging flower baskets swinging. We make our way down the pretty main street of Perth, a historic town in the Rideau Lakes district southwest of Ottawa, and stop in front of a slightly incongruent two-storey split-level building with a pink-coloured brick exterior and a retro vibe. It's most recently been a Salvation Army church, but it's had other incarnations as well. The latest will be the first of our two pilot projects launching the Community Food Centre into the world.

It's all happened relatively quickly. With funding from those progressive foundations as well as government health agencies, Kathryn and another staff member spent much of the spring touring the province to talk to people and organizations who'd read our Metcalf paper and contacted us about setting up a Community Food Centre in their neighbourhood or town. After months of discussion and thought—evaluating need, philosophical alignment, fundraising capacity and leadership, potential partnerships and existing infrastructure—we narrowed it down to this site in Perth and one in Stratford, Ontario, home to the well-known summer theatre festival. The plan is to launch the two new Community Food Centres within the year.

Though I've seen pictures, met some of the key leaders, and spent time thinking and talking about the pilot sites, I'm not entirely sure what to expect today. Perth couldn't be more different from our inner-city, immigrant-rich, low-income neighbourhood. A sleepy riverside town that began as an early military settlement, Perth is a community of only 5,800 people. It's considered a regional hub, though, which means nearly twenty thousand people use the town's services regularly. In the summer, the population swells even more thanks to tourists and cottagers in the region. There are deep agricultural roots in the area, a regular farmers' market and a keen food community. I can already see why, with its meandering river and historic town centre, it's been named one of the best places in the province to retire.

Yet, the Perth and District Food Bank—the organization we are collaborating with for the pilot—knows it also as an area in dire need of supports for the poor. Low-income people make up more than 10 percent of the town's population, and slightly more in nearby Smiths Falls, where the three largest employers all shut down a few years ago. There is no public transportation, and nearly 60 percent of residents in the region are obese or over-weight. Half of households spend more than 30 percent of their income on housing, higher than the average in Ontario. Many of the seniors are living on small pensions and caring for partners with health issues. The food bank does its best, but it's open only three days a week for two hours at a time, and it's run by a single part-time staffer with a team of almost fifty volunteers.

When Kathryn came to visit the first time she was impressed by the organization's articulate leadership, who clearly under-stand the inadequacy of the food bank approach and are com-mitted to reimagining access to good food in their town. Before we were involved, they'd raised the money and bought this building to house a centre with multiple programs. Since then, they've received a provincial grant to renovate and buy commer-cial kitchen equipment.

Still, I'm nervous standing here. In some ways, this is the culmination of all our work shaping and honing The Stop into a Community Food Centre over the last decade. We're betting that every community will benefit from what we've created, and that other neighbourhoods will experience the transformative impact The Stop has had in Davenport West. But it's here and in Stratford where we'll find out whether our model is more than a one-off, neighbourhood-specific success.

Nancy Wildgoose, the sixty-something former government bureaucrat who is heading up the process in Perth, holds open the front door as Kathryn and I step inside. We head directly down the stairs to a large, open space where the food bank will be. There's bare drywall everywhere, but even amidst the dust and debris it has a bright, airy feeling. They've got a large walk-in fridge and have carved out separate office spaces, as well as an area for food demos based on a seasonally appropriate food-of-the-month. The plan is for the food bank to be set up grocery-store style so people will be able to choose their own food from the shelves using guidelines suited to individual or family needs.

Upstairs, the community kitchen and drop-in are taking shape, as well. The space will be open concept, with the kitchen running along one side, two big commercial stoves, stainless shelving and prep stations, an industrial dishwasher and a movable island separating the kitchen from the dining space. Large, round tables and comfortable seating will be spread out over the rest of the upper level.

It's a far cry from most food organizations Kathryn visited over the spring. She saw food banks operating out of sketchy storefronts and offices tucked into a cubby at a local hockey arena; she met with beleaguered staff forced to decide between buying fresh food and fixing their photocopier. Having spent the first part of her career scrambling to source space and money for food programs like community kitchens for homeless people, Kathryn felt like she was right back where she started.

It was a major reality check for all of us. The Stop has come a long way from those early days of mouse turds and stained, wobbly fabric dividers, of rotten lettuce and an executive director working part-time in the food bank while trying to raise money, fix broken technology and run the rest of the organization. We have a well-resourced and active Community Food Centre with adequate staff numbers and the ability to look beyond the panic of emergency food delivery. We also have welcoming, multipurpose physical spaces. The Stop is, at its heart, a place-based centre. What we do is inextricably intertwined with *where* we do it—whether it's the Green Barn or the main site in Symington Place. Ensuring the space is functional and dignified, that people feel good there however desperate their need, is essential to the success of our programming. So is the fact that we have gardens and kitchens, meeting places and dining spaces, offices and education areas all under one roof. We think this multifunctionality is a fundamental ingredient of the Community Food Centre, helping create synergies between programs, staff, volunteers and community members.

Seeing this fresh, emerging space in Perth—to be called The Table Community Food Centre—is thrilling. There is so much possibility here. Over time, The Table and other future Community Food Centres will incorporate the three program areas that we believe are at the heart of the model: dignified food access, meaning programs like healthy drop-in meals or a healthy food bank; food skills, including cooking and gardening, and food literacy for children; and engagement and education—programs that support low-income community members to have a voice in food and social justice issues. Our role is to provide ideas and best practices for these core programs, and to outline the philosophical approach that we consider essential for the Community Food Centre to work. Equally important, we'll be sourcing significant funding over the years—raised from a range of foundations, government, individuals and businesses—to establish adequately staffed centres. And we'll offer ongoing support and guidance, from programming to staffing and facilities, from governance structures to evaluation systems.

Our aim is to bring the best of The Stop to these new organizations, but we're also keenly aware that each town has unique challenges, resources and history. Part of the first year of our collaboration with new partners is doing a community food assessment so that the region's or neighbourhood's most important issues are clear, potential partners are highlighted, gaps are identified, and the Community Food Centre truly responds to the local needs. In Perth, for instance, staff have highlighted a gap in food programming for seniors, as well as the importance of reaching out to low-income people in the wider rural district, especially those who have trouble getting to the site. In Stratford, a healthy food distribution centre has been identified as a strategic initiative. There were numerous small food banks, food and student nutrition programs, but no central distribution or storage site in the town. Part of The Local Community Food Centre (as the Stratford site will be called), this new distribution system will take in large-scale donations and make strategic purchases of healthy food from local farmers, processors and retailers, store it (with refrigerator and freezer facilities) and distribute it to food banks, community kitchens, student nutrition programs and nonprofits. It's not a food bank; instead, it's an effort to increase capacity and encourage the use of fresh, healthy food in existing programs.

Back in the kitchen, Nancy points out where the ventilation hoods for the commercial stoves will go and says she's already had to talk to several contractors and deal with a slow permits approval process. I commiserate with her. I vividly remember the frustratingly long renovation of our commercial kitchen, not to mention the endless Green Barn development process with its many twists and turns. Nancy's also had to contend with people in the community who aren't sure about the entire project and wonder what was wrong with the food bank in the first place, and why The Table needs such a nice facility. Convincing the community and dealing with renovation surprises have eaten up a lot of Nancy's time. But she's still managed to get many people onside. Her savvy about how to connect with those who use the programs as well as businesses, foundations and individuals who will help fund it was one of the reasons Perth made so much sense as a pilot site. Earlier today, Nancy and her board hosted a large group of supporters at a pretty farm site just outside of town. We all ate an outdoor farm lunch before she and I both spoke about what we imagine for The Table. Her willingness to engage with fundraising is key, because she and other Community Food Centre leaders will have to source some funds in order to maintain their organizations into the future. The Table doesn't need to be as big or complex or costly as The Stop, but it will require ongoing financial support from the community to ensure it thrives and survives.

This flexibility within the established core framework—some centres can be small, with only five or six staff; others could be much larger to meet the needs of their area—is part of the reason the model makes sense to so many people. We've had queries about it from places as diverse as Stevens Point, Wisconsin, Washington, D.C., and Wellington, New Zealand.

In Wellington, the food bank contacted us to say they've been inspired by The Stop to create an organization modelled on ours, with a vegetable garden and fruit trees on site. They plan to get food bank recipients into the plot volunteering and learning new skills. The people in Corvallis, Oregon, rolled out the red carpet for one of our staff when she visited while on vacation in the area. She did a presentation that was attended by local politicians and gave an interview to a local radio station. The South Corvallis Food Bank is hoping to raise money to add new programs and services similar to The Stop's.

The open-source Learning Network, an internet-based support system, is another big part of the appeal. We're developing video learning modules on topics ranging from fundraising issues to running community kitchens. There will be blog postings from the pilot projects sharing their highs and lows, and community forums where people can connect with others interested in Community Food Centres.

Nancy leads us to the front door and back outside. We trace the edge of the building to a muddy patch of grass where a garden will take shape over the summer. It's small but there's talk about the town offering a larger plot nearby where The Table will be able to grow more produce. We're hoping we might even be able to build a wood-fired bake oven here like the one behind The Stop. I breathe deeply, taking it all in. Even unfinished, the place is way beyond my expectations. I'm already wondering if they might be able to rent the house next door and use the building for offices, the long green lot for a good-sized garden. The wind whistles at us through the driveway, and I have to hold onto my baseball cap so it doesn't blow away.

TEN

FOOD IS A
PUBLIC
GOOD

JULY 2011. There are days at The Stop when I wonder what it all adds up to. When a young mom we've been working with for a long time to get her life on track goes back to her abusive partner. When there's a fight in the community space or Bobby gets hauled away by the police again. When two of our staff spend an entire workday attempting to make habitable the cockroach-infested, bedbug-ridden rented room of one of our community members so she can get in the door after a hospital stay. When we battle a devastating flood caused by an overflowing sink in the apartment building above our office space—in an area staff already call the swamp.

The swing of the political pendulum also makes me pause. Promised poverty reduction strategies that we cautiously allowed ourselves to anticipate are crushed by austerity measures as the world economy shrinks and shudders. The push for a nutrition allowance for social assistance recipients—or any other forward-thinking, prevention-focused social policy—is lost in the fray. And the hopeful air of progressive city-building that Toronto cultivated for a few years is swept into the lake when a new cost-cutting mayor rides into town.

But, thankfully, there are also days when things come together and all that we have built here at The Stop makes sense to me. When I see with my own eyes that what we are doing is transforming people's lives and the life of our community, providing an alternative vision of what our city can be.

I know it's one of those good days when I arrive and turn on my computer to a Google alert letting me know that one of our Civic Engagement staffers was on a panel last night advocating with low-income community members about woeful social assistance rates. I head out to look for her to find out how it went and make a quick tour of the drop-in. People are taking their spots for breakfast at the round tables. Sharon is standing near the coffee machine, giving last-minute instructions to the volunteers. Rather than asking everyone to line up, volunteers stand behind the large island; some fill the plates while others serve food to those at the tables. Just like eliminating lineups in the food bank brought greater dignity to that space, serving people at their tables helps shape the positive atmosphere here.

Nicole is in the drop-in, too. After working part-time for us for a few years, she was hired permanently as a community and advocacy worker. Part of her job has been the challenging task of connecting the Wychwood and Symington Place communities through their two social justice and advocacy groups. In preparation for an upcoming provincial election, Bread & Bricks and the Wychwood group are planning get-out-the-vote actions, including "vote mobs" that will canvass both neighbourhoods, encouraging people to cast their ballot and asking them to consider poverty issues when they do. Our former civic engagement coordinator, Jonah, is running in the election. After a narrow defeat in a municipal campaign last year, he's got a good chance of taking this neighbourhood, thanks in part to the strong relationships he's built in the community. Support for low-income people, food access issues and mobilizing government in the fight against bedbugs are key parts of his platform—and a big part of his work at The Stop. It's amazing to hear people in Davenport West say that for the first time in their lives they see themselves and their issues in a politician's words and promises.

Over in the corner by the window, one of our urban agriculture staff is setting up a couple of trays of free plants. She has small, folded handouts about how to care for them ready to tuck into the pots. The food bank doesn't open until noon, but preparations are already being made for a cooking duel between Scott MacNeil and Carlos, an active volunteer who is also a great cook. They'll be battling it out with hot plates, showing people what they can do with food from the hampers. Community members will have a chance to taste the results and vote for their favourite dish.

We've just completed another renovation of the food bank. There's more space and efficient storage; we've built an area where we can wash and prepare fresh vegetables. There's better lighting, new tiles on the floor and a fresh coat of paint. It's cleaner and more inviting. Jeremiah, a young man in a wheelchair with severe global disabilities who can't walk or talk, is in the back storage area. His caregiver is breaking down boxes while Jeremiah watches and expresses himself with loud squeals and grunts. The only person missing in this bustling spot is Cliff. Those of us who knew him feel his absence everywhere.

Cliff died of cancer in May. The tumours spread from his arm to his lungs and then his brain. When I saw him in hospital a few days before he died, he was thin and pale, his face drawn. True to form, he told me he was hopeful that he'd get better. He and his girlfriend had planned to wait until he was well to get married, but then, when things weren't looking great, they decided to do it anyway, right in the hospital. Her kids were there; so were some Stop staff. Cliff died a few days later. He was only thirty-nine years old.

We held a celebration of Cliff's life in June. People from every part of his world turned up to toast the life of this big-hearted young man with the crazy laugh and goofy sense of humour. It was standing room only. People who used the food bank and other Stop programs, neighbours, former colleagues and friends all offered up their memories in speeches, music and pictures. They talked about how he grew up poor, but was proud that he'd made something of himself. They said he was a generous man who tried to help others do what he had done, who never stopped learning and had a joke for anyone, no matter where they came from. People recalled the four-finger salute we all offered up in a morbid show of solidarity when his finger was amputated. They giggled about his unreformed love of Kentucky Fried Chicken.

A documentary filmmaker showed a partly edited version of a film she was making about Cliff negotiating the health care and disability system. They'd met when she was working on another film about poverty, and he'd helped her connect with Stop community members. After years of supporting others, he'd found himself dealing with the runaround on his disability benefits, forced to pay out of pocket for some of the expensive drugs he needed. It was hard to see him on the big screen still relatively healthy, the way he said tough things and told his difficult story with a little hint of mischief in his eyes.

We all cried and laughed and after the film and the speeches, headed outside to plant a cherry tree in his memory near the bake oven. A laminated poster announcing the celebration of his life is still up in various places around The Stop. On it there's a picture of Cliff wearing a silly, green jester's hat and standing in front of the bouncy castle at our annual Good Food for All festival. He was a big kid at heart and we all knew that each year Cliffy would be good for a few hours working the castle. In the picture, his hands are stretched out on either side like a hug, and he's got a smile as wide as his arms.

Rekha Cherian, our new food bank coordinator, had some big shoes to fill and she's proved herself more than up to the task. She's at the counter now continuing the never-ending work of organizing food and forms. Rekha is warm and engaging, but she's also tough and has a singularity of purpose that people sense right away. We hired her because she understands intuitively what we are trying to do, and embraces the contradictions of her job—heading up a food bank inside an organization that sees food banks as part of the problem.

Over the years, we've all had to come to terms with the fact that we haven't shuttered the food bank. That doesn't mean we think there's no other way to do things, or that food banks are any answer at all to hunger or poverty. We accept that for the moment the food bank is one way to meet the immediate needs of our community. But we are continuing to fight for alternatives and are constantly working toward a day when food banks won't be necessary.

Rekha's set up a big chalkboard leaning against the new stainless steel counter that separates the food shelves from the tables where people gather to have a coffee and wait their turn. The chalkboard is loaded with information about strawberries, the food of the month. I can see boxes of fresh greens from the community garden, multicoloured carrots from The New Farm, garlic hanging from the ceiling to dry. It's so different from those days when I began at The Stop, even from the time of the Eat the Math campaign. But Rekha is still trying to improve it. She says she's glad to hear the feedback from community members, and doesn't even mind when it's negative. It means people feel confident enough and respected enough in the space to voice their concerns. She's been mulling over the idea of eliminating unhealthy products altogether, and making sure 30 to 40 percent of the food available is Local Food Plus certified. She's even been talking lately about changing the food bank's name and calling it a Free Store. I want to talk to her about all of these ideas but we don't have time to chat today. Rekha's got shelves to organize and I'm expected at the Green Barn for a meeting with Rhonda.

I cycle east across Davenport and find the Green Barn equally busy. The food education crew are in summer camp mode. The kids have their hands in vermicompost buckets in the greenhouse, some squealing at the sight of the red wigglers, others quiet and fascinated. One of the interns tells me they're going to be stilt walking in the afternoon. Some of our food enterprise chefs are in the kitchen prepping for Saturday's Market Café, and an urban agriculture staffer is pulling together information packages for the Global Roots gardeners. We still don't have an aquaponics project, but it could definitely happen here.

When my own meeting with Rhonda is finished, I'm invited to join the staff lunch co-op. Most Mondays and Fridays, one person makes a big meal and the staff all sit down together to enjoy it. We eat together at the main site as well. Staff either bring their own lunch or pay a small fee to The Stop and have the same delicious food as the people at the drop-in. It reminds me of those prescient public health nurses and their communal lunches. It changes everything when you sit down together and share a meal.

I head back to my office at Symington Place to find the food bank and lunch drop-in in full swing. Haircuts are on offer, and the community advocates are offering assistance to anyone who needs help with housing or welfare, health care or landlord issues. I wind my way to the front of the building through the kitchen and see some Healthy Beginnings moms and staff who've started a cooking group called Food, Family and Fun. The kids are in another room with childcare, and everyone has a job prepping the meal. They stand around the island and at the counter chatting as they pull together their lunch of grilled chicken breast, green salad and warm bread.

When I finally get back to my office, it's a relief to sit down. I try to take in all this action and activity, the bombardment of programs and ideas, people and activities. I never did find the Civic Engagement staffer to ask her about the panel. Kathryn leans in my office, knocking on my open door at the same time. There's a group from a nearby city touring The Stop to learn more about what we do and how we do it. Can I come and talk to them? I take a deep breath. I know exactly what I'll say: I'll tell them about my day.

✦

ANYONE WHO KNOWS ME KNOWS that I'm an optimist by nature. I think it comes from my parents, who are in their mid-seventies and still haven't tired of imagining and working toward a better, more equal society. It's become my way of looking at the world. I can't imagine doing what I do without this belief that if we fight for it, things can and will get better. At its heart, I think The Stop's story is also one of optimism—and, most importantly, hope.

As we've worked over the last few years hammering out the Community Food Centre model—expressing what exactly has made The Stop a vital force in our neighbourhood so we can pass this knowledge on to others—it is hope that we always return to. People who come to The Stop feel hope and self-worth when we listen to their needs and concerns, treat them with dignity, and offer support and care, connection to others, and opportunities to speak out themselves. There can be no substantive change in people's lives or in the life of a neighbourhood without this baseline sense that things can and will improve and that as individuals and citizens we are worthy of it.

Of course, hope is not always easy to unearth in families and communities that experience the humiliations of poverty, racism and inequality. But the power of hope is clear at The Stop. It's clear in the Spanish-speaking couple Antonio and Gladys, who, after divorce and widowhood left them both using our food bank and drop-in, met and fell in love at our Sabor Latino community kitchen. It's clear in the experience of Nicole Mitchell, Theora Spooner, Gord Bowes and Tania Julien, who found a community here. Or in the continuing story of my old friend Glenn Kitchener who, after working for us part-time for a while, ended up getting a job at FoodShare. He took the wheel of one of their delivery trucks in January 2009 and has been with the organization ever since. Feeling respected in his volunteer and then paid work at The Stop, he says, made him able to move forward, made it possible to imagine something better for himself.

If it is hope that is the common denominator in the trans-formation of people's lives and the life of this community, food is its vehicle. I see how powerful food can be at The Stop every day. It brings people together, breaks down differences and can act as a tool for change.

Of course, not everyone believes this. Gene Kahn—organic food pioneer and founder of Cascadian Farm, which he sold to General Mills—famously told Michael Pollan in *The Omnivore's Dilemma*, "This is just lunch for most people. *Just lunch*. We can call it sacred, we can talk about communion, but it's just lunch." Fuel for the body, sure, but most importantly, a simple com-modity on the world market.

Nowhere was this sentiment more in evidence than at a recent conference I attended called the Canadian Food Summit. Hosted by the Conference Board of Canada and sponsored by many major players in the food industry, it was held over two days at a big downtown convention centre. The subject was the challenges and opportunities presented by a changing food system, and I was asked to respond to a panel speaking about national food policies.

I talk a lot about The Stop and Community Food Centres these days, but I spent more time than usual thinking about what I'd say—as well as asking colleagues from Britain, Australia and Brazil about their own national food policies. The preparation was partly because the subject is not my area of expertise. But I also knew I wouldn't be preaching to the choir—the audience would be full of representatives of big food companies and cor-porate agriculture. I figured I would need to marshal as much hard information as possible to convincingly tell our story and that of other organizations with a vision for change.

I sat in on the first day and a half of speakers and breakout groups before my own panel was scheduled to speak. Though

there was an attempt by organizers to surface alternative views—
inviting *New York Times* food columnist Mark Bittman and a
small handful of others—the overwhelming tone in the talks
I attended and of the people I spoke to was self-congratulatory,
even triumphant, about the ascendance of industrial food. The
idea that bigger is better, that price is king, that industrial agriculture and factory farming are necessary—that lunch is just
lunch—seemed to go unquestioned. The dominant message in
the talks I attended was that government should get out of the
way and let big food and agriculture companies run the show.
When the idea of "food security" came up, it referred not to the
right of everyone to access healthy, culturally appropriate food,
but to the importance of traceability, safety concerns, even
national security. There were breakout groups that explored
diet-related health issues, sustainability and the environment,
but they were the sideshow, not the main event.

When I spoke, following several international experts talking about food policy in their countries, I opened with my
bewilderment at attending a food conference where the growing problem of hunger in our affluent society wasn't even on
the table. In fact, it seemed to me as if all the pioneering and
inventive work I have seen across the country and around the
world, all the interesting and engaged people working to change
the food system—bringing equity, sustainability and health to
the fore—weren't on the radar of the participants at all.

So I took the opportunity to talk about the alternative food
system that I've witnessed emerging over the last decade or so,
the efforts of organizations like the ones I saw in Oakland as well
as those closer to home. I talked about our work at The Stop and
that of our friends at FarmStart, a nonprofit focused on training
and educating a new generation of small-scale sustainable

farmers, especially immigrants. I mentioned the co-operative model of farmer-owned Organic Meadow, and the excellent work of Food Secure Canada, which initiated a citizen-generated national food policy called "Resetting the Table: A People's Food Policy for Canada." Despite the focus of the conference, this People's Food Policy—created through a two-year-long collaborative process and based on the views and values of 3,500 Canadians—wasn't officially acknowledged at all. And yet, it's an impressive document looking at food from the perspective of farmers and fishers, Indigenous people, nutritionists, public health professionals, gardeners, cooks and entrepreneurs. "In the absence of strong food policies and regulation in the public interest," the report argues, "corporations and global capital have undue influence and control . . . operating beyond the reach of government or public oversight. . . .

"It is time for strong citizen and civil society involvement in the construction of a new food policy . . . which places the well-being of the majority and the health of our planet at the centre of all decisions."

I spoke about all of this to illustrate what I've come to realize is *the* major fault line in the debate about our food system, and what I believe is the most serious barrier to real change. It is the philosophical divide between those people who see food as a pure commodity, something simply to be bought and sold, and those like The Stop and many others who view food as imbued with cultural, social, health and environmental significance.

The audience at the conference was largely made up of the former; and the truth is, I was genuinely surprised by their triumphalism, by the sense conveyed in presentations and on the floor of the convention centre that these large, industrial food players feel they are completely in control. Every fibre of my being was saying: What are you talking about? What about the problems, the costs, the consequences—environmentally, health-wise and socially—of industrial food and agriculture? What about the worldwide obesity crisis, an issue intimately connected to the growth of the fast-food and processed food market and the powerful effect of junk food marketing? Or food safety scares like mad cow disease and listeriosis, E. coli in hamburger meat and bean sprouts that are forcing people everywhere to question industrialization, centralization and the speed and efficiencies demanded by a system that is focused on profit alone? What about arable land all over the earth being destroyed by monoculture and poisoned by chemicals, forcing farmers and their families into poverty and debt? Or environmentally vital rainforests being razed to make way for pasture land for cattle? What about the way that cheap processed food is making people everywhere sick? What about the one billion people in the world who are hungry?

After my own talk, I went and listened to several others. Eventually, I couldn't take it anymore. "What about full cost accounting?" I asked a speaker, the head of a large food retailer, during the Q & A period. If cost is king, shouldn't we be taking into consideration the cost to our health care system and the impact on the environment of industrial processed food? I told him I think that big food companies are privatizing profit and socializing cost—reaping the monetary rewards of cheap, processed, fuel-intensive food and passing the cost of the health and environmental fallout on to the public purse.

The speaker listened to me politely. He even said it was a valid point. But it was instructive that he didn't need to bother refuting it and could proceed with a shrug. The message to me and everyone there was that the world of big food is so powerful, the system so pervasive, it's easy to ignore a few pesky questions.

Still, I left the conference feeling not demoralized, but revivified (didn't I say I'm an optimist?), understanding more clearly than ever just what we're up against in trying to change the food system. My father is right: the other side is trying, too. And the battle for the hearts, minds and stomachs of people everywhere is very much on.

The good news is, those of us who look at food more holistically have thousands of years of history on our side. The rituals of food and its growth, preparation and consumption have played a central role in defining human society as it has evolved, helping establish ours as a social existence. In relative terms, the corporate agri-food world that sees things like health, equality and the environment as "externalities"—unconnected to the real work of buying and selling food commodities—hasn't been around for very long. My own parents' generation still remembers what it was like to eat with the seasons, to eat whole foods— not unpronounceable processed food products—to sit down for meals with family, to consider sugary drinks a rare special treat. Even now as we have become so disconnected from food production, as well as the act of eating (think of all that fast food scarfed down in the car), food cannot be utterly disentangled from social relationships.

Given the opportunity, people leap at the opportunity to reclaim good food—growing it, cooking it and sharing it. I won't easily forget the joy at the table when Herman's callaloo came out piping hot from the kitchen, or the pleasure and pride of those kids in our After School Program showing off their knife skills to superchef Jamie Oliver, or the comfort and sustenance so many people take in sharing a home-cooked meal at our breakfast and lunch drop-ins. I think, too, of the generous spirit that buoys everyone, like a giant inflatable castle, at our Good Food for All festival or our two food markets. If food is a commodity, it certainly is an intimate one.

And because it is so intimate, it is too important to our health, the health of the environment and our social relationships to be defined entirely by profit. I think the way we must begin to reclaim food and the food system from corporate control is by reframing the conversation and claiming food as a public good. By that I mean access to good food makes our society stronger, healthier and happier, and it is good for everyone when we all have adequate food. Most democratic societies believe that education, health care and housing are essential to the public good. I think we need to expand that idea to include food.

I'm not talking about taking food entirely out of the marketplace—though I think there is an important place for growing and producing your own food and reclaiming food skills that can make families and communities more self-sufficient. Instead, this approach is about demonstrating that the interests of people and the planet are as important as the bottom line. And it means waking up about food and seeing ourselves as more than just consumers. We must reimagine ourselves as food citizens—aware and engaged about how good food is produced, distributed and consumed, pushing for policies and programs that promote sustainability and equity. Food citizenship is about insisting that food is viewed by policy-makers and average people as such a key element of who and what we are that it cannot be left to the market. It means marrying thoughtful individual consumption with advocacy for change to the system as a whole.

Middle-class people are already combining their consumer power with their politics, participating in alternative food distribution networks such as community shared agriculture or farmers' markets, planting home veggie gardens, buying organic, lobbying for healthy changes to their kids' school lunch and advocating for urban agriculture. Innovative organizations and businesses such as The New Farm, FarmStart or Off the Hook, a project of the Ecology Action Centre in Nova Scotia, are doing it as well. Atlantic Canada's first community-supported fishery, Off the Hook uses only bottom hook and line fishing—rather than dragnetting that has caused so much damage to the seabed and fish habitats—and they sell directly to consumers. These consumers and fishers support sustainability and the health of the ocean, and the fishers get a fair price for their labour.

But to create long-lasting, sustainable change, low-income people need to be included in the conversation and the fight must be pushed into the public realm. That's where Community Food Centres come in—combining the energy and passion of the consumer side of the good food revolution (through farmers' markets and foodie events) with a justice perspective and an eye to social, political and economic policy that benefits everyone. With the Perth and Stratford pilots off the ground, we're looking at creating fifteen Community Food Centres across Canada over the next five years. It's an ambitious project, but the way we see it, the potential for transformation is enormous. Like The Stop, these new centres will offer dignified food programs and services for low-income people, as well as advocacy support, and as a group, the communities will have the ability to help reshape and redefine the food system.

As The Stop has done in Davenport West, Community Food Centres elsewhere will remind people of food's power to bring disparate groups and people together. They will prove food's position as a public good, showing tangibly how adequate access to healthy, sustainable food can make our cities, towns and rural areas better for everyone. These Community Food Centres will be a platform and a voice for the food movement, joining with thousands of individuals and organizations around the world already engaged in the fight. And by building a big tent, one created with the goal of forging links between low-income people and the rest of society, this collaboration will be a powerful force.

Moving beyond the individual to acknowledge the collective consequences of the current system and the collective benefit of a more equitable and sustainable one, the goal will be to generate the political will to invest our tax dollars (they are ours, after all) in the kind of food system we'd all like to see. We can begin by insisting governments protect the health of citizens and the environment through adequate minimum wages and benefits for low-income people, regulation of harmful processed food products and support for sustainable food producers. But we also need government bodies with genuine powers—like Brazil's Ministry of Food Security—and the ability to bring together all the players. We have to ensure government food planning structures are transparent and truly democratic so that big food and agriculture corporations aren't the only ones at the table. Such an approach also demands using integrated thinking when it comes to food—making the links between what people eat and their health, how we produce food and the state of the environment, how governments subsidize farmers and what that means to the rest of us. It might mean mandating and supporting municipalities, regions and institutions to source their food from sustainable local producers—with all the positive ripple effects such a move would mean up and down the supply chain. It would definitely see us starting early with children, providing adequately resourced national school nutrition programs

(Canada is one of the few industrialized nations in the world without one), and integrating food literacy into curriculum, making sure every child understands the links between what they eat, their own bodies and the world around them.

We are at an important moment. Despite their power and influence, both corporations and governments lag behind civil society in thinking about these issues. I was reminded of this when grocery magnate Galen Weston Jr. of the Loblaw chain put his foot in his mouth during an off-the-cuff moment at the Food Summit. "Farmers' markets are great," he said. "One day they're going to kill some people, though." He immediately said he was just being "dramatic," but the response online and in the media was swift and ferocious. There are stringent food safety rules applied to farmers' markets, the outraged said. Meanwhile, rats and mice had caused the shutdown of a Toronto Loblaws store and, only the month before the summit, rancid baby food from the chain's in-house label had been voluntarily recalled. Commentators vented about the near-constant contaminated food recalls in the industrial food world in general—including a listeriosis outbreak a few years before that killed over twenty Canadians.

His comments, though, were revealing about just how slow-moving large corporate or government bodies can be. They're happy to make small changes, create spaces in their stores that evoke farmers' markets, hug a farmer for the cameras, throw a legislative bone to noisy people here and there. But government and big food corporations are waiting to make sure the interest in food that's been growing over the last decade is real and long-lasting before committing to substantive change. They need to know people are serious.

Of course, the concerned citizens who sat around kitchen tables, went to workshops, wrote discussion papers and told their stories to create the People's Food Policy are serious. So are the committed food activists and communities I've met in Oakland, Boston, Brazil, Stratford, Winnipeg, Calgary and elsewhere. The thousands of community members at The Stop who've found better health, a sense of community and hope for the future at our Community Food Centre are also serious. So are the cities and towns and neighbourhoods calling for us to expand our model on their turf. There is a thirst for engagement and for change. The time is right for all of us to take charge of our food system and make it work for everyone.

DECEMBER 2011. White cloths are draped over the round veneer tables in the drop-in space, pretty centrepieces made of evergreen branches and ribbon placed in the middle. There are water glasses and cutlery, linen at each place. Staff are hustling around, making sure everything is ready to go. I see Mary Milne and Rosa and Tony Lamanna already sitting at a table not far from the kitchen with a couple of other regulars. I can't think of an annual general meeting they've missed.

Staff wearing Stop aprons are standing in a cluster near the doors that lead to the kitchen. They're waiting for their cue to begin serving. Tonight, it's staff who will bring out the food to community members, donors, volunteers, board members and friends seated at the tables. I walk through the kitchen to say hello to Scott and the others. Everything is running smoothly. Up until a few years ago, I was involved in every part of planning the AGM, from renting plates to finding a speaker to crafting the wording on the plaques we give our volunteer of the year. I worried about every detail and probably drove people crazy. I was always a bit concerned that someone in the audience would go rogue, stand up and challenge the slate of board members we'd already recruited, or complain about some issue they had with staff or one of our house rules. Nothing like that ever happened, but I worried about it all the same.

Tonight, I'm confident that we know our community well and have built up a sense of trust and solidarity. I think anyone with an issue would speak to staff or me before raising their concerns in a large public forum. And with so many events under our belt and excellent people whose job it is to organize them, I don't worry about the details quite as much anymore.

Looking around at all the familiar faces, I actually have a pang of nostalgia. Though not many people know it, tonight will be my last AGM as executive director at The Stop. We haven't announced it publicly yet, but I'll be leaving next summer to take the helm of a new national organization that we're calling Community Food Centres Canada (CFCC). With so much interest, we couldn't continue to build this new organization off the back of The Stop. Kathryn, who has been deeply involved and without whose intelligence and leadership the entire project wouldn't even exist, will be leaving, too. We're bringing a small team with us and heading to a new office not far from Symington Place. CFCC will be an umbrella organization that develops Community Food Centres across the country and acts as the national voice of the network. We'll work with local communities to raise the money to fund new sites, supporting their operations and programs; we'll collaborate with prospective centres as they organize and build their capacity; and we'll build and promote the Learning Network to connect with other food organizations and individuals interested in our work and in food system change more generally. Our aim is to use CFCC to strengthen the entire sector—supporting organizations to increase their ability to advocate for and with low-income people and integrate the idea of food as a public good into our collective consciousness. We're already working on raising the twenty million dollars we need to achieve our goal of fifteen Community Food Centres by 2017.

The pilot projects in Perth and Stratford have spent the past year consulting with their communities to determine the kind of programming that will best serve their area. In Perth, The Table Community Food Centre has completed its renovation and set up the shiny new commercial kitchen and drop-in space, as well as the grocery store–style food bank. They're starting community kitchens and an after-school program, as well as a gardening project. They've built raised beds and created a demonstration plot in the back. I'm still hoping for the lot next door to become available.

In Stratford, the group has been doing similar work and is renovating an old garden warehouse store that will become The Local Community Food Centre. There will be a state-of-the-art kitchen, a food distribution warehouse and a large garden, and there are plans to fix up the greenhouse already on site.

We're also continuing to develop the Learning Network and connect with organizations interested in The Stop's model. Our free webinars are invariably booked, and monthly tours of The Stop's facilities have long waiting lists. But even with all these developments and the exciting birth of a new organization, it's not going to be easy for me to leave here. I've grown up at The Stop. I know everyone. They know my strengths and my quirks. They remember when I dressed up for Halloween as Veggie Man in running tights, a Speedo and a red cape (and love to tease me about it). They've seen me at my best and my worst. They know Andrea and my parents. They've seen my boys grow from babies to big kids, watching them at annual meetings and Christmas breakfast in the drop-in. They've seen my hair turn grey. The community members and staff are my giant extended family.

When I leave the kitchen, I make a beeline for Joe Virgona, the owner of Fiesta Farms, and his wife, Judy. They're standing off by the window that looks out at the Symington Place townhouses and they seem a bit uncertain, not knowing anyone. Joe and Fiesta are going to be honoured tonight with our partner of the year award.

Gillian Hewitt Smith puts her hand on my shoulder. She's now chair of The Stop board, and she wants to talk quickly before the business part of the evening begins. She, too, has grown up at The Stop. Just twenty-three when she started volunteering, she's now part of our institutional memory, one of our most experienced board members and running a nonprofit herself called the Institute for Canadian Citizenship. Gillian's turned into one of the best connectors I've ever met. As her mother says, she's a "forty-eight-hour person packed into a twenty-four-hour day." She's helped me a lot as we've talked about managing my transition out of The Stop.

The fact that I'm leaving after nearly fifteen years at The Stop really sank in for me and some of our board members at a recent meeting. I told the group that my intention was to leave by the end of next summer for Community Food Centres Canada. There was a long pause, as if people were surprised, though they all knew it was coming, and in the silence, the reality of the move hit me. As people at The Stop know well, I have a tendency to get choked up at emotional public moments, and I had to swallow my tears.

Coincidentally, on my way home that night, I ran into Glenn Kitchener. I was on my bike and he was walking from the streetcar to the bus in his usual loping way. We stopped to chat and he told me he was coming home from a photography class at a local college. He was tired after a long day, but as he showed me his very professional digital camera, a bag full of other lenses across his shoulder, he got more and more excited. He told me that he'd recently been given a promotion and wouldn't have to be driving a truck anymore. He's thrilled to have a desk job. He's planning to become a photographer in his retirement. To hear a guy who just a few years ago was living in a bedbug-ridden rooming house and struggling to eat healthily on welfare talk so enthusiastically about planning for his retirement nearly opened the floodgates all over again.

When I finally reach the Virgonas, their food has arrived and they've struck up a conversation with Renee, a resident of Symington Place and former Bread & Bricks member now working full-time as a community advocate at another nonprofit across town. I welcome Joe and Judy, but I don't need to say much. They're already feeling comfortable.

Recently, Dan Yashinsky, a well-known Toronto storyteller and old friend of mine, has been working at The Stop as our first-ever storyteller-in-residence. Funded by an arts grant, he's been sharing stories with Bread & Bricks, Sabor Latino, the After School Program and the Global Roots gardeners, among others. He's also collecting the stories they tell him. He's heard Yoruba folktales from Africa and stories from El Salvador, the Philippines, China, Jamaica, Mexico, Canada, Pakistan and more. Sometimes he drops into my office and tells me the stories he's heard, and what he's observed about how the organization and programs work. He talks often about the sense of generosity he has witnessed at The Stop, and the way he sees what we're doing as "revillaging the city"—creating pockets of care, mutual assistance and connection, as one might see in a village, within the urban setting.

At its best, I think that's exactly what The Stop aims to do. It doesn't always work without a hitch. The lives of many, many people in our neighbourhood continue to be unrelentingly difficult. But anyone who spends time here understands that it *is* a kind of village. We have our community elders and our comic relief, we have celebrations and rituals, we have familiar faces and new ones mingling together. We have our share of difficulties—like any place where people know each other well—but there is a true spirit of generosity and connection at The Stop. It is built into the programs, the philosophy and the interactions between people—whether they're staff, volunteers, donors or community members.

When dinner is finished, Gillian and I each address the crowd. I can see Cliff's widow and her children sitting up on the small, raised stage on the east side where we've squeezed in two more tables. I barely make it through my tribute to Cliffy.

But before the meeting gets too maudlin, a young gay couple who live in the building and are active in Bread & Bricks present a slide show of images they've taken over the past year. The pair were married the same weekend as our Good Food for All festival, and the whole wedding party came out to cheer on our parade through the streets. A young girl from the community wore Rhonda's carrot costume; a small band with a trumpet and trombone played as we sang along, handing out apples to people on the sidewalk. The couple's slide show is a joyous celebration of the wild and wonderful community they have joined here at The Stop.

It's Dan's turn at the podium. He tells two stories himself, and then introduces Margaret, a farmer from Zimbabwe who sells her organic veggies at the Green Barn farmers' market. She and her husband have a two-acre organic plot at FarmStart's farm north of the city. They grow a variety of vegetables, with an emphasis on produce that is native to Southern Africa. Margaret is wearing a traditional African cloth turban and dress. She has a beautiful speaking voice that carries through the room. According to traditional Shona custom in her homeland, she tells the group, chiefs were required to set aside land for growing food in case of a shortage in the community. This land was known as *Zunde raMambo*. Everyone in the area would volunteer to tend the land, taking turns preparing, sowing, weeding and harvesting—though not everyone would necessarily benefit in a direct way. The harvest would be stored in granaries on the chief's property and saved to be distributed in times of difficulty or on special occasions. Priority for this communally grown food was given to the elderly, widows, orphans and those with disabilities, though soldiers—who protected the community—would also be fed from the chief's granary.

The community's participation in *Zunde raMambo* was important, Margaret told the crowd, because it helped ensure everyone had adequate food. But growing, weeding and harvesting the food also helped ensure people felt connected to each other and to their community.

It occurred to me as I listened that it's this kind of connection I've spent my entire adult life fighting to assert—pushing against what has become the dominant narrative in our society, against those who would say that we are only individuals, not communities. Looking around the room, I can see exactly how wrong they are. The battle isn't over, of course. As the freedom fighters in Mozambique would say: *a luta continua*, the struggle continues. But the very existence of The Stop and other like-minded organizations around the world, as well as the growing embrace of our Community Food Centre model, is a victory in itself.

In fact, I think that The Stop is my *Zunde raMambo*. It is this neighbourhood's, too. We need more of these precious places. In all of their beautiful, imperfect, noisy generosity, they are proof that we are all connected, and that we are better for these bonds.

WE HAVE MORE BOOKS ON FOOD than actual food in our home. But one book more than any other has shaped our view of the problems with food banking. It is *Sweet Charity? Emergency Food and the End of Entitlement* by Janet Poppendieck (Penguin, 1998).

A number of other works on the food system have also been influential, including: Michael Pollan's *The Omnivore's Dilemma: A Natural History of Four Meals* (Penguin, 2006) and *In Defense of Food: An Eater's Manifesto* (Penguin, 2008); Frances Moore Lappé's *Diet for a Small Planet* (Ballantine Books, 1999); Marion Nestle's *Food Politics: How the Food Industry Influences Nutrition and Health* (University of California Press, 2002); *Fast Food Nation* by Eric Schlosser (Perennial, 2002); *Real Food for a Change: Bringing Nature, Health, Joy and Justice to the Table* by Wayne Roberts, Rod MacRae and Lori Stahlbrand (Random House, 1999); *Stuffed and Starved: The Hidden Battle for the World Food System* by Raj Patel (Melville House, 2012); as well as Mark Bittman's *Food Matters: A Guide to Conscious Eating* (Simon & Schuster, 2008) and his invariably timely and tough *New York Times'* opinion columns.

The following is a selective list of written material that was used in researching this book. Sources are listed, as much as possible, according to the subject's appearance in the text. While we relied on others for background and insight, any errors are the authors' own.

For the history of food banking in Canada, Graham Riches' *Food Banks and the Welfare Crisis* (Canadian Council on Social Development, 1986), as well as *First World Hunger: Food Security and Welfare Politics* edited by Riches (University of Toronto Press, 1997) provided key background information. There were also several government papers on the early days of food banks that we found useful: "Not by bread alone: a strategy to eliminate the need for food banks in the GTA" (April 23, 1991); and the Ontario Standing Committee on Social Development's "Report on Food Banks" (April 1990). "Reverend Rick," an article by David Olive (*Toronto Life*, April 1989), offered insight into The Stop's early years as a food bank and antipoverty agency. For background on John van Hengel, we looked to the St. Mary's Food Bank Alliance. Janet Poppendieck's essay, "The USA: Hunger in the Land of Plenty," published in *First World Hunger: Food Security and Welfare Politics*, edited by Graham Riches (Macmillan Press, 1997), offered background on the proliferation of emergency food providers in the U.S. during the 1980s and '90s.

The conversion of Alexandra Park into a co-op is chronicled in Jorge Sousa and Jack Quarter's "Converting a public housing project into a tenant-managed housing co-operative: A Canadian case study" (*Journal of Housing and the Built Environment*, 2004) and "Canada's First Public Housing Conversion into Co-operative Housing" by the same authors (*Cooperative Housing Bulletin*, 2005).

The "Report on Food Access in West Davenport Area" was prepared by Janet Maher for the Davenport Perth Neighbourhood Centre in May 1996.

The literature on urban agriculture is vast and growing. Our own reading includes the excellent Metcalf Food Solutions paper "Scaling up Urban Agriculture in Toronto: Building the Infrastructure" by Joseph Nasr, Rod MacRae and James Kuhns (June 2010); *Carrot City: Creating Places for Urban Agriculture* by Mark Gorgolewski, June Komisar and Joe Nasr (Monacelli

Press, 2011); Lorraine Johnson's *City Farmer: Adventures in Urban Food Growing* (Greystone Books, 2010); and *Locavore: How Canadians are Changing the Way We Eat* by Sarah Elton (HarperCollins, 2010).

Tracking the evolution of the notion of "community food security," we turned to Wayne Roberts' *The No-Nonsense Guide to World Food* (New Internationalist and Between the Lines, 2008) and *Closing the Food Gap: Resetting the Table in the Land of Plenty* by Mark Winne (Beacon Press, 2008). Toronto's place in the emerging food movement has been ably recorded in *The Edible City: Toronto's Food from Farm to Fork*, edited by Christina Palassio and Alana Wilcox (Coach House, 2009). Toronto's influential Food Charter can be found at www.toronto.ca/food_hunger/pdf/food_charter.pdf. For background about La Via Campesina, the rise of the industrial food system and its relationship to the global food crisis, see *Food Rebellions: Crisis and the Hunger for Justice* by Eric Holt-Giménex and Raj Patel (Pambazuka Press, Food First Books and Grassroots International, 2009).

We found interesting information on the early days of Healthy Beginnings in the minutes of a Canadian House of Commons Standing Committee on Health report from May 30, 1996. The link between poverty and poor health is well documented, including in *Social Determinants of Health: Canadian Perspectives* edited by Dennis Raphael (Canadian Scholars' Press, 2004). We refer in the text to the excellent report, "Poverty is making us sick: A comprehensive survey of income and health in Canada" by Ernie Lightman, Andrew Mitchell and Beth Wilson (Wellesley Institute, 2008). Investigating the costs of poverty in general, we turned to "The Dollars and Sense of Solving Poverty" from the late, lamented National Council of Welfare (2011); "The Cost of Poverty: An Analysis of the Economic

Cost of Poverty in Ontario" (Ontario Association of Food Banks, 2008); and *The Spirit Level: Why Greater Equality Makes Societies Stronger* by Richard Wilkinson and Kate Pickett (Bloomsbury Press, 2009). We also refer to "F as in Fat: How Obesity Threatens America's Future 2012," a report released by Trust for America's Health and the Robert Wood Johnson Foundation regarding the economic impact of obesity.

Researching the history of NENA (NorthEast Neighborhood Alliance), the urban agriculture group from Rochester, we read the article "Urban farms transform city's landscape" in *American City & County* (January 1, 2003) by Lindsay Isaacs, and *A Guide to Community Food Projects* by Maya Tauber and Andy Fisher (Community Food Security Coalition, 2002).

We refer to Mark Bittman's September 27, 2011 *New York Times* column regarding the importance of food skills.

Daily Bread Food Bank and Food Banks Canada do excellent yearly reports on food bank use in Toronto and across the country, respectively. We have relied on their research for food bank statistics. Oxfam and Church Action on Poverty produced an excellent report on emergency food aid in the U.K. called "Walking the breadline: the scandal of food poverty in 21st century Britain" (May 2013). Feeding American also releases regular status reports on hunger in the USA. "Food Banks: Hunger's New Staple" draws on data from its *Hunger in America 2010* study. The relationship between corporations and food banks is highlighted in Graham Riches' article "Why Governments Can Safely Ignore Hunger," from the Canadian Centre for Policy Alternatives journal, *The Monitor* (February 1, 2011). Sue Cox's views on food banking and the inadequacy of gardens as a response to food insecurity are recorded in the *Toronto Star* article "'We've Been Institutionalized' Food Banks

No Longer Just Short-term" by Jennifer Quinn (September 30, 2000), and "Toronto food charter aims to cut hunger" by Marissa Nelson in the *Globe and Mail* (June 15, 2001).

Since visiting Brazil, we've read as much as possible about the integrated approach to hunger and poverty in that nation. Cecilia Rocha's work on Belo Horizonte has been particularly influential, especially "An Integrated Program for Urban Food Security: The Case of Belo Horizonte, Brazil" (2000) and "Belo Horizonte social club: where food is treated as a right, both farmers and urban residents benefit" (*Alternatives Journal*, September 2003). We've also consulted several sources on Brazil's food procurement strategies, including Kei Otsuki's "Emerging Governance in the Transition to a Green Economy: A Case Study of Public Sector Food Procurement in Brazil" (United Nations Research Institute for Social Development, 2011) and "Supporting Food Production and Food Access through Local Public Procurement Schemes: Lessons from Brazil" by Darana Souza and Danuta Chmielewska (International Policy Centre for Inclusive Growth, 2010). Lula's story can be found in *Lula and the Workers Party in Brazil* by Sue Branford and Bernardo Kucinski with Hilary Wainwright (The New Press, 2003). We also discovered relevant background on Lula and Brazilian politics in hard-hitting articles in *Red Pepper* magazine, especially "An exception to Lula's rule" by Sue Branford (March 2009). Wayne Roberts' *NOW* magazine article "Loving Lula" (April 8–15, 2004) helped supplement Nick's own memories of the Brazilian hunger conference.

In trying to understand complicated government regulations on charitable organizations engaging in political activities, we have been impressed by the work produced by the Institute for Media, Policy and Civil Society (IMPACS), especially Richard Bridge's

"The Law of Advocacy by Charitable Organizations: The Case for Change" (2000). We have also referred to the Calgary Chamber of Voluntary Organizations' "Advocacy Rules for Charities" (updated 2012), the U.K. Charity Commission, and the Internal Revenue Code [section 501(c)(3)] of the IRS.

Neighbourhood activism around the Wychwood Barns area has been explored in numerous articles, including the *Globe and Mail*'s "The quixotic fight against drive-throughs" by John Barber (April 30, 2002); John Lorinc's "Greened Acres" (*Toronto Life*, July 2002); as well as Jody Berland and Bob Hanke's "Signs of a New Park" (*Public*, 2002). The Wychwood resident who objected to the Barns because of the parking problems it might cause was quoted in Brad Mackay's "Compromise or betrayal?" in the *National Post* (Toronto edition, February 16, 2002).

Michael Pollan's "vote with your fork" mantra appeared in a *New York Times* column on May 7, 2006. Our thinking about the limitations of a consumer-led revolution of the food system has been influenced by *Stuffed and Starved: The Hidden Battle for the World Food System* by Raj Patel (Melville House, 2012) and *Food Movements Unite!* edited by Eric Holt-Giménez (Food First Books, 2011).

Storyteller and author Dan Yashinsky has been an important guide for us on the emerging shape and narrative of The Stop's community. It was he who first suggested that The Stop has community elders and that the bake oven is our hearth. We are indebted to him for this insight. His book, *Suddenly They Heard Footsteps: Storytelling for the Twenty-first Century* (Vintage Canada, 2005), is a wonderful read about the power of stories.

Figures used in the Eat the Math chapter are based on 2009 welfare rates in Ontario; the cost of a nutritious food basket, as calculated by Toronto Public Health, are also based on 2009 numbers. The reporter who named the project "Survivor: Ontario Welfare Edition," was Sean Kelly Keenan in *Eye Weekly* (April 13, 2010). Some of the ideas expressed in the "Eat the Math" chapter first appeared on Andrea's blog, where she chronicled the daily experience of living on a food bank hamper (www.unpackingschoollunch.wordpress.com).

Our reading on the plight of farmers and farmworkers in the industrial food system includes Wendell Berry's beautiful essay "The pleasures of eating" in *What Are People For?* (North Point Press, 1990) with its influential *cri de coeur*: "eating is an agricultural act." *Tomatoland: How Modern Industrial Agriculture Destroyed Our Most Alluring Fruit* by Barry Estabrook (Andrews McMeel, 2011) is required reading on the subject. Anyone interested in the future of agriculture must also pay heed to the prescient words of philosopher and activist Vandana Shiva, especially *Earth Democracy: Justice, Sustainability, and Peace* (South End Press, 2005). For statistics about the economic status of farmers in the U.S. we looked to the United States Department of Agriculture's Economic Research Service on Farm Household Income from February 2013.

Michael Pollan's essay for the *New York Review of Books* called "The Food Movement, Rising" appeared on June 10, 2010.

"Life and Death from Unnatural Causes: Health and Social Inequality in Alameda County" (Alameda County Public Health Department, 2008) is the report on health disparities in the Oakland area.

The challenges faced by the Immokalee Workers are carefully chronicled in Barry Estabrook's *Tomatoland* (see above). Mark Bittman has also written numerous times about the labour action in the *New York Times;* we have quoted his column from

May 12, 2011. We also consulted Beth Kowitt's "Inside the secret world of Trader Joe's" in *Fortune* magazine (August 2010) for background about the grocery chain.

In thinking about the shape and future of the community sector, we have been inspired by numerous books, including *The Samaritan's Dilemma: Should Government Help Your Neighbor?* by Deborah Stone (Nation Books, 2008); *Five Good Ideas: Practical Strategies for Non-Profit Success* (Coach House, 2011) based on Maytree foundation's lunch-and-learn series (Nick is also a contributor to the book); and *On Not Letting a Crisis Go to Waste: An Innovation Agenda for Canada's Community Sector* by Tim Brodhead (J.W. McConnell Family Foundation, 2010).

The story of Campell Canada and Nourish is based on interviews and materials produced by Put Food in the Budget, especially the summer 2011 *Bulletin*, as well as emails sent to Campbell Canada President outlining the organization's concerns about the product claims (www.putfoodinthebudget.ca). We also consulted the article "Campbell's cans hunger" by Jennifer Bain in the *Toronto Star* (March 18, 2011).

Will Allen's autobiography, *The Good Food Revolution: Growing Healthy Food, People, and Communities* (Gotham, 2012), is a compelling account of this important leader's life and work. We have quoted former executive director of the Community Food Security Coalition Andy Fisher about the Walmart donation to Growing Power from an article he wrote for *Civil Eats* website on September 16, 2011. Public health lawyer and author (*Appetite for Profit*, Nation Books, 2006) Michele Simon weighed in on the controversy on her blog on September 18, 2011.

Statistics on charitable giving are from Martin Turcotte's Statistics Canada report "Charitable Giving by Canadians" (April 16, 2012).

Details about food security and poverty in Perth, Ontario, are taken from "A Community Food Security Profile of Perth and District" produced by the Perth and District Food Bank (2011), now The Table Community Food Centre.

Galen Weston Jr.'s remarks about farmers' markets at the Canadian Food Summit were reported by Wency Leung in the *Globe and Mail* on February 9, 2012. The vermin infestation at the Toronto grocery store was reported in the *Toronto Star*, January 28, 2009. The voluntary baby food recall by Loblaw Companies Limited occurred January 18, 2012. The listeriosis outbreak occurred in August 2008. "Report of the Independent Investigator into the 2008 Listeriosis Outbreak" was released by the Government of Canada in July 2009.

The documentary on poverty and homelessness featuring Stop members is Laura Sky's *Home Safe Toronto* (SkyWorks, 2009).

We are indebted to University of Guelph scholar Anthony Winson for the notion of food as an intimate commodity. See, especially, *The Intimate Commodity: Food and the Development of the Agro-Industrial Complex in Canada* (Garamond, 1993). The idea of food citizenship has also been used by others before us. We have been particularly inspired by Rod MacRae and Jennifer Welsh's "Food Citizenship and Community Food Security: Lessons from Toronto, Canada" (*Canadian Journal of Development Studies*, 1998).

For the story of *Zunde raMambo* land, we have looked to the following articles for background: "The revival of *Zunde raMambo* in Zimbabwe" by Edwin Kaseke (VOSESA *Focus*, 2006); and "Community-based food and nutrition programmes: what makes them successful. A review and analysis of experience" by Suraiya Ismail, Maarten Immink, Irela Mazar, Guy Nantel (FAO, 2003).

EVERY BOOK IS A COLLABORATION—between writer and subject, editor and writer, writer and reader—but this book perhaps more than others. Though the experiences it describes and the vision it espouses are Nick's and it is written in the first person in his voice, the book is also Andrea's. As a writer and editor, she has helped shape The Stop's identity and story from the beginning. As a collaborator and advocate for good food, she has been an equal participant in the book-making process. Having shared our lives for seventeen years, raised two great boys and joined forces frequently on work with The Stop, we were not new to the challenges and pleasures of shared labour; but, writing this book was different. It was more fun, more intense, more challenging and more rewarding than anything we've done before.

The Stop, itself, has also been a collaboration of epic proportions. This vibrant and innovative place is the result of the sustained effort, great passion and profound commitment of many, many people. But The Stop would simply not be what it is today without the compassion and intelligence of Celia Harte, Gillian Hewitt-Smith, Sandy Houston, Charles Lennox, Cheryl Roddick, Father Cam Russell, Kathryn Scharf and Rhonda Teitel-Payne. Thank you to The Stop staff and board members present and past, for your friendship, support and belief in the power of food to transform individuals and communities. Our tremendous gratitude to Stop community members, whose resilience and dignity in the face of difficult circumstances inspire us to continue the fight for greater justice and equity. To volunteers, supporters and donors, thank you for your ongoing commitment, ensuring The Stop remains a responsive, effective and caring organization supporting thousands of people every year. To the small but mighty staff of Community Food Centres Canada, our humblest thanks for taking this leap into the unknown with such spirit and decisiveness.

Special thanks must also be extended to the people who agreed to interviews and follow-up emails, who allowed us to follow them around and inspired us with their stories and their lives: Gordon Bowes, Rekha Cherian, Marie Diaz, Nadia Edwards, Sharon Francis, Laura Garrido, the late Cliff Gayer, Tania Julien, Rumana Khalifa, Glenn Kitchener, Rosa and Tony Lamanna, Andrea Maldonado, Mary Milne, Sonja Nerad, Brent Preston and Gillian Flies, Gilberto, Delmy and Ariana Rogel, Jonah Schein, the late Theora Spooner, and Dan Yashinsky.

A special shout-out to fellow travellers with whom we've worked over the years and who've made the journey such a rewarding and enjoyable one: Alan Broadbent, John Broley, Eileen Coulton, Ruth Crammond, Debbie Field, Bryan Gilvesy, Nadien Godkewitsch, Brian Green, Stephen Gregory, Kirsten Hanson, Tim Jones, Scott Lamacraft, Joe Lobko, Lorenzo Loseto, Michael MacMillan and Cathy Spoel, David McKeown, Joe Mihevc, Raj Patel, Janet Poppendieck, David Reville, Wayne Roberts, Bruce Rosensweet, Bill Saul, Juliana Sprott, Joe Virgona, Samara Walbohm and Joe Shlesinger, Mary Lou Walker, Bill Young and Ted Zettel.

Thanks to Jackie Kaiser and Chris Casuccio of Westwood Creative Artists who embraced the idea from the beginning and held our hands along the way. The good people at Random

House Canada were passionate about the project from the start. Thanks to Anne Collins and Louise Dennys for their enthusiasm, and to Craig Pyette, for his patience and his thoughtful, discerning eye. We are also grateful to editors Amanda Lewis, Tilman Lewis and Liba Berry, as well as designer CS Richardson for their precision and attention to detail, helping move this book from words on the screen to a beautiful, tactile object. We are delighted that Kirsten Reach at Melville House saw the international potential of The Stop's story and that she and the team at this feisty independent press have worked so hard to get it out into the world. Thank you also to Christina Palassio who helped us source images and to photographers Zoe Alexopoulos, Matt O'Sullivan and Anna Prior who allowed us to use their remarkable photographs taken at The Stop.

This book would not have been written at all were it not for the kindness, love and childcare of our parents, James and Erica Curtis, and Pat and John Saul. They inspire us with their generosity, dedication to community, family and to a better world. We have also leaned heavily on Joanne Saul, most excellent first reader, sister and cherished friend. A thousand thanks for friendships that sustain us: Shanthi Aranha and Art Sharp, Steph Garrow, Bronwen Low, Robin MacAulay and Charles Gane, Sophie McCall, Janet Nicol, Katrina Onstad, Rosemary Renton, Lorraine and Oliver Sutherns, Patrick Thoburn, Peter Wall and Lisa Werlich.

Finally, all love to Ben and Quinn Saul, whose wise counsel, intrinsic sense of justice and great compassion make us ever hopeful for the future.

NICK SAUL was executive director of The Stop Community Food Centre in Toronto from 1998 to 2012, and is a recipient of the prestigious Jane Jacobs Prize and the Queen's Golden Jubilee Medal. He is now president and CEO of Community Food Centres Canada, an organization that will bring the innovations of The Stop to communities across the country. **www.cfccanada.ca**

ANDREA CURTIS is an award-winning writer and editor. Her family memoir, *Into the Blue: Family Secrets and the Search for a Great Lakes Shipwreck*, won the Edna Staebler Award for Creative Non-Fiction. Curtis's first children's book is *What's for Lunch? How Schoolchildren Eat Around the World*. **www.andreacurtis.ca**

SAUL AND CURTIS live with their two boys in Toronto.